The Tyranny of Generosity

The Tyranny of Generosity

*Why Philanthropy Corrupts Our
Politics and How We Can Fix It*

THEODORE M. LECHTERMAN

OXFORD
UNIVERSITY PRESS

Oxford University Press is a department of the University of Oxford. It furthers
the University's objective of excellence in research, scholarship, and education
by publishing worldwide. Oxford is a registered trade mark of Oxford University
Press in the UK and certain other countries.

Published in the United States of America by Oxford University Press
198 Madison Avenue, New York, NY 10016, United States of America.

Library of Congress Cataloging-in-Publication Data
Names: Lechterman, Theodore M., author.
Title: The tyranny of generosity : why philanthropy corrupts our politics
and how we can fix it / Theodore M. Lechterman.
Description: New York, NY, United States of America : Oxford University Press, [2022] |
Includes bibliographical references and index.
Identifiers: LCCN 2021022644 | ISBN 9780197611418 (hardback) |
ISBN 9780197611432 (epub)
Subjects: LCSH: Charities—Political aspects. | Charities—Moral and
ethical aspects. | Wealth—Political aspects. | Wealth—Moral and
ethical aspects. | Political corruption. | Political culture—Economic aspects.
Classification: LCC HV41 .L385 2022 | DDC 361.8—dc23
LC record available at https://lccn.loc.gov/2021022644

DOI: 10.1093/oso/9780197611418.001.0001

1 3 5 7 9 8 6 4 2

Printed by Integrated Books International, United States of America

Contents

Contents

Acknowledgments

This book began as a doctoral dissertation at Princeton under the supervision of Charles Beitz, Melissa Lane, and Philip Pettit. Many of my thoughts about these topics developed through conversations with Chuck on the nature of our duties to strangers. Perhaps more than anything else, Chuck's philosophical method—an ecumenical and empirically rich version of social contract theory—has helped to shape my own treatment of these issues. Melissa deepened my appreciation of the historical context of ideas about philanthropy and its institutional configuration. I also relied on her for incisive criticism and steady guidance during the project's critical phases. Philip's systematic perspective first helped me to appreciate some of philanthropy's distinctive philosophical challenges. But it was also the conviction that Philip's noted theory of freedom can't easily account for some of these challenges that encouraged me to pursue this study.

The inspiration to expand the project into a book came from Rob Reich, who's dedicated much of his career to making philanthropy a legitimate object of philosophical study and supporting early-career researchers with interests in this area. The book itself took shape under Rob's mentorship during a postdoctoral fellowship at Stanford. There, I was fortunate to have two academic homes, the McCoy Center for Ethics in Society and the Center on Philanthropy and Civil Society, and I cherish the hospitality I received from each. Rainer Forst and Stefan Gosepath fostered the ideal intellectual environment for completing the manuscript during a postdoctoral fellowship at the Centre for Advanced Studies Justitia Amplificata, while the Forschungskolleg Humanwissenschaften at Goethe

University Frankfurt and the Institute for Philosophy at Free University Berlin provided ideal settings for writing. Thanks to the support I received from Johanna Mair and John Tasioulas, I was able to complete revisions in between other projects during respective fellowships at the Hertie School and the University of Oxford.

Many people have had a hand in improving the manuscript. I'm especially grateful to Emilee Chapman, Nan Keohane, Minh Ly, Debra Satz, and Leif Wenar, who participated in a workshop of the manuscript at Stanford in June 2018. Penetrating criticism and generous guidance from anonymous reviewers for Oxford University Press helped me tremendously in refining, framing, and assembling the book's arguments. At OUP, Lucy Randall's early enthusiasm for the project was a great source of encouragement, and her patience a great source of relief.

For advice or comments on other occasions, I thank Calvin Baker, Brian Berkey, Bob Brecher, Paul Brest, Jon Bruno, Mark Budolfson, Hannah Carnegy-Arbuthnott, Eamonn Callan, Lindsey Chambers, David Ciepley, Emily Clough, Chiara Cordelli, Julian Culp, Prithvi Datta, Chiara Destri, Claire Dunning, Gideon Elford, Johann Frick, Iason Gabriel, Laura Gillespie, Greg Gotimer, Peter Hägel, Marcus Häggrot, Dirk Hartog, Lisa Herzog, Johannes Himmelreich, Louis-Philippe Hodgson, Ben Hofmann, Waheed Hussain, Des Jagmohan, Jennifer Kagan, George Kateb, Rob Katz, Stan Katz, Steven Kelts, Tom Kleven, Trevor Latimer, Isi Litke, Désirée Lim, Steve Macedo, Amanda Maher, Alison McQueen, Jason Millar, Darrel Moellendorf, Jakob Moggia, Maribel Morey, Oded Na'aman, Anne Newman, Fay Niker, Woody Powell, Lucia Rafanelli, Emma Saunders-Hastings, Guy Schultz, Jiewuh Song, Kai Spiekermann, Lucas Stanczyk, Richard Steinberg, Annie Stilz, Mark Stuckel, Marty Sulek, Steven Teles, Toshiro Terada, Caleb Yong, John Young, Bernardo Zacka, and Jake Zuehl.

A version of Chapter 5 appears in *Giving in Time*, a volume edited by Benjamin Soskis and Ray D. Madoff and published by

Rowman and Littlefield (forthcoming). I'm very grateful to Ben and Ray for their careful editorial work, and to Rowman and Littlefield for granting permission for republication. A version of Chapter 6 appears in *Polity*, a journal published by the Northeastern Political Science Association and Chicago University Press. I'm grateful to the journal's editors and three anonymous reviewers for considerable assistance in improving the piece. I also thank Chicago University Press for granting copyright permission.

Over the course of the project, I received valuable feedback from audiences at American University of Paris, University of Brighton, Boston College Law School, Free University Berlin, Goethe University Frankfurt, Harvard University, IUPUI Lilly Family School of Family, Princeton University, Technical University Munich, Stanford University, Wharton School of Business, and Yale University, as well as at conferences hosted by the American Political Science Association, the Association for Research on Nonprofit Organizations and Voluntary Action (ARNOVA), the Braga Meetings on Ethics and Political Philosophy, the International Society for Third-Sector Research (ISTR), the Midwest Political Science Association, the Northeast Political Science Association, and the Western Political Science Association.

At Princeton I received additional assistance from the University Center for Human Values (UCHV) Laurance S. Rockefeller Graduate Prize Fellowship, the UCHV's Political Philosophy Graduate Student Research and Travel Fund (endowed by Amy Gutmann), the Politics Department's Stafford Fund, and the Graduate School Dean's Fund for Scholarly Travel. I also received travel assistance from the Society for Applied Philosophy.

I owe significant debts to Eric Beerbohm, who first introduced me to political philosophy and has remained a dependable source of guidance since; Shmulik Nili, who read and improved countless early drafts with relentless kindness and wisdom; and Geoff Sigalet, whose surfing companionship and free spirit supplied welcome relief from the travails of academia. I couldn't have completed this project without the support and care of Sarah Kozloff, Bob Lechterman, Jeremy Lechterman, Bonnie Kozloff, Lloyd Kozloff, Dan Kozloff, Fred Struthers, Nerses Chopurian, Sylvia Chopurian, Tamara Chopurian, and my dearest Vivien Chopurian. Their love could underwrite many books. I'm so lucky they chose mine.

1

Looking the Gift Horse in the Mouth

On September 13, 2018, Jeff Bezos took to Twitter to announce a bold new initiative: a $2 billion commitment to address homeless-ness and preschool education in the United States.[1] As beneficent declarations from billionaires become increasingly commonplace, one could easily be forgiven for passing over this one. Yet Bezos's announcement stood apart for several reasons. The Amazon founder had become the world's richest person less than a year earlier, but unlike previous bearers of that title, Bezos had so far indicated strikingly little inclination to share his fortune. There was no foundation to his name; no record of noteworthy donations on his résumé. For many of his billionaire peers, signing the Giving Pledge—a pact among many of the world's wealthiest people to give away most of their wealth—had become a rite of passage into ranks of the superrich. But Bezos had shown scant interest in adding his name to that distinguished list.

The Bezos Day One Fund parted ways with another trend in elite philanthropy by eschewing a technocratic strategy. For two decades, billionaires concerned with poverty and education have sought to disrupt existing practices by injecting them with the kinds of strategies that have won success in business management.[2] In his announcement, Bezos couldn't resist comparing his new commit-ment to children to his enduring commitment to customer service at Amazon. ("The child will be the customer," he declared.) But the plans for the Bezos Day One Fund conspicuously avoided any more substantive connection to market-driven competition, promising instead to support respected organizations and strategies that al-ready exist.

If Bezos's announcement was remarkable, the public response was anything but that. Over the past two decades, we've grown accustomed to these kinds of announcements, and reactions now cluster into familiar camps. Political pundit Donna Brazile reflected a common sentiment when she praised Bezos for recognizing his *noblesse oblige* by tackling an urgent social crisis.[3] Bezos could have spent the money on space yachts, invested it in his children's trust fund, or donated it to a museum. That he chose to give it away, and to direct it to some of society's neediest, deserves our praise and encouragement. Supporters of the Effective Altruism movement were quick to point out how Bezos's pledge was neither as effective nor as altruistic as it could have been.[4] The evidence suggests that spending $2 billion on mosquito nets, alternatives to factory-farming, or cash transfers to families in Rwanda would add significantly more to global well-being than investing in affordable housing and preschool education in the United States. And while Bezos's $2 billion might be an incredible amount of money, it was only 1.25 percent of his $160 billion fortune—far less than the 10 percent that effective altruists consider the minimum to be expected from a financially comfortable person.[5] Meanwhile, the columnist Anand Giridharadas lambasted Bezos for helping to create the very problems that he was now pledging to solve.[6] Amazon had helped to kill legislation proposed by the City of Seattle to increase the supply of affordable housing with a tax levied on large employers. And Bezos's ruthless management tactics had left many workers in Amazon warehouses too poor to afford either housing or preschool. Before considering how he can do more good, Giridharadas proposed, billionaires like Bezos should ask themselves how they can do less harm. Yet others insisted that judgment of the announcement was inappropriate. How Jeff Bezos chooses to spend his money is nobody's business but Jeff Bezos's, retorted Vinod Khosla, the billionaire cofounder of Sun Microsystems.[7]

As the debate played out, many commentators sounded variations on these themes, which roughly reflect concerns for generosity, effectiveness, justice, and liberty. To be sure, each represents an essential ingredient in the ethics of philanthropy. While we might disagree about how each of these values should be ranked, interpreted, or applied, most people would agree that each supplies a relevant set of considerations. When forming judgments about philanthropic donations, reflecting on our own giving decisions, or evaluating policy options for regulating the broader practice, we ought to account for each of these values.

Suppose, however, that conditions had been otherwise. Imagine that Bezos had committed a far greater share of his fortune, that he had selected causes and strategies based on the best evidence for accomplishing the most good, and that he had amassed his fortune through equitable treatment of his company's stakeholders. The criticisms we've considered suggest that such a scenario, if somehow possible, would be beyond reproach. Had things unfolded in this way, common standpoints on the ethics of philanthropy indicate that public gratitude would be the only appropriate response. Should we find this conclusion satisfying? To do so, this book contends, would be to neglect an essential set of concerns that have so far struggled to find their voice.

Philanthropy that comes with good intentions, careful strategy, and impressive results can often flout and even corrode another crucial value: the value of democracy. As we'll see, democracy supplies powerful reasons to ensure that goods like affordable housing and preschool education are governed collectively, on equal terms. Sharing responsibility and control of matters of basic justice is essential to treating one another as free and equal members of society. By flooding these policy areas with private resources and ideas, the Day One Fund serves to colonize what are essentially democratic responsibilities. But philanthropy and democracy are not irreconcilable. To live up to the demands of democracy, this book contends, donors like Bezos must often take different courses of action than common evaluative standpoints recommend. As admirable as it is, private generosity should not, and need not, purchase undue public power. More importantly, this book argues, the duty to reconcile philanthropy with democracy doesn't lie with donors alone. It falls to all of us to ensure that the practice of philanthropy and the laws that structure it work to support the democratic ideal.

The need for reconciliation between philanthropy and democracy couldn't be more urgent. In a world ravaged by greed, inequality, and government dysfunction, we increasingly look to private philanthropy to rescue and redeem us. Private wealth deployed for public purposes fills gaps left by the market. It solves problems where the state can't or won't. And it fosters virtues of generosity and gratitude, necessary components of a good life and a healthy society. Philanthropy is growing by almost every measure of scale and scope, as donors ramp up their outlays, target new areas, and pilot new strategies. Even countries with no tradition of private philanthropy are beginning to welcome it with warm embraces.

For many observers, the central challenges in the ethics of philanthropy are to encourage people to give more, to give more selflessly, and to give more effectively. Some regard investing one's wealth in the advancement of the common good as the noblest use of capital.[8] For others, philanthropy is a stringent duty for those who benefit from economic inequality.[9] Some bemoan the priorities of donors who support high culture and pet causes in the face of urgent needs.[10] Others excoriate attempts by individuals accused of wicked behavior to launder their reputations with good deeds.[11] And many warn of the massive inefficiencies that result when honorable intentions substitute for careful strategy.[12] Meanwhile, a long tradition of cynicism has regarded philanthropy as a handmaiden of capitalist exploitation, a strategy for pacifying resistance to unjust institutions.[13] The best philanthropy, this view suggests, is none at all.

This book seeks to upend these ideas. Parting ways with certain cynical treatments, it reaffirms that philanthropy does indeed possess considerable virtues. But faith in philanthropy's virtues often blinds us to another problem: that philanthropy as we know it threatens critical foundations of a democratic society. What we frequently fail to see is that philanthropy is too often a form of private power wielded on inequitable terms.

Of course, the power of those who give can sometimes invade the autonomy of those who receive. The overbearing donor and the vulnerable recipient is a familiar drama in fact and fiction alike. Less obvious, however, is that permitting private property to promote public purposes allows parts of a society's common life to be defined by private wealth. For better or for worse, philanthropy takes certain decisions about public matters out of public hands. And, in societies characterized by wide disparities in wealth, philanthropy combines with background inequalities to make public decisions overwhelmingly sensitive to the preferences of the richer. Allowing private wealth to control social outcomes collides with core commitments of a democratic society, a society in which persons are supposed to determine their common affairs together, on equal terms.

But why exactly is democracy valuable? How should democratic values be weighed against the liberty of donors and the many social benefits that philanthropy promises? Observers who have appreciated these questions have tended to find their answers elusive.[14] Reconciling philanthropy and democracy requires that we engage the tools of political philosophy, which provides analytical bases for justifying and appraising social practices. Political philosophy helps to disentangle concepts and values, allowing us then to reassemble them into principles that balance the considerations that compete for our judgment. Armed with these tools, this book reaches a surprising conclusion: the success of the democratic ideal may actually require certain forms of philanthropy—but making philanthropy safe for democracy also requires radical changes to policy and practice.

The next section explains more precisely what I mean by philanthropy and describes recent trends that make this phenomenon worthy of deeper reflection. Section II details how this study builds

on and departs from other attempts to analyze and evaluate philanthropic giving. Section III then sets out the plan for the book with a
brief summary of each chapter to come and some guidance on what
to expect.

I. The Social Practice of Philanthropy

The term "philanthropy" often means different things to different
audiences.[15] One might think that by "philanthropy" I mean to
refer to a specific legal device, that is, the private grant-making
foundation, whose influence in this area looms large. Indeed,
foundations raise many interesting and important issues. While the
project certainly entails implications for the evaluation and regulation of foundations, it rarely addresses foundations directly. The
foundation helps to concentrate and extend certain powers of donation (an issue taken up in Chapter 5), but it doesn't create them.
Focusing on foundations can artificially limit our view of other and
more fundamental normative issues. One might also think that by
"philanthropy" I mean to refer exclusively to the donative activity
of the superrich, whether through foundations or by other means.
Indeed, the relationship between economic inequality and philanthropy is a theme that courses through each chapter. To focus only
on elite philanthropy, however, inhibits us from considering other
basic questions, such as how opportunities for philanthropy should
be distributed and what kinds of activities ought to be left to private
donation in the first place. Thus, this book also pays attention to
the donative activity of people of modest means. Finally, one might
think that by "philanthropy" I mean to reference something distinct
from "charity," which specifically involves donations for the benefit
of the disadvantaged. Certain historians characterize philanthropy
as oriented toward solving social problems, in contrast to charity,
which they define as addressing the symptoms of these problems.[16]
While this may be a useful distinction for historiographical

purposes, it leaves us without a term to describe a broad array of contemporary phenomena. Most donations undertaken under the auspices of philanthropy or charity today target neither root causes of social problems nor their symptoms, serving instead to express individuals' commitments to religious, cultural, and scientific endeavors.[17]

By "philanthropy," I mean to refer to a general social practice, a pattern of social interaction, regulated by formal and informal rules, that occurs in various forms across national and historical contexts.[18] As I construe it, the social practice of philanthropy can be distinguished initially by the particular type of economic transaction that sustains it: the donation, or what theorists of property call a *gratuitous transfer*.[19] A transfer of property is gratuitous when it is neither compelled by law (like taxation) nor offered in return for goods or services (like market exchange). But further reflection reveals that not all such transfers operate within a distinguishable practice of philanthropy. Interpersonal gift-giving and contributing to a private club of which one is a member represent different and, in my view, nonphilanthropic forms of donation. Birthday presents and country club dues can hardly count as philanthropic. I take it that what renders the practice distinct is the fact that it transfers resources more impersonally. We might say that philanthropic donations are therefore *impersonal gratuitous transfers*, directed at an indefinite number of persons who are mostly or entirely unknown to the donor.[20] This definition comes close to a more elegant description favored by contemporary sociologists, who often define philanthropy as the *voluntary commitment of private property for public purposes*.[21] Though this definition is limited by the essential ambiguity of the meaning of "public," for simplicity I often appeal to it in what follows.[22]

Armed with this conceptual understanding of the phenomenon, we can say that an individual engages directly in philanthropy when they donate resources that they own to a public purpose or to an agent entrusted with carrying out such a purpose. Under modern conditions, this primarily means transferring money to an incorporated nonprofit organization.[23]

So-defined, philanthropy today is expanding by nearly every conceivable measure. This expansion is felt most acutely in the United States, where donations supply 2.1 percent of gross domestic product (GDP).[24] Over the past 25 years, rates of donation from all sources (individuals, foundations, corporations, and estates) have increased at an average pace of 3 percent per year in the United States.[25] Outside the United States, philanthropy's contributions to GDP remains strongest in commonwealth countries: New Zealand, Canada, and the United Kingdom.[26] But recent trends indicate that other countries may be catching up. Europe's philanthropic foundations now surpass those of the United States in terms of number and spending rate.[27] Giving in China increased at a rate of 18.6 percent per year between 2008 and 2017.[28]

Aggregate statistics also mask distributional trends. In the United States, foundation giving has grown at double the rate of individual giving for the past 25 years.[29] Although giving by individuals far outstrips the amounts given by other sources in the United States, estimates suggest that as much as 30 percent of dollars contributed by individuals come from the ultrawealthy, a group that composes less than 0.03 percent of the population.[30] In Europe and China, meanwhile, a substantial proportion of donations comes from corporate foundations.

These facts challenge a critique I often receive when presenting research on this topic to international audiences: that philanthropy represents a quintessentially American practice, raising issues of limited relevance to other national contexts. Philanthropy does indeed enjoy a particularly prominent role in the contemporary United States, and in what follows, I will often draw on examples from the American experience to motivate and illustrate various theoretical issues. As the role and scale of philanthropy expands in many societies, however, it can't simply be dismissed as an American peculiarity. Those who wish to preserve a more limited role for philanthropy must supply arguments to justify these restrictions, as must those who wish to encourage philanthropy's growth.

II. Philanthropy in Moral and Political Philosophy

When philosophers and political theorists take interest in philanthropy, they tend to do so from the first-personal perspective. They ask whether and how giving can be part of an ethical life.[31] They consider the particular values that donation might implicate and debate the boundaries between beneficence and justice.[32] They explore the nature of duties to donate and assess the merits of different potential causes.[33] The history of ideas is replete with illuminating perspectives on these and many related questions.[34] But the focus on the individual giver, and, to a lesser extent, the relationship between giver and receiver, are all too often hamstrung by their neglect of the institutional conditions that make philanthropy possible. To treat institutions as exogenous to the ethics of philanthropy is to fail to appreciate the essentially political character of philanthropic giving.

As generic practices of gift-giving appear across all human societies on record, one might think that philanthropy is a natural or "preinstitutional" feature of social life.[35] If philanthropy didn't depend on political institutions in any significant way, political philosophy would have relatively little insight to contribute to this topic. But in fact, philanthropy is inextricably embedded in political choices, with its role and attributes varying widely across different theories and historical settings. This is so for three main reasons.

First, a social practice of donating property for public purposes depends on laws of property and contract that determine what may be owned, how it may be owned, who may own it, and how it may be transferred. Different configurations of these laws can give radically different opportunities for gratuitous transfers—including none at all. And, as each configuration will empower and advantage some while disempowering and disadvantaging others, these laws stand in need of justification.

Since regimes that forbid private property will effectively eliminate the possibility of philanthropy, philanthropy's existence presupposes that private property can be justified.[36] Few modern readers will find this a difficult concession. While thoroughgoing rejection of private property has animated many thinkers and communities, it is an increasingly uncommon position. Nowadays, most avowed socialists tend to reserve at least some space for private property.[37] But property regimes that uphold private ownership need not necessarily protect philanthropy. Even the United States, renowned for its particularly strong protection of private property, has not always regarded philanthropy as a necessary or desirable consequence of this institution. In the early days of the American republic, several states restricted philanthropic donations, viewing them as tinder for civic faction.[38] Similarly, theorists who defend the institution of private property have not always extended this defense to philanthropy. For John Locke, according to one prominent interpreter, gratuitous transfers of property are illegitimate because they are not received on the basis of labor; barring certain exceptions, it is only through laboring that one can permissibly acquire a property right.[39]

Second, the role available to philanthropy depends in large part on the roles that a society assigns to other mechanisms for financing economic activity. A society that chooses to furnish higher education through market exchange (as Brazil and China increasingly do) will effectively limit opportunities for philanthropy in this area; likewise for a society that chooses to furnish military defense through taxation.[40] Societies that choose otherwise may carve out a larger or different role for philanthropy. Private education is virtually nonexistent in contemporary France; privately funded military campaigns were commonplace in classical Athens.[41] How a society configures its institutional division of labor raises controversial issues. Each configuration will advance certain interests and values at the expense of others, resulting in different distributions of benefits and burdens and different civic cultures. Political theorizing is essential for assessing which configurations are permissible or optimal.

Third, in many modern societies, it turns out that the state generously promotes the practice of philanthropy and steers it in particular ways. Using tax privileges, matching grants, special restrictions, and unique legal devices, the modern state gives the practice of philanthropy its particular strength and texture. Which if any of these regulatory strategies can be justified requires careful analysis and evaluation.

In sum, political institutions necessarily enable, circumscribe, and structure any recognizable practice of philanthropy. Each configuration of these institutions advances certain interests and values at the expense of others. These configurations, moreover, are not natural facts like glaciers and gravity. They are the products of political choices. While we may not be responsible for bringing these institutions into existence, whether to maintain or reform them is, in some sense, up to us. How these political questions are resolved also has massive implications for the practical ethics of philanthropy. The moral prescriptions that apply to donors under favorable conditions may be drastically different under conditions that are unjust or illegitimate.

In the last few years, a small number of philosophers and political theorists have begun to evaluate philanthropy's political dimensions. Most prominently, they have addressed the tax treatment of philanthropic donations,[42] the role and conduct of elite donors,[43] the duties of nonprofit organizations,[44] and donating in contexts of injustice.[45] This book seeks to build on these existing studies in two primary ways. One is by probing aspects of the practice that have so far generated little attention, such as the intertemporal dimension of philanthropic giving and philanthropy by commercial corporations—topics on which I elaborate in what follows. Another is by examining philanthropy particularly through the lens of recent advances in normative democratic theory.

In evaluating social conditions, political philosophy sometimes distinguishes principles of *justice* (standards for evaluating social conditions) from principles of *legitimacy* (standards for evaluating the processes that shape these conditions).[46] *Liberalism* names a family of conceptions of justice that enjoy wide support among contemporary theorists. In the abstract, liberalism holds that coercively imposed arrangements must be justifiable to each of their subjects, taking equal concern with each person's interests.[47] More concretely, liberalism typically recommends (a) the protection of a robust slate of basic liberties, such as conscience, speech, association, and movement, and (b) a set of economic policies— public goods provision, a decent social minimum, and limits on inequality—designed to ensure fair opportunities to enjoy these liberties. Liberal theories diverge on precisely how to fill out these categories and the relationship between them. Important for my purposes is that much existing work on the political theory of philanthropy has been devoted to whether and how philanthropy might satisfy the requirements of liberal justice. It has sought to articulate how the policies that structure philanthropy, and the decisions of individual donors, can simultaneously protect individual liberty and promote a fair distribution of resources.

Recent work from this perspective has yielded critical insights on numerous questions, such as whether tax subsidies for charitable donations are fairly designed and whether it's permissible for donors to support pet causes in the face of staggering poverty and inequality. But this work has left us ill-equipped to evaluate other controversial aspects of contemporary practice, aspects that have more to do with the distribution of power than the distribution of wealth. Neglecting to evaluate the power that typically comes with philanthropic donation deprives us of sufficient theoretical resources to evaluate philanthropist-led interventions in education policy, the privatization of foreign aid, and the accelerating efforts of business firms to solve social problems, among other trends. Serious attention to these kinds of issues requires venturing into another area of political philosophy.

While liberalism provides a common anchor for many conceptions of justice, theories of *democracy* animate many contemporary conceptions of political legitimacy. Democracy refers to a process of collective decision-making that treats members of the collective as equals in some way. To be fully legitimate, according to several influential views, coercively imposed decisions must come about through democratic processes.[48] Individuals are entitled to determine their common affairs collectively, through processes that afford each affected person an equal say. Focusing on democratic legitimacy thus prompts some different questions about the role of philanthropy. It invites us to consider not only how philanthropy can assist in the pursuit of just outcomes but also the conditions under which philanthropy represents an appropriate method for doing so. Philanthropy might be a way of supplementing or supporting democratic processes; it might also be a way of circumventing or subverting them. Philanthropy might provide means for political expression and participation in democratic deliberation; it might also provide means for richer citizens to dominate the public sphere. Philanthropy might help to redistribute resources to disadvantaged individuals; it might also subject recipients to objectionable forms of power. Although principles of justice enter into the picture at many points throughout this study, the book seeks to give greater attention to overlooked questions about philanthropy's relationship to the democratic ideal.

The limited philosophical attention to philanthropy's relationship to democratic theory has a simple explanation: the common presumption that philanthropy represents a problem of "nonideal justice." Most liberal theories of justice regard limitations on economic inequality as a moral imperative. Since many of the objections to the contemporary practice of philanthropy are tied to unprecedented levels of economic inequality, one might easily think that objectionable features of this practice simply illustrate the failure of contemporary societies to live up to familiar ideals. If societies just did more to rein in inequality, this reasoning holds, philanthropy would no longer stand in conflict with political morality. In other words, the practice of philanthropy raises no unique philosophical puzzles.

This view is surely correct that economic inequality exacerbates the conflict between philanthropy and principles of political morality. But as this study shows, it's a mistake to presume that the challenges that philanthropy raises carry no independent philosophical significance. For instance, the question of how wealth should be distributed is entirely separate from the question of which elements of public life a society can permissibly finance by donation (and a question that no major contemporary theory of justice has directly addressed).[49] And, since most liberal theories of justice permit some degree of economic inequality, it remains to be shown how such differences in wealth can be consistent with equal citizenship.

III. The Plan of the Book

The book is roughly structured into three main parts. Following this introductory discussion, the first part consists of Chapter 2 ("Of Sovereignty and Saints") and Chapter 3 ("A Farewell to Alms"). It tackles the question of philanthropy's justification—what role, if any, such a practice should play in societies that recognize individuals as free and equal moral persons. Having clarified philanthropy's proper role, the second part of the book asks how power within this practice should be distributed. Chapter 4 ("Donation and Deliberation") considers the distribution of donative opportunity, while Chapter 5 ("In Usufruct to the Living") examines the temporal limits of donors' power. The book's third part attends to more applied questions, considering what these conclusions about political morality entail for practical ethics. Chapter 6 ("The Effective Altruist's Political Problem") demonstrates how a democratic political morality provides guidelines for individual donations. Chapter 7 ("Milton Friedman's Corporate Misanthropy") considers the unique challenges that giving by corporations raises for democratic legitimacy.

Although the chapters work together to develop a general theoretical perspective, they were originally written independently of one another, and the connecting threads between different chapters' arguments are not always as strong as I'd like. Nonetheless, readers with particular topical interests may appreciate that each chapter offers a self-contained argument, allowing them to engage with the material selectively. A more detailed chapter summary follows presently.

What's the point of philanthropy? To address this question, it can be helpful to distinguish forms of philanthropy according to the different functions that donations might serve. Donations might operate in a *productive* mode, to finance goods and services. They might also operate in an *expressive* mode, to finance the expression and dissemination of ideas. Chapter 2 ("Of Sovereignty and Saints") examines philanthropy's productive function. It asks which kinds of goods and services a democratic polity should furnish via donation. Donations are a well-known solution to the problem of "public goods." So-called public goods are goods with characteristics that prevent markets from providing them reliably. They must either be supplied by taxation or by donation if they are to be provided at all. But are all such goods appropriate objects of philanthropy? The chapter considers a variety of perspectives in political philosophy on the responsibility for providing public goods. Though certain views contribute helpful criteria toward a normative theory of public goods provision, these arguments fail to appreciate a central component of the value of democracy. A significant part of democracy's value lies in its assignment of certain decisions to collective control. Democracy, I argue, makes citizens sovereign over the legislation and administration of matters of basic justice. Our interests in democratic sovereignty supply a strong reason to maintain public control over public goods that are intimately linked to fundamental rights, duties, and opportunities. The argument helps to justify and explain discomfort that many share about privately sponsored social assistance and private funding of public schools. It also indicates that philanthropy for goods more distant from basic justice—such as the arts, research, sport, and religion—may be easier to justify in democratic terms.

Having considered why a democratic polity might have reason to limit philanthropy's reach, Chapter 3 ("A Farewell to Alms") considers the conditions under which such a polity might have reason to offer donations affirmative support. Policies that subsidize philanthropic donations are a fixture of the public finance regimes of most democratic societies. Most instantiations of this policy make subsidies available on a neutral basis, with no special priority accorded to specific categories of nonprofit activity. Numerous critics find this policy wanting, contending that public support for philanthropy can only be justified as a way of responding to poverty. The chapter affirms that a society's least advantaged members have powerful claims on collective resources but notes serious limitations with using philanthropy to satisfy them. Meanwhile, it proposes that public support for citizens' varied philanthropic commitments is valuable as a way of mediating the limitations of majority rule and securing the organizational foundations of democratic deliberation.

But there are alternative ways of providing this public support, and unfortunately, common practice in many societies falls short. Charitable tax deductions serve to amplify the voices of the wealthy at the expense of the less advantaged. Under conditions of economic inequality, subsidizing donations on formally equal terms allows wealthier citizens to augment their influence over public affairs, further marginalizing poorer citizens. Chapter 4 ("Donation and Deliberation") contends that this state of affairs is ultimately incompatible with the requirements of political equality, and I consider various policy proposals for redressing this problem. In the process, I reexamine and rearticulate the nature of political equality and what it demands.

An especially underappreciated problem regarding philanthropic power concerns the way in which charitable gifts exercise control over future generations. Charitable bequests and trusts, which are popular instruments of donation, bind future generations to respect the wills of past donors. Chapter 5 ("In Usufruct to the Living") draws on views of Thomas Jefferson—noted critic of institutions that favor the dead over the living—to illustrate the problem of "dead-hand control." Jefferson's perspective helps us to appreciate that donations meant to benefit future persons may also mistreat them by imposing conditions on their use of resources. The chapter argues that generations have an interest in sovereignty over their common affairs that qualifies how resources can be donated across time. Though it ultimately defends the practice of intergenerational philanthropy, the chapter also shows how taking the value of sovereignty seriously recommends restrictions on the duration that donors can expect to have their wills honored.

What does it mean to give well? Chapter 6 ("The Effective Altruist's Political Problem") argues that political considerations are essential—though often neglected—ingredients in the practical ethics of giving. The argument develops through an examination of effective altruism, an increasingly popular and sophisticated perspective on the ethics of philanthropy. A core component of effective altruism is the relief of poverty through targeted interventions in the developing world. The chapter rearticulates and expands on the moral challenges of relieving the symptoms of poverty through philanthropic interventions. I counter, however, that redirecting philanthropists to institutional reform—as effective altruism's critics often advocate—falls unwittingly into some of the same traps. Namely, an unqualified recommendation for diverting more money into politics stumbles right into the challenges of political injustice that I raise in Chapter 4. I offer some ways in which individual donors can overcome these challenges, such as by making assistance projects self-consciously transitional and investing in community organizing rather than direct policy change. The value of democracy can't tell us where to give, but it can tell us how to give more respectfully.

Chapter 7 ("Milton Friedman's Corporate Misanthropy") considers how the foregoing arguments might inform the ethics of corporate philanthropy. It also recruits an unlikely ally for this task: the libertarian economist Milton Friedman. Friedman is notorious for his opposition to corporate philanthropy, which follows from his conviction that a corporation's sole purpose and obligation is to maximize profits. This is an extremely unpopular view today. But Chapter 7 argues that Friedman's position is substantially more attractive than many may realize—when treated as a democratic critique. A firm's shareholders, managers, and employees are already free to make donations in their individual capacities as citizens. To allow firms to donate in addition serves, in effect, to multiply the public influence of its stakeholders. This is deeply prejudicial to citizens who can't call on a firm to multiply the effects of their own donations. The concentrated wealth that firms typically command can also afford them domineering influence over receiving communities. And the inherent conflict between a commercial firm's acquisitive and altruistic motives exposes vulnerable beneficiaries to heightened risk of mistreatment. Nonetheless, the chapter argues that certain kinds of corporate philanthropy can overcome this criticism. It also shows how new developments in business that blend commercial and nonprofit aims suggest a need for further research. Businesses are increasingly pursuing social ends through means other than donation. Although this study focuses specifically on the phenomenon of donation, future work might show how the principles uncovered here might extend to address broader challenges of private power.

A brief concluding chapter summarizes the study's main conclusions, clarifies its upshots, and identifies outstanding questions. Certain outstanding questions will already be obvious, as many interesting and controversial aspects of the practice of philanthropy go unaddressed in this book. These omissions do not reflect a judgment of the relative importance of different topics. I have chosen to focus on the issues I have mainly because they are areas where I thought I had something original to say. As political theorists and philosophers take increasing interest in philanthropy, I remain optimistic about the prospects for more brightly illuminating its many puzzles and promises.

Finally, a disclaimer about the intended audience and approach. The topic of philanthropy matters to many scholarly disciplines, practitioners, and the general public. In writing this book, I have learned much from exploring diverse perspectives, and I have sought to present material in ways that are sensitive to the interests and expectations of various audiences. I take pains to avoid jargon and assume no prior familiarity with current philosophical debates and methods. I try wherever possible to use real-world examples and illustrate my points concretely. Nonetheless, some readers may find the argumentation in certain chapters denser and more laborious than they may like. Likewise, while some of the resulting discussions yield fairly determinate suggestions about how to reform policy and practice to address the concerns I identify, this is ultimately a work of theory and not of policy design, management strategy, or personal advice. Often, rather than specific actions to take, the arguments point us to general principles, values to account for, or shifts in orientation. This is as it should be, as my aim is ultimately not to dictate conduct or offer silver bullets for enormously complex problems, but to enliven debate and advance ideas that others may develop further.

2

Of Sovereignty and Saints

If we gauge generosity by the size of philanthropic gifts, the past decade has been one of humankind's most generous periods. Some of the largest gifts have come from Facebook founder Mark Zuckerberg, who committed $100 million to Newark Public Schools in 2010; financier Steven A. Cohen, who pledged $250 million in 2016 to provide free mental health care for military veterans; entertainment mogul David Geffen, who gave $150 million to the Los Angeles County Museum of Art in 2017; and financier Raymond Dalio, who (along with his wife Barbara) offered $100 million to the State of Connecticut in 2019 to reduce poverty and improve education.

The public reception of these saintly acts follows a familiar script. A majority of commentators gape at and gush over the magnitude of the donors' magnanimity. Meanwhile, a minority of skeptics impugn the donors' motivations and deny that the money will achieve its intended aims. Neither of these reactions is entirely unreasonable. The individuals in question could have chosen to purchase luxury goods or top up their heirs' trust funds. That they chose instead to benefit others, some of whom are desperately underserved, does indeed deserve admiration. It's also worth asking, with the skeptics, whether gifts like these represent conflicts of interest. Since philanthropy often serves as a tool for whitewashing questionable behavior in a donor's career or personal life, observers should be cautious about assigning accolades too hastily. Given the complexities of the problems that some of these gifts are meant to address, and the vulnerability of some of their intended beneficiaries, it's also important to scrutinize the plans in place for spending the funds.

What common reactions to major philanthropic gifts share, however, is a reluctance to ask the deeper question that lurks beneath these debates. Few if any commentators openly question whether gifts like these have a legitimate place at all in a liberal democracy. Should these transactions be protected by law and encouraged by public policy and social norms?

To some, the question may at first sound bizarre. Acts of donation represent transfers of private property. The right to give property away is typically considered a central incident of ownership.[1] If property is mine to consume or exchange, how could it not also be mine to donate? But a moment's reflection reveals that limitations on property's donation are consistent with the institution of private ownership. No one would argue that donations to criminal enterprises should enjoy legal protection; few would support donations for malicious or harmful ends. Most people regard limitations on political donations as essential to protecting the integrity of the democratic process; most also accept limitations on donations within families as essential for protecting equality of opportunity. To question the justification of philanthropy, therefore, is neither to misunderstand nor to reject the justification of private property.

In what follows presently, I argue that philanthropic donations for some of the most laudable causes are in fact some of the hardest to justify. No matter how well-intentioned or effective, certain kinds of donations are objectionable from the standpoint of political morality. This is so because they undermine a key constituent of the democratic ideal, a notion I call democratic sovereignty. Democratic sovereignty holds that, to be fully legitimate, major social outcomes must issue from collectively authorized decisions. Certain forms of philanthropy violate this standard, privatizing decisions that properly belong to citizens collectively.

While this chapter reaches a generally negative conclusion, the chapter that follows complicates this picture by defending other aspects of the practice from skeptical challenges. Not only are certain aspects of philanthropy morally permissible, it argues: these aspects also deserve state subsidies.

The present chapter proceeds, in the next section, by introducing the concept of public goods and the question of who has the legitimate authority to provide them. Section II examines leading philosophical perspectives on the legitimacy of public goods provision, including utilitarian, republican, communitarian, and egalitarian treatments of the topic. While several of these views contribute key principles toward an account of public goods provision, I show how these principles are insufficient to justify and explain common intuitions about the exercise of power. Section III contends that the value of democracy supplies the missing puzzle piece. A core constituent of this value is collective self-determination, or what I call democratic sovereignty. Section IV argues that democratic sovereignty hems in the legitimate role of philanthropy by entitling citizens to collective control over certain public goods. Section V replies to some potential objections, while a concluding section distinguishes the account from recent alternatives and clarifies its practical consequences.

I. Public Goods, Private Funds

So-called *public goods* possess some peculiar qualities. While widely desired or desirable, these goods exhibit economic characteristics that prevent them from being produced adequately by ordinary market mechanisms.[2] The conventional wisdom in economic theory identifies these characteristics as *nonrivalry* and *nonexcludability*. A good is nonrival if one person's consumption of the good doesn't interfere with anyone else's ability to consume it also. Think of a fireworks display, which you can enjoy without diminishing the quantity or quality of the experience available to me. A good is nonexcludable if, once provided, it can't be withheld from those who haven't paid for it. Think of national defense. Once a society has established a system of national defense, tax evaders can still enjoy the benefits of national security without contributing to its production. Standard economic theory holds that markets fail to supply public goods efficiently. Nonrivalry makes a good difficult to price; nonexcludability makes payment collection difficult. These qualities render public goods unprofitable and thus irrational for profit-seekers to produce.

The observation that important public goods don't emerge spontaneously but require more complex forms of collective action has led many theorists to regard the provision of public goods as a central function of government. Indeed, for some schools of thought, such as the classical utilitarian tradition, the ability to provide public goods is what justifies the state in the first place.[3] Despite the importance of public goods for political theory, however, political theorists addressing the topic of public goods have tended to focus their attention on a limited number of related controversies. The philosophical literature on public goods has been almost singularly concerned with the question of when it's *permissible* for the state to provide public goods.[4] And, to be sure, this is an important question. Although many believe that the legitimacy of state power hinges on its being justifiable to each citizen, not all citizens stand to benefit from any particular public good. Or, even if all stand to benefit from the state's provision of a public good, some might benefit much more than others. Citizens may also disagree about the value of different public goods, or the optimal qualities and quantities of these goods. Any state-provided public good will all but inevitably involve taxing some citizens to subsidize the preferences of others. As Robert Nozick provocatively mused, is this not akin to forced labor?[5]

The current consensus in liberal theory holds that states are permitted to provide public goods under two broad conditions.

First, a state may provide public goods when doing so is a prudent way of facilitating conditions of background justice.[6] For instance, the protection of basic liberties, including expression, religion, conscience, association, and movement is generally regarded as a fundamental requirement of justice. Thus, the state is permitted to provide goods and services that protect these liberties from standard threats. A legal system, police, and national defense fall naturally into this category. Liberal theories also uphold a decent social minimum as one of justice's most basic requirements. This requirement can be defended as a prerequisite for equal citizenship, an implication of the justification for private property, and a matter of basic human rights.[7] Public goods that sustain a decent social minimum, such as emergency services, social insurance schemes, and basic education, are thus permissible for the state to provide. Liberal theorists disagree about whether justice requires provisions that go beyond a social minimum to protect against unfairness in the distribution of resources or to promote values of other kinds. But they do generally agree that the state can legitimately offer a wider range of public goods that satisfy an additional condition.

This second condition holds that the state may provide discretionary public goods (i.e., those goods not required by justice) if these goods are "presumptively beneficial" to most citizens.[8] This condition reflects the idea that many public goods not required directly by justice may nevertheless yield extensive benefits. Examples might include telecommunications infrastructure, certain investments in research and development, and cultural or leisure institutions like monuments or parks. The benefits of these goods may be so substantial, or so widely distributed, that virtually no citizen has grounds to object to the state's provision of them.

How best to determine whether a good is presumptively beneficial still presents some considerable challenges. Because people can reasonably disagree about theories of value, they can also

reasonably disagree about what makes a given public good beneficial.[9] And even those who share a theory of value may disagree
about whether a particular public good proposal satisfies the
requirements of that theory. So, arguments for state provision of
discretionary public goods still have some hurdles to overcome.

In any case, the narrow focus on the permissibility of state action
has left us ill-equipped to evaluate historical shifts in the landscape
of public goods provision. Indeed, the question of whether it's permissible for the state to provide public goods has greatest practical
relevance in a world in which the state is in fact heavily involved
in providing public goods. Much of the initial theoretical work on
public goods took place under such a condition, and this seems to
have steered the debate down a particular path. But a retreating
welfare state and rising inequality have conspired to change this
landscape, prompting some different questions. As the familiar
narrative goes, since the 1980s, governments in many high-
income countries have been withdrawing from and decentralizing
the provision of many public goods. Meanwhile, soaring wealth
among top income earners has made it possible for economic elites
to fill some of this void. This civic-mindedness isn't limited to the
wealthy, as many individuals of more modest means routinely contribute private funds to disaster relief efforts, booster campaigns,
and cultural initiatives. But the towering wealth and influence of
large donors, whose fortunes increasingly overshadow state and
municipal budgets, attract the most attention.

The private provision of public goods takes four principal
forms: (1) public financing with private administration; (2) private
financing with public administration; (3) private financing with
constrained public administration; and (4) private financing with
private administration.

In the first kind of case, the state raises the requisite funds but
outsources the administration of the goods in question to a private organization. This is in fact the dominant mechanism of
social service provision in the United States, where government

bodies provide grants and contracts to nonprofits to assist the poor and disadvantaged.[10] Such a practice raises many important issues, but most exceed the scope of this book's focus on private donation.[11]

In type-two cases, private donors provide funds to supplement or replace government outlays. The gifts in question aim to replenish depleted government budgets without influencing the direction of policy. In 2019, financier Raymond Dalio and his wife, Barbara, offered $100 million to the State of Connecticut to reduce poverty and improve education. The Dalios left existing policies on these matters untouched; they simply sought to fill a gap in funding. Think also of the trend among some rich persons toward sponsoring national monuments.[12] Like adopt-a-highway programs, these gifts seek to provide maintenance without dictating content or direction.

Cases of the third type involve donations to state agencies on the condition that officials promote the donors' policy objectives. In 2010, Mark Zuckerberg notoriously offered $100 million to Newark Public Schools, a distressed urban education system, on condition that the district embrace a slate of market-friendly reform proposals—tactics originally pioneered by the Gates and Broad foundations.[13]

However, of the cases that involve private financing, most common are the fourth type: philanthropic initiatives that bypass the state entirely, providing public goods directly to citizens without channeling resources through government agencies. Consider the 2016 pledge from financier Steven A. Cohen, who promised $250 million to provide free mental health care for military veterans. Consider also the 2017 gift from entertainment mogul David Geffen, who offered $150 million to the Los Angeles County Museum of Art (a private organization). These kinds of initiatives seek to provide a public benefit without relying on the state's administrative channels at all.

Proponents of these varieties of private provision may argue that relying on private solutions to public problems promises greater efficiency, better respects our liberty interests, and fosters aspects of individual virtue. Privately led initiatives are often nimbler and more innovative. They can harness the knowledge of successful entrepreneurs and deploy that knowledge creatively, short-circuiting the bottlenecks that clog up a government's administrative channels. Relying on donations rather than taxation also means relying less on the coercive power of the state. Since government coercion is presumptively objectionable, donative financing schemes would appear to offer superior protection to citizens' liberty interests. What's more, encouraging donors to make sacrifices to meet public needs promotes a virtue of beneficence or magnanimity—a valuable asset in any society.

For many people, however, examples of private provision may also trigger some unsettling intuitions. While we may applaud innovative and effective initiatives, we may also worry about the reliability or accountability of these efforts. Can such diffuse and episodic initiatives really meet their beneficiaries' needs reliably? How can beneficiaries contest adverse conditions when those conditions result from free gifts? And while we may be grateful for someone else picking up the tab, we may also think that certain goods are inherently public responsibilities to which all of us must contribute our fair share. Bailouts from billionaires seem to let governments and their citizens off the hook too easily. At the same time, we may also think that these intuitions only arise or intensify in some cases. Private financing of an art museum raises fewer hackles than private financing of public education. Donations that exploit recipients' financial vulnerability to impose the donors' policy preferences seem to invite stronger objections. How can a moral theory of public goods provision account for all of these considerations? The next section considers some answers from leading schools of thought in political philosophy.

Before proceeding further, however, I want to stave off some potential conceptual worries. Although initial work on this topic assumed a rigid distinction between public goods and private goods, further work has shown that almost none of the goods we commonly regard as public entirely fit the traditional criteria.[14] In practice, nonrivalry and nonexcludability manifest as scalar qualities, and the degree to which a good exhibits these qualities can also depend on background social conditions. We often think of museums as public goods, but museums can easily exclude nonpayers. We also think of welfare payments as public goods, but welfare payments are excludable by means-testing, and their rivalry depends on the scarcity of government revenue. Attempting to accommodate this variation, some scholars have suggested referring to the full spectrum of goods that cause market failure as "collective goods."[15] "Collective goods" include pure public goods as well as goods that exhibit nonrivalry or nonexcludability to more limited degrees. And it's the broader category of collective goods that I mean to discuss in this chapter, as all such goods are inadequately provided by markets and must be provided by taxes or donations if they are to be provided sufficiently. But because this term has yet to catch on, in what follows I continue to use the term "public goods," in the full recognition of its limitations.

Another conceptual challenge lies in the fact that some public goods lack any clear material substrate. Innovation, language, and social trust all meet the technical definition of a public good. A social norm of trustworthiness doesn't diminish when spread over greater numbers of people, nor can deviants be prevented from enjoying the general benefits of trust once this norm takes root in a society. Although virtues like social trust clearly depend in some distant way on the distribution of resources, they can't come about through discrete acts of *provision*. Rather, they tend to be byproducts of complex institutional conditions and social practices, which depend more or less equally on state and nonstate activity alike. Suffice it to say, here I'll only be discussing public goods with discrete material bases.

II. What's Wrong with a Free Gift?

The classical utilitarian argument for state provision of public goods sees the state as the technical solution to collective action problems. The incentive to free-ride makes it the case that, without coercion, essential public goods will go undersupplied. I know that as long as enough people contribute to raising an army, I can still enjoy the benefits of national defense without paying my share. But because many people reason this way, many also withhold payments and the army never gets raised at all. Forcing everyone to pay taxes solves this problem. Although this view traditionally regards the state as the default provider of public goods, as Eric Beerbohm observes, nothing in the view actually picks out the state for this role.[16] Since it values the state only for its technical capacity, the view is in principle just as friendly to private providers if and when they can find ways to overcome the collection action problem. Indeed, modern conditions have shown clearly that the prospect of coercion isn't always necessary to get various public goods up and running. Those with deep coffers and a modest sense of generosity, for instance, don't need to rely on the cooperation of others to fund the provision of public goods. So long as private providers can find ways to supply essential public goods at the proper level, the view implies that there should be no objection to allowing them to do so. Beerbohm challenges this implication. Even when private providers could or do succeed in providing an essential public good in an efficient manner, Beerbohm holds that an intuitive "moral remainder" often lingers. And I find this suggestion compelling. If a consortium of philanthropists banded together to provide a spectacular new military for the United States, we would sense that something was amiss. An attractive theory of the responsibility for providing public goods should be able to tell us what (if anything) explains this moral residue.

Perhaps some neorepublican resources can fill in the gap.[17] Neorepublicans argue that we have reason to object to private provision insofar as private providers stand in relationships of domination to recipients. Here, domination means the capacity to withdraw essentials goods and services at will. Since philanthropy is by definition voluntary, domination presents a standing worry for any scheme of private provision. But there are also ways of avoiding the domination complaint. As Beerbohm points out, a perpetual charitable trust can be designed to limit the discretion of those who administer its funds. If a private provider lacks the power to withdraw resources at will, recipients don't have a valid complaint against domination. Recent work also indicates that private provision can be reconciled with nondomination in a more general way. If there are many private providers that recipients can freely patronize, recipients can exit or preempt arbitrary exercises of power.[18] Furthermore, insofar as public agencies afford officials discretion over how and whom to serve, worries about domination aren't limited to private benefactors. Bureaucrats, especially those on the front lines, can be capricious, too.[19] In sum, neorepublicanism suggests that there's nothing in principle to object to about the private provision of public goods. Private provision will be objectionable when it's dominating, and only then.

Not everyone will be satisfied by this explanation. Imagine a scenario in which so many philanthropists are offering educational services in a community that the domination objection doesn't apply. Because students face numerous options and can enter and exit schools at will, they are not dominated by the caprices of the schools' funders. In response to such cases, some may worry that private provision changes or perverts the "social meaning" of certain public goods.[20] Students may not be dominated, but perhaps they will receive a qualitatively different form of education than they otherwise would. The community may come to view education as a commodity rather than a civic exercise, or a privilege rather than a right.

An account of privatization premised on associating public goods with specific social meanings faces some well-known challenges. First is the problem of identifying a singular social meaning, particularly in a pluralistic or polarized society, where there's widespread and (sometimes) reasonable disagreement about the point of education, welfare, military power, and everything else. How would we know the true social meaning when we see it? Second is the more general problem of cultural relativism. Social meanings are relativistic concepts: they depend entirely on the judgments of a community's members. But public opinion can be deeply misguided. If the social meaning of property in a given society involves property in human beings, does justice require slavery? Most of us will think that a view that makes space for this possibility can see itself out the door.[21]

Even if these challenges can be met, the communitarian argument can only get us so far. Offhand, it would seem that thoroughly transforming a good's social meaning can't occur without a wholesale transformation in the mechanism of a good's provision. A drop of privatization here or there won't fundamentally shift the public culture around a good. A social-meanings account might explain the wrong of total privatization, but it seems to exaggerate the worry if it rebukes privatization in limited form. Consider, for instance, cases like the Dalio donation, in which philanthropists shore up public school systems without demanding any change in curriculum. These cases don't change the social meaning of public schooling. And yet the sense of a moral remainder persists.

Beerbohm's proposed corrective appeals to the notion of agent-relative duties.[22] He argues that distributive justice is an agent-relative duty, one that applies to specific agents rather than serving as a general ideal that anyone and everyone ought to promote. Namely, it's the responsibility of citizens collectively to preserve justice, or fair terms of social cooperation, among themselves. We can see Beerbohm's point by way of a slimmed-down analogy. If I cause damage to your person or property, I and I alone owe you restitution. If a stranger offers to pay you back on my behalf, you might feel partially restored, but the stranger's beneficence can't entirely cancel out the wrong done. You would be justified in continuing to resent me. In this case, our intuitions suggest that justice "names" me as the obligation bearer, and Beerbohm believes that this naming function is an inherent property of justice. As with interpersonal morality, claims Beerbohm, so with political morality. If there are certain public goods that are required as a matter of justice, justice names the citizenry as their rightful providers. Since the state is the only entity that serves as our collective agent, this responsibility normally falls to the state. It's wrong to offload these responsibilities to private benefactors, no matter how generous or technically proficient they may be. Beerbohm calls this the "free-provider" objection to private provision, a designation that plays on the "free-rider" objection that motivates the classic account.

In my judgment, Beerbohm's free-provider argument can account for the moral limits of private provision in particular cases—cases in which private providers offer funds but defer decisions about spending to state officials. But this account fails to capture a distinctive objection to the more common phenomenon whereby private individuals bypass the state altogether. What's troubling about these cases is not, or not only, that we are prevented from discharging a shared obligation. Rather, many of these cases raise a unique kind of democratic objection, rooted in a concern for the way in which saintly generosity purchases sovereignty. By offering to finance a public good, philanthropists buy the authority to shape the content and distribution of that good. This grates against the sense that this authority belongs to all of us, equally. To see this, we'll need to consider why we have reason to care about democratic governance in the first place.

III. The Democratic Ideal and
Its Components

Democracy might be thought to comprise four values: collective self-determination, political equality, deliberative justification, and substantive reliability.[23] *Collective self-determination* (sometimes called "popular sovereignty") refers to the idea that the "makers" and "matter" of the laws, the rulers and the ruled, are one and the same. Democracy is valuable in part because it affords us a measure of control over our common affairs. Forms of authoritarianism—dictatorships, oligarchies, epistocracies, theocracies, and so on—serve as natural contrasts. *Political equality* refers to the idea that citizens ought to enjoy this control on equal terms. One interpretation of this is that citizens ought to enjoy equal opportunities to influence their common affairs. Equally weighted votes are an important mechanism for assuring this condition, though they are not necessarily sufficient. *Deliberative justification* refers to the idea that decisions must follow a process of reflective reason-giving rather than a simple tallying of exogenous preferences. Deliberation helps to protect against the possibility that outcomes will reflect ignorance or prejudice. That decisions can be defended with reference to sound arguments also enhances their justifiability to those who fall subject to them. Finally, *substantive reliability* is the idea that a system of government ought to generate high-quality outcomes over time. Democracy achieves this partly due to the epistemic properties of deliberation, which, in its best forms, can draw out the judgments that most closely track the truth.[24] Democracy also tends to generate high-quality outcomes because of the ways that it aggregates the wisdom of the multitude,[25] appoints competent officials through institutions of representation,[26] and reproduces itself stably over time.[27]

Recent work has had a lot to say about the distinctive value of political equality.[28] This literature has shown convincingly that deliberative justification and substantively good outcomes don't ultimately lie at the core of the democratic ideal. This isn't to say that deliberative justification and substantive reliability lack significant value. Rather, it's to say that these values travel with democracy only contingently. Nondemocratic forms of government could incorporate deliberative justification in various ways. A despot could consult deliberative bodies and offer good reasons for policies. And well-designed forms of authoritarianism could, in theory, produce outcomes that are substantively better than what democracy can generate. A true philosopher-king (or -queen) could very well deliver, and fairly distribute, everything we might want.

What makes political equality valuable, according to Niko Kolodny, is the necessary contribution it makes to relationships of social equality.[29] Political inequality inevitably creates or consecrates relationships of social hierarchy and subordination. This is most obvious when opportunities for political influence draw on ascriptive characteristics like caste, race, gender, nobility, or class. Such characteristics are entirely unreasonable grounds for distributing power, authority, or consideration. Consequently, coercive power that heeds these distinctions, or even simply turns a blind eye to them, reinforces unjust social asymmetries. But even in the absence of preexisting social asymmetries, the unequal distribution of political influence can work over time to create such asymmetries. Anointing a diverse group of wise individuals as overlords will very likely lead that group to enjoy a status of social superiority that solidifies and reproduces as time passes. The equal opportunities for political influence that democracy demands are thus necessary for restraining objectionable social hierarchies.

This account helps to explain what goes wrong in the type-three cases we considered earlier, where philanthropists seek to push their policy preferences on state bodies. In those cases, individuals are seeking to obtain greater consideration for their political preferences on the basis of their wealth—a paradigmatically antidemocratic practice, according to the social egalitarian view. But whether political inequality explains objections to more common cases that sidestep the state altogether is less clear. Objections to political inequality draw much of their strength from the fact that subjection to political decisions is nonvoluntary. A society can't achieve or maintain relations of social equality without ensuring equal opportunities for influence over coercively binding rules. Equality in this domain may not be sufficient for realizing social equality. But if the demands of political equality are to extend further than this, further distinctions are necessary to determine where exactly those demands stop. For democratic governance isn't necessarily a requirement of all domains of social life. In a society that governs itself democratically, why shouldn't citizens enjoy the liberty to form or join associations that run themselves by different processes?

Perhaps homing in on the value of collective self-determination can help us locate the boundaries of political equality's demands. Collective self-determination gets much less attention in contemporary democratic theory. More often it appears in discussions of international justice, serving to anchor arguments against foreign intervention or control.[30] Colonial rule, for instance, is objectionable in part because it violates a society's right to govern itself on its own terms. The objection remains even if the colonial power were to rule wisely and benevolently. Although the claim to exclude foreign intervention may be defeasible, the autonomy it seeks to protect can't be ignored. Recent work has suggested that this logic might also carry implications for the qualities of domestic governance.

According to Jake Zuehl, collective self-determination is valuable because it allows us to identify with our social world.[31] Even if a benevolent despot, a council of geniuses, or artificial intelligence could track justice's demands more reliably than democratic processes, we would have grounds for a strong objection. The objection is that such conditions prevent us from seeing ourselves in the decisions that affect our lives. We would feel like guests in a hotel room rather than residents of a home. The social world would confront us as other and alien. A central component of the value of democracy is that it puts us in charge of our society's design and development.

For Zuehl, members of a society can reasonably feel at home in their polity when their institutions are causally responsive to their will.[32] Controlling collectively doesn't require that each member gets their way over everything. That's impossible. Rather, collective control is satisfied simply by a well-functioning democratic process, one that incorporates representation and majority rule. We can reasonably see ourselves in collective decisions when we're bona fide participants in the process, even though the outcomes may sometimes depart from our preferences. And, to be self-determining doesn't require that members of a collectivity control each individual law and policy, or that they do so in the most direct way. What's essential is that citizens can give direction to, and effectively contest, the agents who govern. Thus, collective self-determination may be consistent with certain varieties of judicial review. Democratic control can also be filtered down a ladder of accountability in a series of principal–agent relationships. Perhaps there's some point at which that ladder becomes too long, or the connections between the rungs too tenuous. But the mere existence of mediating institutions isn't in itself an objectionable setback to our interest in collective self-determination.

IV. Control over What?

Collective self-determination thus helps to fill out what's distinctively valuable about democracy. In short, democratic governance is uniquely valuable because it affords all members of a community a measure of control over their common affairs, and it does so on the basis of equal say.

But accounting for the value of collective control still leaves underspecified who or what exactly we have an interest in controlling by way of our representative institutions. A natural thought—and indeed, perhaps the most common thought in the history of democratic theory—is that collective self-determination entitles us to control the machinery of government. Through our representatives or otherwise, we the people are to enjoy equal opportunities to exert control over formal laws and their enforcement, administrative policies and their funding, and at least certain aspects of the judiciary. As we'll see, however, this approach leaves something wanting. Collective control over the machinery of state is necessary but not sufficient for enjoying collective self-determination. Cases in which the machinery of state is underdeveloped, crippled, or constrained make this clear.

Imagine a small democratic society grappling with the consequences of a massive natural disaster. Foreign agencies, NGOs, and local elites rush to the rescue, assuming responsibility for healthcare, nutrition, rebuilding, and much else, too. Days stretch to months, and then to years. The democratically controlled government still maintains law and order, but its influence over other aspects of society remains very weak. We can suppose further that, in many respects, conditions in this society are now better than they were *before* the disaster. Economic and social indicators all show noticeable improvements. But it should be clear that residents of such a society would have reason not to let this situation drag on indefinitely and to insist, with all due respect, that their benefactors hand back the reins promptly. Though the residents of this society can effectively control their state, they can't collectively control most of their common affairs. They may take some comfort in the fact that conditions in their society are improving, but they'd also be justified in feeling alienated by these circumstances. The conditions of justice don't reflect their affirmative choices. The tendency of these conditions to reflect their preferences is at best a happy coincidence.

When social outcomes are good enough, why should we care if they don't bear the imprint of our conscious direction? One might protest that we don't have an interest in controlling things that already satisfy our substantive interests. To claim otherwise reflects the vice of the "control freak," the kind of person gripped by a compulsion to master all potential variables in their environment. But this objection misfires. As we saw before in the elaboration of the value of collective self-determination, it's hard to deny that it would be in one sense better for us to control the features of our world, at least those that matter most to us. We can't feel fully at home in our social world unless its features are responsive to our choices.

We must recognize, furthermore, that social choices have effects that go far beyond their distributive consequences. They inevitably give rise to ancillary practices that condition a society's culture. Think, for instance, of the esteem in which many British citizens hold their National Health Service, and the culture that surrounds this particular way of providing medical care. A well-managed system of private provision could arguably do just as well at generating decent health outcomes. But it would reflect different cultures in the workplace, different tenors in the doctor–patient relationship, and a different sense of national pride. When we choose, or omit to choose, alternative policies, we are also choosing or omitting to choose a cascade of remote effects. These effects may be only obliquely related to fundamental principles of justice, but they clearly matter in numerous other ways.[33]

This all goes to show that control over the machinery of state doesn't fully satisfy our interest in collective self-determination. There must be more to it. A more promising possibility is that we have an interest in controlling the "basic structure of society." One entry on the long list of John Rawls's contributions to political philosophy is the argument that principles of political morality apply to a society's major social and political institutions, those that exert a pervasive impact on our life prospects.[34] These institutions certainly include the formal machinery of the state, which comprises the constitution and system of government. But the basic structure extends further than this. Notably, we are not to take the property regime and design of markets as lying somehow outside of justice's purview. Rather, because property and its exchange will inevitably condition our life prospects, these institutions are necessarily subjects of justice.

The basic structure argument suggests that we have an interest in controlling these kinds of major social and political institutions. They should be sensitive to our collective decisions. But whether this response exhausts the moral remainder may depend on how we further characterize the basic structure. To treat this structure as a static list may lead us right into the same kind of problem we face in limiting the subject of collective self-determination to the machinery of state. Evolving societies breed new forms of power. Witness the creeping power of algorithms and computing platforms. Their influence over our lives grows by the day, transforming the ways we exchange goods and ideas. Technological infrastructure doesn't appear on any canonical list of basic structural institutions. Yet, a democratic society that failed to regulate these developments could easily and quickly come to find itself alienated from its social world. Citizens of such a society might still be able to modify the rate and direction of social investment, the public finance regime, property rights, and everything else we might ordinarily consider a major social institution. But characterizing the basic structure in static terms leaves us unable to account for historical changes that allow new forces to exert pervasive influence over our lives.

How, then, should we define the scope of the value of collective self-determination? I propose a more dynamic conception, inspired partly by Elizabeth Anderson's account of the value of civic equality.[35] Let *basic principles of justice* refer to the terms that underwrite free and equal citizenship. These principles define and distribute the rights, duties, and opportunities necessary for sustaining social cooperation and preventing relationships of oppression, domination, and subordination. Whether, why, and to what extent justice also contains more demanding principles are questions I deliberately set aside. I submit that a minimal criterion for the satisfaction of collective self-determination is shared control over the specification and administration of these basic principles of justice. Given the monumental importance of the interests these principles protect, it's essential that the ultimate authority for their protection lies with the bearers of those interests.

To summarize this idea with a slogan, we can say that democracy makes us *sovereign* over matters of basic justice. Democracy requires equal opportunity for political influence, and the scope of that influence extends at least to matters of basic justice. As discussed earlier, this influence needn't always be direct or absolute. But our interest in collective self-determination is frustrated in situations where the conditions of basic justice are authored by third parties. What goes wrong, then, in many cases of the private provision of public goods, is the fact that some other agent has assumed the power to select and interpret basic principles of justice, matters that should be up to us.

V. Objections and Replies

Let's take stock of the argument so far. We began by noting a particular class of goods that ordinary market exchange fails to provide. These public goods must either be provided by taxation or donation if they are to be provided at all. Does the identity of the provider matter? A long tradition of philosophical scholarship has sought to explain when the state might be permitted to engage in taxation and spending for these purposes and the risks that come along with this power. However, this tradition has largely failed to scrutinize the credentials of private agents to engage in similar behavior.

We encountered several arguments against leaving the provision of public goods to private benefactors. While these positions revealed various pertinent objections to private provision, they overlooked an important set of considerations related to the value of democracy. What makes democracy valuable, I argued, isn't only that it affords us equal opportunities for political influence, but that it makes us coauthors of major social conditions. Democracy requires that citizens enjoy sovereignty over the specification and administration of basic principles of justice. Outsourcing decisions about essential public goods to private agents is incompatible with democratic sovereignty.

One might wonder why democracy's sovereignty, as I've termed it, doesn't extend further than I've claimed. Why limit democracy's sovereignty to the basic properties of justice, and not, say, to a thicker notion of the common good? As I elaborate in the next chapter, a strong justification for the private provision of certain public goods lies in the fact of reasonable pluralism about questions of the good life. Citizens can reasonably disagree about a panoply of evaluative questions, including which religious traditions deserve allegiance, which forms of artistic expression or scientific innovation merit support, and which aspects of cultural heritage need preservation. If the state were to provide all discretionary public goods, it would struggle to do so in a way that reflected the diversity of reasonable preferences for public goods. Leaving public goods provision entirely up to majority vote would tend to satisfy only mainstream tastes, leaving those with alternative reasonable preferences in the lurch.[36] Delegating public goods provision to state officials would place officials in the difficult position of justifying their own judgments about public goods to a diverse polity.[37] Those goods that aren't essential to the project of justice are therefore fit for individuals and groups to provide of their own accord.

Some qualifications follow. First, to say that the private provision of discretionary public goods can be legitimate isn't to say that the state can't permissibly supply any discretionary public goods on its own, or that the state can't regulate the private provision of these goods. Although liberty interests may tell in favor of allowing democratic minorities to supply the public goods they find valuable, in some cases at least, the values of efficiency and fairness may tell in favor of a larger state role.

For instance, one might think at first that the state has no comparative advantage in funding works of art, and that these goods are precisely the kinds of things that should be left to private individuals and groups. But agencies like the National Endowment for the Arts provide an important counterweight to a system of private arts funding. A public agency may have greater resources than private entities that allow it to fund larger projects. More important, perhaps, is that a public endowment for the arts is bound to public norms for the distribution of funding. This helps to ensure that access to the arts isn't dominated entirely by a society's most advantaged members. Aside from providing goods directly, the state might also apply regulations to private provision to prevent corruption, inefficiency, discrimination, and domination.

Second, one might wonder why the ineliminable fact of reasonable pluralism doesn't also tell in favor of the private provision of justice goods. Surely, disagreement about the best conception of justice is widespread. Doesn't the logic of liberal neutrality also tell in favor of allowing private persons or groups to provide for their own conceptions of justice?[38] Previously, I argued that democratic sovereignty applies at least to basic principles of justice that maintain the terms of free and equal citizenship. This account leaves open whether justice's demands extend further, and whether political legitimacy requires that these demands be decided democratically. Consider luck-egalitarian conceptions of justice, which involve insuring individuals against unchosen misfortunes and make much more extensive claims on the distribution of resources. A society deeply fragmented over the nature and extent of these more demanding criteria might indeed have grounds to welcome private efforts to satisfy them. But disagreements about the essential elements of free and equal citizenship must ultimately be settled by law. Accommodating deep divisions about the reigning conception of basic justice requires systems of federalism that create separate jurisdictions or entirely separate polities that run themselves according to their own rules. In a single jurisdiction, however, we should think of basic justice as a natural monopoly good.

Finally, one might protest that this argument fails to appreciate the ways in which the private provision of public goods might represent a democratically authorized decision.[39] The prevalence of this phenomenon in places like the United States might be taken as evidence of a revealed popular preference. While the United States falls far short of meeting the demands of the democratic ideal, one might believe that conditions are democratic enough to permit citizens to limit the role of philanthropists in public life—if they truly desired to do so. This reasoning holds that the continued tolerance for this phenomenon shouldn't strike us as a violation of democratic sovereignty but rather an embodiment of that value.

Of course, one might respond by denying that the United States satisfies the conditions necessary to impute a popular will to these trends. Over the past several decades, political inequalities have arguably grown too extreme. But I think there's a more fundamental reason to reject this line of argument, a reason that may be familiar from discussions of voluntary slavery. A regard for liberty might seem to entail a right to alienate our own liberty by selling ourselves into slavery. Most people, of course, find this implication thoroughly disturbing. The typical justification for limiting or outlawing these kinds of contracts is that ongoing control of our lives is a precondition for enjoying liberty itself.[40] Advocating voluntary slavery on grounds of liberty reflects a fundamental misunderstanding of that value. Something similar, I think, is true of democratic sovereignty. While we might authorize private agents to administer the provision of essential public goods in light of our wishes, ongoing control over the terms of authorization is inalienable. Ceding control to the wishes of others is incompatible with the value of democratic sovereignty itself.

VI. Conclusion

It pays to demonstrate how this account of democracy's sovereignty departs from a few other ways of objecting to the private provision of public goods. Emma Saunders-Hastings has drawn attention to the fact that private providers of public goods often enjoy, and take advantage of, opportunities to exert paternalistic control over the recipients of these goods.[41] Among equal moral persons, paternalism is presumptively objectionable. Those who wish to defend policies with paternalistic qualities must ordinarily show how the evils of denying beneficiaries' autonomy can be undercut or outweighed. Perhaps the moral remainder we observe in the private provision of essential public goods can be cashed out in terms of paternalism. I believe, however, that paternalism constitutes an independent concern.

In cases of paternalism, the objection lies exclusively within the relationship between the provider and the recipient. For instance, we rightly take concern with employers who demand that their employees adopt specific diets or exercise regimens as a condition of receiving fringe benefits. Or we worry about religiously inspired charities demanding displays of religious devotion from vulnerable populations in exchange for food or shelter. We object here from the standpoint of the recipient. In cases of nondemocratic sovereignty, meanwhile, the objection extends to the general community of persons who aren't themselves providers or recipients. We object to the blocked opportunity to administer conditions of justice, whether or not we stand to benefit directly from the policies in question. We object, for instance, to a foundation that controls education or health policy in a particular area—despite the fact that we may be bystanders rather than students, parents, or patients. Instead, we object as citizens.

Another possibility is that democratic sovereignty is merely a semantic variation of the time-honored principle of *quod omnes tangit, debet ab omnibus approbari* ("what touches all must be approved by all").[42] This principle has recently come to be known by English speakers as the principle of all-affected interests (AAI). In its bare form, it states that all individuals whose interests are affected by a decision ought to enjoy opportunities for influencing that decision. The AAI comes in numerous varieties, depending on how we construe "interests" and what it means to have one's interests "affected." Do the interests in question concern merely our self-regarding interests (interests in having our own lives go well) or also our moral interests (interests in satisfying our duties with respect to others)? Am I affected by a decision when the decision actually affects me, or also when it fails to have any impact on me but otherwise could have done so?[43]

There are clearly some similarities between democratic sovereignty and the AAI. Perhaps we can understand democratic sovereignty as fleshing out the "interest" dimension of the AAI. Democratic sovereignty claims that the relevant interests are interests in matters of basic justice. That is, decisions that involve matters of basic justice must give all persons affected by those questions opportunities for influencing them—whether or not those decisions are coercively imposed.[44] But democratic sovereignty has nothing to say about the metaphysics of affecting.

In closing, I wish to note some important limitations of the argument for democratic sovereignty. The argument applies only to a central range of cases, namely those where the provider in question assumes the authority to make decisions about the quantity or quality of relevant public goods. The argument doesn't apply to cases in which the private party merely provides supplemental funding to a public provider—at least insofar as this funding comes without strings attached. If we object to cases of supplemental private funding, those objections are likely best accounted for by Beerbohm's free-provider argument.

More important, perhaps, is that the argument has relatively little to say about the government outsourcing of public goods and services. If a duly constituted democratic state opts to contract out the administration of certain goods, such policies don't necessarily frustrate the opportunity for popular control. These situations occur, for instance, when a state supplies grants to nonprofit organizations to provide various goods and services. We might worry about the extent to which these kinds of outsourcing agreements maintain clear chains of accountability. Perhaps state agencies possess certain structural features that tend to make them more sensitive to collective self-determination. But, for the most part, these are contingent empirical questions that can't be answered in advance by conceptual or moral argument.[45]

This isn't to say that such cases may not be objectionable for other reasons.[46] We might think, for instance, that contracts with profit-seeking providers in matters of incarceration raise distinctive worries, due to the conflict of interest between the profit motive and the aims of incarceration.[47] But there are also many cases in which outsourcing policies seem to raise no objections of deep principle, and the democratic sovereignty argument helps to explain why this is so. We may think that every citizen is entitled to essential medical care as a matter of justice. But do we have strong reasons for thinking that this care should be provided exclusively by public hospitals? Why not provide this care indirectly by furnishing citizens with insurance that they can then use to purchase medical care in a market? In such a case, the decisions to offer and implement the relevant insurance scheme, along with decisions about the regulation of the healthcare market, ought to respect the principle of democratic sovereignty. Beyond this, it's difficult to identify a principled case against such mechanisms of welfare provision.

The main consequence of this view for a theory of public goods is that the state isn't simply *permitted* to supply certain public goods— it's positively *required* to provide public goods that are instruments of basic justice and to discourage alternative forms of provision. From this perspective, what goes wrong when private benefactors provide these goods isn't always that citizens are underserved, exposed to domination, served in the wrong way, or prevented from contributing their fair share to the project of justice. Rather, what goes wrong in many cases is that citizens are deprived of the equal opportunity for influence over matters that affect their most basic interests.

In practice, the view implies that a state is required to furnish not only the standard list of public goods like national defense, a legal system, and public health measures, but also goods directly related to the provision of a decent social minimum, such as basic education, health insurance, legal insurance, and unemployment insurance. A society that relies on private initiatives to produce and distribute these essential goods fails to treat its subjects as citizens and fails to treat its citizens as equals. This failure is possible even in societies that honor other democratic criteria, such as free and fair elections and majority rule. The argument implies that the private provision of public goods is unobjectionable only insofar as those goods are supplemental. Either they are supplemental alternatives to robust public options, or they address matters that are distant from those of basic justice. Festivals, museums, literary magazines, space exploration, and research into rare medical conditions, therefore, are all items fit for private provision.

Another important implication is that the argument applies to all sources of philanthropy—not only philanthropy by the superrich. While I've often illustrated the argument with examples of superrich individuals, the private provision of essential public goods is no less objectionable when it draws support from the pooled donations of less wealthy persons. Any agent or group that lacks the possibility of universal membership necessarily undermines democratic sovereignty if it controls decisions about essential public goods. The objection will be weaker if a large number of individuals pool their resources to provide a collective good in their own community.[48] But the objection will be just as strong if those same individuals seek to provide a collective good in some other community.

Finally, it's crucial to note that democratic sovereignty's value isn't absolute; precisely how to account for it will often depend on contextual judgments.[49] In situations where the state is unwilling or unable to provide essential justice goods, temporary assistance from private benefactors may be absolutely vital. In other scenarios, short-term sacrifices may be necessary to ensure the long-term realization or stability of democratic sovereignty. Democratic sovereignty shares this practical indeterminacy with other constituents of the democratic ideal. When judging the legitimacy of a law, defects in the deliberative process won't necessarily provide us with sufficient grounds to disobey that law. We will want to consider other qualities of the process, as well as independent reasons that count in favor of the law. But an account of the value of deliberation nonetheless supplies us with an essential consideration to weigh in deciding how to react to such a situation, as well as a target for institutional reform. The same is true of democratic sovereignty. How exactly to account for the value of democracy in policy and practice is a theme to which we'll return in subsequent chapters. For now, what's important is that democratic sovereignty provides us with a key ingredient in the moral evaluation of acts of private philanthropy and a regulative ideal toward which to strive.

3

A Farewell to Alms

In a property-owning society, we tend to agree at least that individuals should be generally free to give their property away. When it comes to various uses to which we might put our assets, the ability to donate them to others is a distinctly valuable option. This is most obvious in the case of interpersonal gift-giving, which facilitates our ability to perform favors and show concern for friends and family. In their impersonal variety, gratuitous transfers also enable us to sponsor agencies that respond to the needs of strangers or express our conceptions of the common good.

Appreciating the value of making donations doesn't entail that a society must enforce or protect donations for all possible ends, or in all possible forms. The previous chapter argued that donations for a particular class of goods—essential public goods—sit uneasily with the political morality of a democratic polity. The question I consider presently addresses an issue from the opposite direction: whether such a polity ought to provide affirmative support for citizens' donative decisions. That is, under what conditions, if any, are we justified in using public resources to promote private gift-giving?

This question becomes more pressing when we realize that many contemporary societies do in fact sponsor private philanthropy in significant ways. Typically, the state provides public subsidies to citizens' gratuitous pursuits when the intermediaries of donation satisfy the legal definition of "charity."[1] The contours of this definition vary across jurisdictions, but the core remains the same. Most societies consider a donation charitable if it both (1) benefits an "indefinite number" of persons (the "public benefit" test) and (2) doesn't return a profit to any private shareholder (the "nondistribution constraint").[2] Donations to entities that satisfy these criteria will ordinarily qualify for public subsidy. Primary modes of administering subsidies include tax deductions (in the United States and Australia), tax credits (in Canada and New Zealand), and matching grants (in the United Kingdom). These differences notwithstanding, policies for subsidizing philanthropic giving share certain essential features: each makes public subsidies available to a wide range of purposes; they do so without any attempt to prioritize some purposes ahead of others; and the level and direction of subsidies depend entirely on citizens' individual choices.

This policy treatment of impersonal gratuitous transfers raises numerous principled questions. Without questioning its justification or wider consequences, some point out that several versions of this policy tend to advantage high-income earners disproportionately, raising a problem of tax equity.[3] For instance, American low- and middle-income taxpayers face strong incentives against using the charitable tax deduction at all—unless their donations are larger than the "standard deduction" (currently $12,550 for individuals). Both Canada and the United Kingdom increase the value of the subsidy if the donor is in the top tax bracket, raising similar concerns about fairness.[4] I argue in Chapter 4 that criticism on grounds of tax equity doesn't go far enough. A more fundamental problem with these policies is that they augment the power of wealthier citizens to control social outcomes by determining the rate and direction of charitable investment. In what follows here, however, I consider a question that lies further upstream: what might justify subsidizing philanthropy in the first place?

Scholars and laypersons alike often claim that if the state is to subsidize charitable giving, it ought to do so specifically for the purpose of relieving poverty. A number of considerations lend support to an *eleemosynary* ("alms-dispensing") rationale for donative subsidies. To lack access to the means of a minimally decent life is a cruel fate anywhere, and it's especially cruel in societies that are relatively affluent overall. Nonetheless, sizable portions of the population in many affluent societies live below the poverty line.[5] In these same societies, large numbers of people are comfortable enough to be in the position to give money away. Many of the other causes that they might support—amateur sports leagues, the performing arts, Philosophy Bites podcasts—reflect no particular moral urgency. It can therefore seem disturbing for the state to support leisure pursuits and high culture precisely at the same rate that it subsidizes donations to necessities like homeless shelters and Meals on Wheels.

The sense of indignation only becomes more palpable when we confront statistics about this policy's effects. Less than one-third of tax-privileged charitable donations in the United States have any discernible redistributive consequence.[6] The majority of these donations support churches, public interest groups, educational institutions, and cultural organizations.[7] Nor is the nonredistributive character of philanthropy a singularly American phenomenon. Troubled by similar statistics in the United Kingdom, the UK High Court has tried to push back, holding that subsidized philanthropic organizations must not exclude disadvantaged populations from their benefits.[8] For instance, to be eligible for state subsidies, a music hall might need to reserve a portion of seats at each performance for low-income patrons. But if we believe that state-subsidized philanthropy ought primarily to serve the poor, provisions to prevent the least advantaged from being excluded from the benefits of philanthropy amount to superficial concessions.

In what follows, I contend that, contrary to its appearance, the failure of current policy to prioritize the claims of need isn't unjust. It might be misguided in numerous ways, but its indifference to poverty isn't one of them. This isn't because the claims of the poorest citizens lack strong foundations. Nothing could be further from the truth. Rather, it's because the nature of those claims demands an entirely different kind of collective response. Meanwhile, as I show, a democratic society has strong independent reasons to subsidize philanthropic pursuits in a way that respects citizens' diverse judgments of value.

The chapter proceeds, in Section I, by further exploring recent normative arguments for what I call the *eleemosynary rationale* for subsidizing philanthropy. Section II contends that the view of justice that underpins these arguments doesn't support a role for donations in meeting claims of need. A right to a decent social minimum is a basic component of any plausible view of social justice. But a policy that made part of the finance of this minimum voluntary and discretionary would be self-defeating. It could not reliably effect the required transfer of resources. Separately, it would subject the least advantaged to forms of control and subordination that are particularly odious among equal citizens. Moreover, as Section III shows, subsidizing a plurality of voluntary pursuits has at least three plausible rationales. Subsidies assist individuals with minority preferences in overcoming collective action problems in the production of certain kinds of goods. They help to expand the range of valuable options available to citizens generally. And they facilitate a diverse and vibrant associational life that underwrites a well-functioning democratic order. Section IV concludes with a cautionary note about endorsing the eleemosynary rationale as a pragmatic compromise under nonideal conditions.

I. The Eleemosynary Rationale for Subsidizing Philanthropic Giving

Several theorists of political morality doubt whether a subsidy policy that ignores claims of need can be justified.[9] As Rob Reich has written, "the philanthropic sector in modern society is justified at least in part because of its redistributive or eleemosynary aims."[10] This eleemosynary focus is warranted, in Reich's view, in part because the conventional meanings of the terms "charity" and "philanthropy" refer to assisting the vulnerable.[11] Common usage distinctly associates these terms with caring for the least advantaged. Besides the words we use to describe it, Reich notes that the historical role of the practice has often taken a redistributive shape. The origins of the philanthropic sector lie in the practice of almsgiving, which began in churches but gradually evolved into a secular form. Reich takes these facts as evidence of a principled justification. It would be surprising if our inherited understanding of the practice of charity was wildly out of step with the demands of justice.

Miranda Fleischer proposes that we apply principles of distributive justice directly to policies toward philanthropy.[12] Because state support for philanthropy triggers distributional consequences, she believes that this support must be defended in light of a theory of distributive justice. Though she endorses no particular theory, she explores how we might apply subsidies to charitable organizations based on their contributions to a utilitarian welfare function, or their value within a scheme that promotes capabilities thresholds, or their tendency to maximize the economic position of the least well-off in accordance with Rawls's difference principle. She believes that this exercise is the first step in properly identifying the regulative ideals of policy toward philanthropy.

Writing with particular reference to the policy of deducting charitable contributions from one's income tax, Liam Murphy and Thomas Nagel note, "The word charity suggests that this deduction is a means of decentralizing the process by which a community discharges its collective responsibility to alleviate the worst aspects of life at the bottom of the socioeconomic ladder."[13] But the justification for such a policy isn't merely verbal, in their view. "Since there is disagreement about what the exact nature of that responsibility is," they continue, "and about which are the most efficient agencies, it is arguably a good idea for the state to subsidize individuals' contributions to agencies of their choice rather than itself making all the decisions about the use of public funds for this purpose."[14] Because, in effect, the current policy doesn't satisfy this collective responsibility to the least advantaged, Murphy and Nagel regard its justification as questionable.[15]

Upon further analysis, I submit that none of these arguments provides a strong case for the eleemosynary rationale. Though we might take some counsel in the observations that the common dictionary definition of charity and the historical role of charitable enterprise both point toward special concern for the least advantaged, whether or how these facts generate normative implications is at best unclear. The words we use in common speech have ambiguous definitions and messy genealogies. Often our moral convictions advance more swiftly than developments in language. It wouldn't be too surprising if the current common meaning of charity reflects crude evaluative notions or makes sense only in the context of a primitive sociology.[16]

Unfortunately, the claim that the historical role of charity constrains the contemporary role of charity fares no better in this regard. Whether and to what extent history can serve as a source of moral authority is itself a contentious question. But even if we accept the premise, we face the problem that the historical role of charity isn't singular: it has varied considerably across time and place, and rarely without controversy. In ancient Rome, philanthropy traditionally focused on gifts to the city and its citizens, rather than the poor as such. According to one prominent historian, the norm of almsgiving only emerged as a result of a divisive political campaign of the early Church.[17] By proclaiming itself steward of the poor and demanding donations in their name, the Church was able to extract rents and consolidate its own power in relation to the declining empire. This account suggests that looking to history for advice on charity policy may raise more questions than it answers.

Fleischer's claim that public policy toward philanthropy must be defended in light of the demands of distributive justice invites no objection, especially when the choice of the particular theory is left open.[18] But it remains to be explained how exactly distributive considerations bear on this domain. For theories of distributive justice needn't hold that principles of justice must be applied directly to each individual policy. In many cases, applying a general principle to an individual act or policy works against that principle's aims. Few utilitarians, for instance, would claim that criminal punishments should be doled out directly according to their tendency to maximize utility. This might require putting less socially useful persons in jail, while letting highly useful murderers go free. A utilitarian is more likely to say that we should apply a principle of utility with regard to the wider institution, or set of institutions, rather than to each policy falling under it.[19] The set of institutions that maximizes utility most likely requires particular policies that take no direct concern with utility at all. This example indicates that a conclusion in favor of an abstract principle of justice generally underdetermines the conditions of its application. With this in mind, we should be wary of oversimplifying the translation from principles of justice to policies regarding charitable giving.

Recall Murphy and Nagel's alternative proposed justification, that support for charitable enterprise can be justified as a way of discharging the collective responsibility to the least advantaged under conditions of disagreement about the nature of that responsibility.[20] Their statement suggests the principle that decentralization is the legitimate policy response to conditions of disagreement. Such a principle is hard to square with Murphy and Nagel's overall view of taxation, in which this discussion of charitable subsidies takes place. When it comes to taxation, disagreement is hardly limited to duties to the least well-off. Citizens disagree profoundly about the purposes of taxation, how to implement it fairly and effectively, and everything in between. In spite of this, Murphy and Nagel don't consider decentralizing other decisions about public finance and administration. Indeed, their general argument mounts a spirited defense of liberal egalitarianism and a particular way of institutionalizing it. If there is something special about the disagreement that surrounds poverty, the authors give no indication as to what that might be.

The eleemosynary critique nevertheless contains some valuable observations. It rightly acknowledges that better-off citizens have a collective duty toward their less well-off compatriots. It also recognizes accurately that most societies woefully fail to appreciate or discharge this duty to the extent that justice requires. In my view, the critique's mistake is to see policies toward philanthropic donations as a fitting response.

II. Voluntariness, Discretion, and the Social Minimum

Part of what makes this general line of criticism philosophically interesting is that it issues from scholars who appear to share a broadly liberal-democratic view of distributive justice. A basic tenet of such a view is that individuals have a right to the material conditions of a minimally autonomous life. Encouraging individuals to respond to circumstances of disadvantage in a voluntary and discretionary way seems more at home in rival philosophical perspectives, perspectives that don't consider poverty a matter governed by justice.[21] For instance, in its most prominent version, libertarianism denies that individuals are entitled to a social minimum.[22] This is because it considers justice to be a function of respecting natural rights to property. Attempts to require property owners to compensate victims of misfortune would seize from them what is rightly theirs. If this is so, responding to suffering or disadvantage can only take the form of an exercise of personal liberty.

By contrast, a liberal-democratic view regards individuals as free and equal citizens, to whom a society's major institutional arrangements must be justified. The prevalence and magnitude of poverty is, if not entirely a consequence of institutional arrangements, overwhelmingly sensitive to those arrangements.

Institutional choices determine the way a society assigns ownership over resources, the way it rewards contributions to social production, the way it makes scarce opportunities available, and the way it insures against misfortune. A determination not to regulate institutions is no less an intentional social decision than an affirmative state program. Those who are directly subject to these institutional arrangements are entitled to a justification of their distributional consequences. As Jeremy Waldron stresses, in the absence of a compelling justification, subjects of social institutions lack sufficient reason to abide by the outcomes of these arrangements, particularly when those outcomes inhibit satisfaction of their most basic needs.[23] The level and specification of the social minimum is a matter of particular urgency, as it protects some of citizens' most vital interests. John Rawls notably treats the establishment of a social minimum as a "constitutional essential," a status that he withholds from more expansive distributive demands covering access to desirable positions and the range of inequalities.[24] He notes that securing a social minimum is an essential demand in a liberal democracy because without certain guarantees individuals can't participate in society as citizens at all. As many others have stressed, formal protections of liberties such as freedom of speech and association offer negligible value to someone who is seriously ill, starving, homeless, or at significant risk of facing such conditions.[25]

Thus, from a liberal-democratic perspective, the eleemosynary rationale for charitable subsidies appears contradictory. On the one hand, by emphasizing the claims of the least fortunate, it acknowledges the special urgency of assuring a social minimum. On the other hand, it suggests that duties to the least well-off are unenforceable and discretionary.

To be sure, a liberal-democratic picture contains much room for debate about the nature of the social minimum and how best to administer it. For instance, should the social minimum be set at a threshold of sufficiency, or should it be maximized in accordance with a difference principle?[26] Another challenge concerns whether the minimum should insure against all possible causes of deprivation, even when they are the result of irresponsible behavior.[27] An undifferentiated policy risks the possibility that able-bodied citizens may take excessive risks or refuse to contribute to the social product. A further challenge pertains to whether the minimum ought to accommodate the fact that persons require different amounts of resources in order to achieve the same level of functioning.[28] That is, we might suppose at first that the fairest standard would entitle each person to an equal share of an index of social resources. But it soon becomes apparent that the same package of resources buys radically different outcomes depending on a person's handicaps and abilities. The dilemma hardens when we realize how demanding it might be to raise all individuals to the same level of functioning. For instance, applying the difference principle to persons with severe disabilities appears to require able-bodied persons to make unlimited sacrifices.[29]

Perhaps Murphy and Nagel have these kinds of challenges in mind when they advocate decentralizing the collective duty to the very least-advantaged members of society. Clearly, resolving these challenges at an abstract level isn't an easy task. Designing policies to reflect the chosen principles also requires complicated empirical assessments regarding likely effects of various alternative packages. But I think it would be a serious mistake to infer simply from the complexity of the issues that the solution must lie in philanthropy. It would be mistaken for at least three reasons, which I stipulate presently and elaborate in what follows. First, outsourcing the definition of the social minimum would be self-defeating, as it would make the satisfaction of subsistence rights unverifiable and unenforceable. Second, whatever justice requires of the social minimum, voluntary and discretionary donations are an unreliable mechanism of administration. Third, making citizens dependent on largesse subjects them to forms of treatment that stand in marked tension with democracy's presumption of equal citizenship.

With the first mistake in mind, note that delegating a social decision to individual discretion is appropriate in a variety of circumstances. Chief among these is when the value of the decision lacks an independent standard: the goodness or justice of an outcome depends primarily on the particular preferences of those affected by it. The value of a new stadium might be "choice-sensitive" in this way, as it depends largely on how many citizens desire this option and plan to take advantage of it.[30] By contrast, the value of "choice-insensitive" issues reflects independent standards, not individual preferences. Certain matters of justice, at least when it comes to fundamental rights, duties, and opportunities, are choice-insensitive. The wrongness of murder doesn't depend on individual preferences. It's wrong regardless of how many people approve of it. Notice that precisely what constitutes murder and precisely why it's wrong might admit reasonable debate. But controversies regarding the specification of the principle wouldn't lead us to conclude straightaway that rights and duties in this area are matters of personal discretion. A large part of the explanation for this would be that a society needs settled, public standards of justice in order to verify and enforce their satisfaction. Within a single jurisdiction, a person can't be both guilty and not guilty of a crime; a victim of mistreatment can't be simultaneously wronged and not wronged. The same things are true of the social minimum. As we saw before, the assurance of a social minimum is one of a society's most solemn duties. It is a constitutional essential that protects the very possibility of citizenship. A guaranteed social minimum is the price a society pays for private property: if subsistence rights are not enforced, the dispossessed lack reason to respect others' claims to property. Without a common standard, there is simply no way to determine whether these rights are satisfied, either in general or in any individual case. While there might be room for principled debate and policy experimentation, therefore, outsourcing the definition of the social minimum itself isn't an option.

We should also recognize that, whatever one takes the social minimum to be, delegating the finance and administration of that principle to voluntary and discretionary donations would be an entirely unreliable way of satisfying it.[31] Focus first on the fact that a donative system allows individual citizens to determine the *amount* of their contribution to the satisfaction of the basic minimum. With each choosing their level of contribution (including no contribution), it's doubtful that the amount of resources transferred would consistently resemble what the minimum requires.[32] Next consider the fact that a donation-based system allows individual citizens also to determine the *direction* of their contributions toward the social minimum, with each choosing based on their own assessment of where needs lie. Without centralized coordination, it's difficult to imagine that contributions will spontaneously reach each person in need in proportion to their legitimate claims. (Indeed, evidence suggests that donations tend to be biased toward novel problems and in service of persons most similar to the donors themselves.)[33] Consider also that such a system encourages individual citizens to determine the *currency* of their transfers to the least advantaged— i.e., whether to assist others with cash or with some in-kind good or service. Donors, however, aren't generally in a position to understand the particular interests of strangers they may wish to assist or the strategies that are most sensitive to those interests. Their judgments of means will often diverge from the judgments of experts or of recipients themselves. In short, however we set the social minimum, a system of voluntary and discretionary financing offers little confidence that the amount, direction, or currency of transfers will correspond to the targets specified by that minimum.

Against these odds, let us suppose for the moment that some kind of voluntary scheme did in fact prove relatively efficient at effecting the requisite degrees of transfer, in the right directions, and in the most appropriate currencies.[34] Even if it could do this, recipients within this scheme would still have grounds for a strong objection, which is that such a system consecrates asymmetries of power and status between citizens of different fortunes. Because the scheme is voluntary, receipt of critical benefits partially depends on the goodwill of better-off citizens. The wealthy can withdraw these benefits if they please. To guard against this, beneficiaries of donations face pressure to ingratiate themselves to the wealthy, by genuflecting, flattering, and dissimulating. Criticizing or contesting the decisions of the wealthy risks cutting off the flow of benefits. This places the better-off in a position of domination with regard to persons in need.[35] Relatedly, because the scheme allows donors discretion over the direction and currency of their donations, it effectively places recipients on trial, subject to invasive investigations of their conditions. It forces the unfortunate to plead their case to wealthy benefactors, who sit in judgment of their honesty and worthiness. This casts recipients in an arbitrary position of social inferiority.[36] These kinds of asymmetries of power and status are objectionable in many circumstances. But they are especially objectionable among citizens of a democracy, where no one is assumed to be inherently worthier of consideration or wiser in judgment. Thus, even if satisfying the social minimum on the basis of voluntary and discretionary transfers somehow proved to be an efficient strategy, it would subject victims of misfortune to forms of control and hierarchy that have no place among free and equal citizens.

A few essential qualifications are in order. First, one might agree that attempting to assure the social minimum *entirely* through subsidized donations would be unacceptable but nonetheless contend that donations could work to supplement other strategies. Supplementation might serve as a hedge against predictable state failures and intractable disagreement about borderline cases. Consider that voters and officials are far from infallible. Statutory definitions of the social minimum may prove less than fully reasonable; strategies for administering it may fall short. Subsidizing donations to eleemosynary charities might serve as a prudent stopgap measure, an insurance device against the realities of state failure. While I've argued against appealing to reasonable pluralism about justice as a justification for outsourcing the definition and satisfaction of the social minimum, I acknowledge that disagreement about the borders of such a minimum may sometimes prove intractable—particularly when it comes to the definition and treatment of medical conditions. Some degree of outsourcing might be warranted to handle abiding disagreement about opioid maintenance therapy, cosmetic procedures, abortion, sex reassignment surgery, and other highly sensitive issues. These considerations indicate why it would be mistaken to *exclude* eleemosynary concerns from the stable of subsidized aims. But they certainly don't support the claim that such concerns demand a privileged or exclusive status.

A second qualification is that the case against decentralized financing of the social minimum doesn't necessarily affect the case for decentralized administration of social services. State-run service provision faces a number of well-known criticisms. For instance, it lacks the incentives to run efficiently or creatively: it offers rigid, cumbersome solutions that are insensitive to local contexts. Separately, state programs are often no better (and sometimes worse) at treating recipients as equal citizens. Means-tested programs may corrode the self-respect of their beneficiaries.[37] Recipients may be dominated by front-line bureaucrats who enjoy discretion over who can receive benefits.[38] Those persuaded by these criticisms may argue that the provision of the social minimum shouldn't occur primarily through direct state services, but rather through a variety of decentralized mechanisms. But it would be a mistake to presume, in turn, that decentralized provision also requires voluntary donation. These two aspects of a social minimum policy aren't intrinsically connected. For instance, publicly financed basic income or publicly subsidized insurance can enable recipients to purchase needed goods and services on the market. Offering state contracts to private organizations to provide certain services in-kind can work to introduce certain incentives and harness the knowledge of local practitioners. Both practices decentralize the provision for basic needs without also decentralizing responsibility for their finance.

III. Alternative Subsidy Rationales

The previous section challenged the common thought that the point of subsidizing donations is to underwrite a just social minimum. Later on, I consider whether greater public support for eleemosynary donations might offer a pragmatic compromise in the event of certain nonideal conditions. In this section, I seek to show how alternative justifications for subsidizing citizens' philanthropic donations might illuminate current policy in a warmer hue.

Further reflection reveals three potential justifications for general state support for charitable enterprise that have little to do with poverty and inequality. The first is that indirect subsidies overcome a limitation of majoritarian decision-making with respect to a certain category of goods. The second is that general subsidies allow the state to support a flourishing culture in a way that's sensitive to reasonable disagreement about evaluative questions. The third is that subsidies of this type promote public deliberation and the stability of a democratic order.

A. Fair Provision of Collective Goods

As we saw in the previous chapter, economists have long noted that certain types of economic goods exhibit some peculiar qualities.[39] Though the good may be highly desirable, or desired by many people, ordinary market mechanisms fail to provide it in proportion to effective demand. One class of such goods is "public goods." In the classic case, a good is "public" if it possesses the qualities of nonrivalry and nonexcludability. A good is nonrival if one person's consumption of it doesn't diminish its availability for consumption by others. A good is nonexcludable if nonpayers can't be prevented from consuming the good. A lighthouse is the paradigmatic example. "Merit goods" provide another cause of market failure.[40] Here, the idea is that consumers may desire or otherwise "merit" a certain good but be unable to pay the market rate. Museums are a case in point. Museums can exclude visitors and thus charge fees for entrance. But a museum that tried to subsist on fees alone would either need to charge exorbitant ticket prices, such that only the wealthiest consumers could afford to enter, or else provide cut-rate exhibits in order to keep ticket prices affordable. As in the case of lighthouses, profit-seeking firms will not generally find it worthwhile to erect and operate high-quality museums. Those who desire such goods must turn to alternative, nonmarket mechanisms for providing them. That is, they must either enlist the state to contribute public funds or convince individuals to contribute private donations.

Though many still use the term "public goods" to refer to both types of goods, some economists now prefer the umbrella term "collective goods."[41] The terminological shift helps to accommodate the observation that "publicness" is neither a binary quality nor indicative of a natural kind. For many such goods, rivalry is a matter of degree. Virtually every good becomes rival at some point. The terminological shift also helps to head off a common fallacy in policy discussions of public goods. Many assume that the "public" in "public goods" refers to the identity of the *provider* of the good. That is, something is a public good if and only if the state provides it. Or, if something is a public good, then the state has a duty to provide it.[42] These statements are understandable, given that the theory of public goods emerged from the study of public finance and has sometimes been used to justify a particular role for the state.[43] However, both statements beg the question. A good can exhibit the technical qualities of "publicness" whether or not anyone is in fact providing it. More importantly for my purposes, the fact that a certain good exhibits "publicness" underdetermines whether any particular entity is morally permitted or required to provide it.

The previous chapter argued that the state is required to provide a society with those collective goods that are essential to realizing principles of justice. But there are also many collective goods that maintain no direct connection to principles of justice. Consider architectural preservation, fireworks displays, exploration of outer space, and sports radio broadcasts. Many citizens may prefer these goods. Perhaps even a majority of them will. But at least some citizens will not prefer these goods or prefer them in precisely the same way. When the state endeavors to provide discretionary goods that only certain citizens prefer, the dissenters deserve a justification for why they must contribute tax dollars to pay for such things.[44] Rawls puts the point starkly when he writes, "There is no more justification for using the state apparatus to compel some citizens to pay for unwanted benefits that others desire than there is to force them to reimburse others for their private expenses."[45]

The solution that Rawls suggests is to appoint a special "exchange branch" of government that will adjudicate propositions for discretionary collective goods on the basis of a unanimity criterion. If a candidate good secures the unanimous approval of all relevant parties, then the state may provide it. Though he doesn't address the scheme in detail, he registers the worry that "very real difficulties stand in the way of carrying this proposal through."[46] Obviously enough, the number of propositions that might secure unanimous approval is extremely small. Another potential solution to the problem (that Rawls doesn't consider) is simply to allow citizens to make donations to organizations that provide the discretionary collective goods that they prefer. Such a proposal doesn't "compel some citizens to pay for unwanted benefits that others desire," and it doesn't give rise to the various implementation problems that beset the idea of an exchange branch. But the proposal also leaves some things wanting. In the first place, it doesn't offer a complete solution to the problem of market failure. For instance, collective goods often have high fixed costs that make them difficult to provide unless they can attract donations from a large number of donors. But without the assurance that sufficient others will contribute to the good that a donor desires to produce, each faces pressure to withhold their donation. Such goods will tend to be underprovided in relation to their demand. Another problem is that simply leaving the provision of collective goods up to donation will favor certain citizens and disfavor others. That is, the main beneficiaries of such a scheme will be citizens who prefer relatively popular collective goods, or collective goods that are relatively cheap to provide.

An alternative solution may lie in another proposal of Rawls's, made for a slightly different purpose. Besides the exchange branch, Rawls also proposes an "allocation branch." One of its primary functions lies in "identifying and correcting, say by suitable taxes and subsidies and by changes in the definition of property rights, the more obvious departures from efficiency caused by the failure of prices to measure accurately social benefits and costs."[47] The passage is ambiguous as to what counts as an "obvious departure from efficiency" as well as the standard for assessing "social benefits and costs." But it provides some modest support for the thought that subsidies in particular provide the state with another potential tool to deploy in the case of market failures. On this reading, subsidizing citizens' charitable donations is a desirable way of facilitating the efficient satisfaction of preferences for collective goods. Amplifying the value of donations can increase the chances that donors reach the threshold required to provide the collective goods that they prefer. And it allows individuals to win public support for their preferences without needing to clear the impossibly high hurdle of securing unanimous approval through the exchange branch.

One might protest that this proposal doesn't entirely overcome the problem that the exchange branch's unanimity criterion is meant to solve. Namely, a consequence of applying subsidies to philanthropic donations is that some are compelled to pay for the satisfaction of others' preferences for collective goods. The mutual benefits that accrue from cross-subsidizing each other's choices might mitigate these concerns, but such benefits will likely be unequally shared. In particular, individuals who forswear ever making philanthropic donations gain nothing from a scheme that uses tax revenues to subsidize donations. It's unclear how such a scheme can be justified to them. In response, I can only note that this kind of "net loser" complaint would appear to apply far beyond the case of philanthropic donations. It seems to apply to any use of subsidies to resolve market inefficiencies. And if we think that subsidies are at least sometimes justified as a solution to market failures in other parts of the economy, the challenge for the critic of applying subsidies to philanthropic donations is to show what makes this case special.

B. Interests in Valuable Options

Of course, a way out of the foregoing problem is to argue that a state's role isn't limited to respecting citizens' existing preferences for collective goods. Rather, in some cases it may have a duty to ensure that citizens possess an adequate range of valuable options. For Ronald Dworkin, this aspect of the state's role owes to a requirement of intergenerational justice.[48] In his view, we owe to it future generations to leave the stock of ideas and experiences no less enriched than we found it, and preserving the richness of a cultural language requires investment in and expansion of its components. For Joseph Raz, controlling aspects of our lives in accordance with our own choices is a large part of what gives value to life.[49] However, exercising this control depends not only on the permission to choose for oneself but also on the presence of an adequate range of options. Both Dworkin and Raz worry that democratic majorities and market forces are insufficient to provide a robust and diverse range of valuable options. Consequently, claims Raz, "The government has an obligation to create an environment providing individuals with an adequate range of options and the opportunities to choose them."[50]

A challenge for both positions is that citizens disagree profoundly about questions of value. If the state were to decide on citizens' behalf what count as valuable options, it would risk denying the equal respect it owes to each of them. A policy that subsidizes citizens' own choices with regard to these questions offers a way out of this dilemma.[51] It allows the state to enrich the cultural language and expand the range of options without imposing a particular vision of the good.

C. Democratic Stability

Indirect state support for philanthropy may also be defended on a different plane. Several commentators have argued that a robust and manifold civil society provides indispensable infrastructure for a stable democratic order and creates the possibility of a more thoroughly deliberative process of self-government. As Jürgen Habermas defines it, "Civil society is composed of those more or less spontaneously emergent associations, organizations, and movements that, attuned to how societal problems resonate in the private life spheres, distill and transmit such reactions in amplified form to the public sphere."[52] The public sphere, for Habermas, refers to the communicative space in which a society registers and debates matters of common concern. It's where citizens formulate public opinions, articulate conceptions of the public interest, formulate social norms, and debate ideals. Critically, it's also a primary way through which citizens can influence the political agenda and contest state action.

Civil society is able to serve these purposes because it's not coordinated primarily by the logics of exchange or command. Rather, as Iris Young notes, civil society operates according to the logic of communicative interaction.[53] It depends, furthermore, on donation for much of its sustenance. But the spontaneous donations it receives may not be sufficient to maintain it. Habermas warns that "the network of associations can assert its autonomy and preserve its spontaneity only insofar as it can draw support from a mature pluralism of forms of life, subcultures, and worldviews."[54] This network of associations risks colonization by market forces, state authorities, or dominant groups within civil society itself. Though Habermas doesn't argue specifically for affirmative state support for civil society, he worries whether legal freedoms are sufficient for its protection.[55] It would seem that affirmative support would provide an important supplement to these constitutional guarantees. And yet, in order to "assert its autonomy and preserve its spontaneity," civil society must remain at critical distance from the state.[56] Were the state to sponsor particular organizations directly, it would risk curtailing the sector's independence.

We can see indirect subsidies emerging as a solution to Habermas's dilemma. They provide a way for citizens collectively to strengthen civil society while preserving its diversity and autonomy.

In sum, fairness in the provision of collective goods, preserving and promoting a rich cultural language, and securing the foundations of democratic deliberation all lend support to policies that offer generalized support to charitable giving. These rationales are not mutually exclusive. Further reflection might even reveal additional grounds for subsidizing philanthropy. Indeed, the case for general state support for philanthropy seems to be overdetermined.[57]

IV. Conclusion

As we've seen, the fact that, and the way in which, the modern state subsidizes impersonal gratuitous transfers puzzles many observers. Using public funds to subsidize private decisions stands in need of justification. A seemingly obvious way of justifying this policy would be if it facilitated the satisfaction of one of a society's most basic duties. A basic component of justice in a liberal democracy is a social minimum that protects against the worst forms of disadvantage. An eleemosynary rationale for subsidizing donations seems compelling in light of the many aspects of the nonprofit sector that are associated with responding to disadvantage. The word "charity" that lingers in our description of the major class of subsidized nonprofit corporations reflects a historical connection to almsgiving. A large number of such organizations continue to play a significant role in providing various forms of support to persons in need. The discovery that the state makes subsidies formally available to a wide range of pursuits may stoke suspicions that the policy has been captured or perverted in some way. The fact that the effects of this policy ultimately steer a greater amount of resources to noneleemosynary aims may work to confirm these suspicions.

I've argued, however, that the eleemosynary rationale doesn't hold up to scrutiny. Precisely because the provision of a social minimum is a matter of basic justice, the parameters of that minimum must be publicly established, rather than delegated to personal discretion. Whatever those parameters turn out to be, attempts to satisfy them on a voluntary and discretionary basis would be entirely unreliable. By making recipients dependent on the largesse of more fortunate citizens, such attempts would also expose recipients to asymmetries of power and status that undermine their standing as equal citizens.

Meanwhile, I suggested that the case for the eleemosynary rationale becomes considerably less compelling when we consider alternative rationales for subsidizing philanthropic donations. I proposed that generalized support for citizens' donative choices can be justified as a way of solving a common failure of markets. The state can also subsidize donations as a way of strengthening or expanding a society's cultural language. A third compelling rationale for subsidizing citizens' donative decisions is to encourage forms of deliberation and civic virtue that undergird a stable democratic order.

A proponent of the eleemosynary rationale might nonetheless respond that the foregoing arguments all miss the point: they presuppose a well-ordered society in which citizens agree on and comply with particular principles of justice. Few if any actual societies are like this. In particular, most citizens are simply not willing to accept the rate of taxation or the shift in state expenditure that would be necessary for realizing a just social minimum. However, a majority of citizens might be willing to accept reforms of the charitable subsidy that would steer greater resources toward the disadvantaged. Given these circumstances, should we not endorse the eleemosynary rationale as a "second-best" policy that better responds to limitations of feasibility?[58]

As Section II acknowledged, prudence may demand casting policy safety nets to cushion against predictable institutional failures. In societies facing extreme polarization or weak institutions, trusting the state alone to bear the burden for meeting basic needs can expose vulnerable persons to significant risk. That risk may be altogether more objectionable than the forms of mistreatment that lie within voluntary and discretionary attempts to satisfy a just social minimum. I take these considerations as sufficient justification for not excluding eleemosynary causes from the stable of subsidy-worthy charitable aims. Policies that encourage some private attention to unmet needs can be a crucial barrier against abject suffering. But these considerations aren't sufficient to vindicate the eleemosynary rationale for charitable subsidies, if that rationale is understood as marking off eleemosynary causes as singularly worthy of support or entitled to greater support than other causes.

A further note of caution comes from recent work on nonideal theory. Sensitivity to the gap between prominent theories of justice and the circumstances of contemporary political life has generated a torrent of competing views on how to narrow it. Some argue for abandoning ideals in favor of feasible local improvements, others argue for abstracting even further from empirical facts, and still others argue for reorienting the discourse altogether.[59] While I can't do justice here to the complexities of these debates, the advice of one particular camp strikes me as especially compelling and directly relevant to this discussion.[60] For this camp, it's a mistake to select policies based simply on whether they improve on the status quo in some way or another, as local improvements may counteract broader or long-term gains. Nor should we endorse policies that split the difference between our favored ideal and what we expect current majorities or other powerful forces to accept. Rather, as A. John Simmons argues, "A good policy in nonideal theory is good only as transitionally just—that is, only as a morally permissible part of a feasible overall program to achieve perfect justice, as a policy that puts us in an improved position to reach that ultimate goal."[61] Policies that we recommend under nonideal conditions must assist (or at least not interfere) with the transition to a well-ordered society. This transitional conception of nonideal theory helps to explain why theorizing about political ideals is a worthwhile pursuit at all. If political ideals weren't reasonably achievable, political philosophy would have no practical point. But in fact, on this way of thinking, ideal theory is necessary for orienting policy choices in the real world—even if it may have little to offer in terms of detailed practical guidance.

Accepting this way of framing policies in nonideal conditions invites us to subject the eleemosynary rationale to a two-part test. The first part involves asking whether the ideal of a just social minimum is realistically achievable. Lowering our sights would be especially compelling if collectively providing a just social minimum were in fact unachievable. But there's no reason to think that a state-guaranteed social minimum is metaphysically impossible or even hopelessly unlikely. Although recent trends are discouraging, several regions in Europe have succeeded in supplying a just social minimum—or come close to doing so—at various periods in the last few decades.[62] The existence of encouraging examples cautions against settling for the putative second-best.

The second part of the test asks whether the proposed policy would assist in a transition to a just state of affairs. Would subsidizing donations to eleemosynary organizations help to generate greater support for collective provision of a social minimum? Or would it make the adoption of collective provision even less likely? Though less than fully conclusive, current evidence tilts toward the latter position. Some historians argue that the creation of the modern welfare state was founded on the work of private charities.[63] The work of many benevolent societies raised public consciousness and eventually generated support for a more coordinated solution as the limits of patchwork efforts became apparent. From this perspective, encouraging private responses to disadvantage may pave the way for a more concerted collective response. Continuing such a policy once a state is established, however, may prove counterproductive. Other historians conjecture that the absence of more redistributive policies in places like the United States owes to the mistaken perception that the many nonprofits that provide social services are funded by voluntary donations.[64] (In fact, the vast majority of their funding comes from state contracts and fees for services, with donations composing only 13 percent of receipts.)[65] The myth of voluntarism hamstrings the development of a more active state. If this is true, applying even greater state assistance to private relief efforts might be thought to harden resistance to a publicly guaranteed social minimum.[66] This hypothesis draws strength from recent experimental evidence: individuals who believe that private philanthropy is significantly invested in a particular cause are less likely to support government spending in that area.[67]

While new evidence might certainly force a reappraisal of these claims, the balance of current evidence is clear. Advancing policies that make the provision of justice even more voluntary and discretionary appear likely to reinforce the status quo and violate the demands of transitional justice.

* * *

In arguing that general public support for citizens' philanthropic donations may be justifiable, I haven't meant to claim that any existing policies are in fact justified. Many have pointed out that whatever the justification for subsidizing donations, the particular design of current policies is seriously flawed. Some charge that states exercise insufficient oversight over the process of incorporation, such that a large number of fraudulent or borderline-fraudulent organizations are able to extract public resources.[68] Others dispute whether religious causes ought to be included among the list of purposes eligible for public support.[69] Tax subsidies for private giving raise challenges of equity in the way they impose costs on taxpayers of different brackets. In the next chapter I consider an additional critique, that by permitting wealthier citizens greater say over the collective features of society, existing practice offends notions of political equality. These challenges notwithstanding, this chapter has shown that private philanthropy has a role to play in a liberal democracy, a role so vital that it merits not only public toleration but also affirmative public support.

4

Donation and Deliberation

For all of their virtues, private acts of public beneficence frequently rankle those who profess allegiance to political equality—the idea that citizens should enjoy political power on equal terms.[1] The claim that philanthropy and political equality stand at odds with one another has been a recurring theme in public discourse at least since the dawn of the twentieth century, when the Walsh Commission mounted a high-profile investigation of philanthropic foundations in the United States. In our own time, handwringing over the role of large donors in public affairs is an almost daily ritual among journalists and social critics.[2]

Recent scrutiny has focused especially on the mechanisms through which philanthropy has reshaped American education.[3] A consortium of extremely well-endowed donors has pioneered strategies for reforming public schooling in line with a particular conception of national education. Generally, these strategies appear to cluster into four types: electioneering, lobbying, advocacy, and independent provision. When it comes to electioneering, members of this consortium have financed campaigns of sympathetic candidates for public office. In a lobbying capacity, donors have offered sizable resources to public schools in exchange for implementing their favored policies. In the mode of advocacy, the movement's financial backers have funded a bevy of sympathetic academic researchers, created think tanks to develop and promulgate policy advice, and forged alliances among activist organizations. These funders have also chartered alternatives to public schooling to operate in place of, or alongside, the publicly provided schools.

One might level various critiques at these strategies. For instance, one might oppose the conception of national education that inspires the reform movement. Or, one might concede the educational philosophy but find their implementation strategies wanting in some respect. One might also contend—along the lines of the argument in Chapter 2—that education is a matter of basic justice whose provision simply can't be legitimately outsourced to private parties. Critics who bemoan the abuse of power, however, seem to indicate a distinctive and no less fundamental objection.

Many people have the sense, particularly when confronted with such cases, that there's something morally troubling about the use of economic privilege to influence public affairs. Though we may admire the donors' civic commitment, and even agree with some of their positions, these cases grate against our sense of fairness in making collective decisions. Still, we find it hard to specify exactly why this is so.

A natural place to look for answers would be the theory of democratic decision-making that's primarily concerned with preventing the conversion of economic power into political power. The family of views traveling under the label *political egalitarianism* holds that rights to political participation are governed by a principle of equal opportunity for influence. We can't fully treat one another as democratic citizens unless we prevent background resource inequalities from contaminating our collective decision-making. A society that encourages differences in wealth to be converted into differences in political influence runs afoul of this principle and fails to live up to the democratic ideal.

Democratic critics of philanthropy may be surprised to learn, however, that authoritative explications of political egalitarianism provide only tepid support for their claims. This is because the standard interpretation of political egalitarianism holds that a principle of political equality applies only to official processes. For those who hold this *official proceduralist* view, the demands that political equality makes on property are exhausted by regulations on the availability of electoral and administrative influence. If and when inequalities in wealth don't translate into differential opportunities to affect electoral and administrative outcomes, political equality imposes no further conditions on attempts to shape public affairs. Thus, official proceduralists would join the objection to major donors' electioneering and lobbying activities, but their view prevents them from objecting to the use of economic power to shape conditions in civil society.

For some partisans of the democratic ideal, the official proceduralist position might seem like something of a straw man. How could any reasonable position deny the reality or significance of political inequalities outside of formal politics? Thanks partly to the contributions of feminist, antiracist, and anticolonialist intellectual and social movements, awareness of the inequities in power within social practices, organizations, and everyday interactions is increasingly a matter of common sense. As reflection on the official proceduralist position shows, however, serious obstacles confront attempts to extend the scope of political egalitarianism beyond its traditional boundaries. The drive to minimize political inequality quickly runs up against countervailing demands from the values of expressive liberty, deliberation, expertise, and economic efficiency. The difficulty in balancing these competing demands helps to explain the absence of comprehensive alternatives to the official proceduralist position.

A necessary first step in moving beyond the official proceduralist position is to locate precisely where it goes astray. As this chapter argues, these deficiencies include (1) an unstable conception of the value of equality and (2) a crude picture of the way influence can manifest outside of official processes. Overcoming these deficiencies leads us to an alternative position on the subject of political equality. According to what I call the *associational proceduralist* view, principles of political equality extend to the process of public deliberation that precedes and encircles electoral and administrative processes. This account maintains that while insulating official procedures from inequalities in wealth may very well take moral priority, a well-ordered democratic society can't permit inequalities in property ownership to colonize civil society. The view suggests, furthermore, that regulatory strategies often taken to apply to political spending might also apply to certain kinds of philanthropic donations. Ultimately, I contend that satisfying the demands of political equality requires a radical transformation in the regulation of philanthropy for expressive purposes. But sensitivity to certain concerns that animate the official proceduralist account impose principled limitations on the extent of this transformation.

The chapter continues, in Section I, by introducing the official proceduralist view and its application to campaign finance. Section II reveals how this position struggles to fully account for the core interests that animate the value of political equality. I consider, in Section III, whether certain features of official procedures nevertheless generate particularly urgent egalitarian concerns or else more easily allow for egalitarian regulation. Section IV shows how an alternative perspective, what I call associational proceduralism, can better address these concerns. I propose a particular mechanism for institutionalizing this perspective—a progressive voucher scheme—that helps to equalize opportunities for financing political expression. This scheme applies to conventional political spending and expressive philanthropy alike. Its advantage lies in satisfying the demands of political equality without imposing intolerable limits on liberty or efficiency.

I. Political Equality and Political Donations

A. Political Egalitarianism

In a democracy, the legitimacy of political decisions is due in significant part to the equal distribution of rights to participation. Collectively binding decisions can't be fully legitimate unless those subject to these decisions enjoy equal rights to contribute to them.[4] In other words, the fact that we enjoyed the same chances to contribute to a decision is part of what makes it permissible for those executing the decision to compel our compliance. Relatedly, this fact about the equality of decision-making procedures is part of what vests decisions with authority, what gives us reason to comply with the outcome of a decision even when we disagree with its substance. Few believe that political equality is all that matters in determinations of legitimacy or authority.[5] One might insist, for instance, that no matter how egalitarian the procedures that lead to them, decisions that deliberately violate basic human rights can't be remotely legitimate. One might also insist that decisions need to exhibit certain virtues associated with the rule of law, such as consistency and publicity. But at least for certain theorists, equality in the distribution of political power is what gives a legitimate decision a distinctively democratic flavor: it's the signal contribution that democracy makes to legitimate governance.[6]

The conception of political equality that I wish to challenge roughly reflects the positions of John Rawls and Joshua Cohen. (Cohen takes himself in large part to be elaborating and refining Rawls's view, which, despite its influence, remains relatively terse and gestural.) Though their general position doesn't enjoy universal support, it both reflects widely shared intuitions among ordinary citizens and serves as a frequent point of departure for numerous philosophical explorations. Indeed, casual usage of the term "political egalitarianism," it seems to me, tends to pick out the particular commitments of this specific conception.

Though every democratic theory incorporates some conception of political equality, not all such theories earn the label "political egalitarian." Explaining some ways in which political egalitarianism differs from other conceptions of political equality will serve to clarify why it holds a certain appeal.

Conceptions of political equality differ across several dimensions. In the first place, they differ over what they take the

grounds of political equality to be. On some views, egalitarian political procedures are valuable instrumentally because they tend
to produce substantively just outcomes. As a matter of empirical
tendency, it turns out that assigning participants equal say in political decisions happens to result in high-quality outcomes, across
numerous conceptions of what counts as a "high-quality" outcome. If some other inegalitarian procedure could reliably generate
better outcomes, those who accept the instrumental justification
for democracy are committed to endorsing it. For political egalitarianism, however, egalitarian procedures are valuable not only
because they tend to produce good outcomes but also because of
qualities inherent in the procedures themselves. We have reasons
to prefer egalitarian procedures even if inegalitarian procedures
somehow proved to be more reliable at generating good outcomes.

Conceptions of political equality also differ over what they regard as the *currency* of equality. One might hold that the relevant
distribuendum in rights to participation is a citizen's *impact* on collectively binding decisions. Impact can be understood as the contribution one's preferences make to a political outcome.[7] For example,
equality of impact obtains in the ideal of simple majority rule: when
a group assigns each member an equally weighted vote and awards
victory to the option that gains the support of a majority, each
voter enjoys equal impact over the resulting decision. However,
if certain common conditions obtain, two individuals who enjoy
the same formal impact on a decision may still enjoy vastly unequal power over outcomes. Suppose that these two individuals are
permitted to express opinions publicly before the vote or to lobby
the implementers of the decision after the vote. If one of the two
individuals possesses greater resources to engage in these activities,
their preferences will enjoy an extra advantage. The consistent supporter of impact as the currency of political equality faces an intractable dilemma. The impact-theorist must say either that these extra
advantages don't matter, or that engaging in political activity outside of voting is impermissible. Political egalitarianism, meanwhile,

claims that what matters here is not impact but rather a broader notion of *influence*. Political influence encompasses voting rights as well as access to other modes of political expression.

Conceptions of political equality also differ over how they accommodate variation in citizens' motivation and talent. Even if citizens enjoy equal external resources to contribute to political decision-making, some will be more motivated to engage in political contestation and some will be more talented at identifying and marshalling convincing political arguments. On certain views, the potential advantages that accrue from greater motivation or talent are unfair: citizens aren't responsible for their motivational sets or their abilities.[8] Such views are particularly compelling against a backdrop of wide resource inequalities, which heavily condition chances to develop and express motivations and abilities. Even so, taking this view seriously entails some troubling implications.

At the limit, a view that insists on strict equality of political influence rules out the possibility of representative government. The ideal of representation depends on the permissibility of sorting citizens with the relevant motivation and talent into leadership roles. The justification for this ideal starts from the observation that governing a large, modern polity is a time-consuming and complex task, and such sorting allows a society to reap the benefits of a division of labor. Citizens with the inclination and talent for other pursuits can specialize in those, leaving all better off than if they had each shared the same tasks. Strict equality of influence, however, must reject the greater influence that representative government affords to representatives.[9]

A principle of strict equality of influence would also undermine the possibility of public deliberation, which naturally favors participants who express the best arguments. Those who express the best arguments are frequently more enthusiastic and more rhetorically skilled. If these advantages are unjust, skilled deliberators must either have their liberties curtailed, or other participants must often be encouraged to ignore what they believe to be the best arguments, lest those arguments issue from someone who is unfairly brilliant.

What does equality demand here? Cohen argues, with some force, that a principle of political equality ought to screen out unequal advantages in access to the political process only insofar as they are "irrelevant to performance."[10] In his view, the motivation to engage in politics and the talent to persuade others are qualities that are relevant to the performance of a citizen's role.[11] Though a society should take measures to redress socially caused differences in motivation and talent, it shouldn't discourage citizens with the strong desire and ability to participate in public life from doing so. Wealth, by contrast, is an arbitrary advantage. Differences in wealth are irrelevant to the performance of a citizen's role and thus appropriate objects of regulation.

In sum, political egalitarianism holds that procedures for making collectively binding decisions must observe a principle of *equal opportunity for political influence*. Behind this principle lie the judgments that egalitarian procedures are valuable apart from the contribution they make to substantively just outcomes; the currency of equality cashes out in terms of influence, rather than impact; and sources of influence that are irrelevant to the performance of active citizenship deserve the most scrutiny.

For those who hold this general view, regulating the flow of resources into the political process is essential for assuring equality of opportunity within that process. Political egalitarians warn that unequal opportunities for financing electoral campaigns and lobbying officials distort fairness in political participation, thereby undermining the legitimacy of subsequent exercises of state power.

B. The Official Proceduralist Interpretation

Because political egalitarianism regards economic advantage as an unjustified source of political power, it would seem to provide principled support to criticism of philanthropy's influence on public policy. This appearance is partly misleading. For both Rawls and Cohen, the principle of political equality applies exclusively to the formal mechanisms of decision-making: elections and administrative procedures. Their position condemns the unchecked ability to convert wealth into influence over the selection of representatives, the passage of ballot initiatives, and the lobbying of officials. This position would also presumably condemn the efforts of wealthy individuals to pressure school boards, as noted above. However, according to this position, political equality doesn't apply to mechanisms that operate at further remove from the electoral and administrative processes, mechanisms that shape the background political culture. This brand of political egalitarianism thus ignores less direct but potentially more insidious efforts to sway public policy: the use of economic advantage to shape civil society.

The insistence that we confine political equality to official procedures may certainly seem strange. We typically think that political outcomes depend considerably on influence from a society's background public culture.[12] Indeed, because the background culture heavily conditions the political agenda, processes of public opinion formation would appear to exercise greater ultimate control over the direction of collective decision-making than campaigns and lobbying.[13] Whatever objections there are to unequal opportunities to influence elections might therefore seem to apply even more strongly to unequal opportunities for shaping the background public culture. Nevertheless, official proceduralism forces us to contend with three serious challenges to extending the scope of political egalitarianism:

1. *The value of equality is symbolic.* A main reason for regulating official processes by a principle of equal opportunity for influence is that this publicly and firmly expresses respect for each member of the polity as an equal citizen. The existence of differences in opportunities for influence outside of the

official processes doesn't undermine the public recognition of
equal citizenship.

2. *Positions of official authority are unique.* Official procedures
   deserve to be singled out because they distribute inherently
   scarce goods, namely positions of coercive authority (and
   access to positions of coercive authority). The goods that
   unofficial mechanisms distribute aren't inherently scarce,
   nor do these mechanisms have direct recourse to coercive
   enforcement.

3. *Regulatory strategies must be workable.* Even if it were true
   that inequalities in the availability of influence over civil society were unjust, a constitutional democracy has no workable way of regulating these inequalities. Applying political
   egalitarianism to civil society would entail intolerable costs to
   our other significant interests in liberty or prosperity.

These claims create significant obstacles for any attempt to extend the scope of political egalitarianism beyond the boundaries of
official procedures. They suggest that inequalities in influence over
civil society are either innocuous or inevitable. As the next section
shows, however, careful analysis of these claims points the way toward an alternative perspective.

II. The Value of Political Equality

A. Symbolic Equality

One argument for confining a principle of equality to the electoral
and administrative processes is that doing so simply exhausts our
reasons for caring about political equality in the first place. The
main interest we have in enjoying equal access to public influence
is the interest in being publicly recognized as an equally valuable
participant in deciding collective affairs.[14] At the extreme, to be

excluded entirely from processes of decision-making can express, or appear to express, profound disrespect. It can express the proposition that one's judgment is worthless, or that one's interests count for nothing. Relative exclusion improves on this situation only by a matter of degree. To be afforded fewer opportunities for influence than others can be taken to express that one's judgments are inferior or that's one's interests count for less.

If the main interest in equal opportunity for public influence consists in this recognition of equal moral status, equal availability of input into official processes may appear to be both necessary and sufficient for satisfying it.[15] This owes partly to the fact that official processes are highly visible focal points for political activity. They constitute the final stages in the determination of laws or in the determination of the identities of those who will make the laws. They are terminals on which all effective input must eventually converge. The contours of these processes have distinct boundaries. What's more, the outcomes of these processes are determinate: someone gets elected, a law gets passed. Arguably, these qualities combine to render official processes the appropriate subject of political equality. Inclusion in the decisive and consequential processes that everyone can plainly see cements one's status as an equal citizen.

Meanwhile, inclusion in background processes of public discussion and opinion formation makes only trivial additional contributions to that status. The focal points of these processes are many, varied, and constantly in flux. (The locus of debate on a given issue might oscillate between television news programs, social media platforms, and outdoor rallies.) The processes through which public influence travels lack clear boundaries and access points. Additionally, the outcomes of the processes of public opinion formation are indeterminate. Whereas one can identify at any given moment which party holds the balance of power, what the public thinks shifts constantly and is difficult to track. The indeterminacy of public opinion diffuses any sense of injury that one might experience as a result of exclusion from the processes that shape it. Thus, one might think it redundant to extend a principle of equal influence to a wider range of decision-making processes. Doing so would contribute little or nothing more to the establishment of a public status of equal respect.

Though this argument exposes some potentially important distinctions between narrowly political processes and others, it ultimately undermines itself from within. For there are good reasons to believe that the interest in equal recognition doesn't actually require equal opportunity for influence over official processes in the first place. Niko Kolodny wonders why, if the interest in political opportunity is merely a symbolic one, we don't simply send a flag to each citizen when they reach the age of majority.[16] Sending a flag to each citizen would express that they are considered equal members of the polity. Surely this would be less costly than regulating access to political processes. Though the flag proposal is probably not meant to be taken seriously, the point remains that there may be other relatively inexpensive methods for securing the public status of equality.

David Estlund challenges the relationship between political equality and equal public status more directly.[17] He argues that political inequality needn't express any disrespect at all. In his view, differences in relative influence only signify expressions of disrespect when they in fact owe to disrespectful attitudes. Justifications for exclusion based on the proposition that some citizens are inherently wiser than others, or that the interests of some citizens count more than others, are "invidious comparisons." They are invidious because they rely on utterly contestable premises. Justifications to exclude citizens from opportunities for influence based on their race or class, for instance, depend on the despicable proposition that race or class determines one's ability to make sound political judgments, or on the repugnant proposition that the interests of persons of certain races or classes count for less. But justifications for political inequality that don't rely on invidious comparisons express no disrespect and do no damage to the interest in public recognition. Estlund thinks, moreover, that there's at least one powerful justification for political inequality that survives this test. To permit wealthier citizens to buy proportionally more political influence leads to a situation in which greater overall input enters into decision-making processes. The greater the quantity of input, the more likely that the truth about justice sees the light, and the more likely that political outcomes are substantively just. Recognizing political equality, meanwhile, requires limitations on the amounts that wealthier citizens are allowed to spend. This reduces the overall quantity of political input and renders outcomes that are, if not substantively unjust, less substantively just than they could otherwise be. From this, one might conclude that substantive political equality not only fails to protect the interest in equal recognition but also undermines other vitally important interests.

B. Social Equality

If substantive political equality isn't even a requirement of official processes, a fortiori it can't be a requirement of unofficial processes. Or at least, this would be a natural implication of the criticism we have been exploring, if the interest in public recognition of equality actually does underlie the principle of equal opportunity for influence. Recent work by Daniel Viehoff, Niko Kolodny, and others indicates, however, that principles of political equality are best understood in different terms.[18] We have reason to care about egalitarian procedures not because they express a public status but because they facilitate distinctive kinds of relationships.

Viehoff observes that being in an egalitarian relationship, such as friendship, marriage, or citizenship, requires that we exclude certain reasons from the domain of eligible reasons when making joint decisions. One important category of excluded reasons are differences in power. A friend or spouse who uses her greater physical strength as a bargaining chip during arguments fails to treat the other party as an equal. The same is true of a citizen who uses his greater wealth as a relevant consideration in political deliberations. Securing an egalitarian relationship requires taking such inequalities of power off the table. Obeying egalitarian procedures prevents us from acting on considerations that would undermine the egalitarian character of our relationships.

I take this idea to show that what's valuable about political equality isn't that it *symbolizes the idea* that members of the polity are equal citizens, but that it *establishes the fact* that citizens do stand in relation to each other as social equals. When wealthier citizens leverage their greater financial means to win for themselves greater chances of determining political outcomes, they subject the less wealthy to their power and treat them as inferiors. Moreover, a simple disposition to refrain from taking advantage of this power is generally insufficient to prevent the development of these objectionable social hierarchies. For it makes the deployment of power depend only on the whims of those who possess it. When available, institutional mechanisms that take this option off the table more firmly protect the standing of each person as a social equal.

This explanation of political egalitarianism in terms of social equality has two important implications. First, it sidesteps Estlund's critique of accounts of political egalitarianism that take their cues from the interest in equal public recognition. Though Estlund's argument for encouraging substantive inequalities in political input might not offend the value of symbolic equality, it surely would offend the value of social equality. The lack of a disrespectful intention doesn't vindicate subordinating relationships. Second, it reopens the possibility that principles of political equality apply not just to official procedures but to other ways of influencing social phenomena as well. If using one's greater power to sway elections objectionably treats one's fellow citizens as social inferiors, it's hard to see how using one's unequal resource advantages to control civil society wouldn't constitute the same form of objectionable treatment. Conceivably, the degree of the injury might be weaker, but the form of the objection is equivalent.

In sum, the value of equality itself gives us insufficient reason to limit the scope of egalitarian regulatory principles to official procedures. But, as I consider in the next section, perhaps certain features of official procedures trigger unique egalitarian concerns or else are easier to regulate.

III. Scarcity, Competition, and Workability

A. Scarcity of Offices

Classically understood, the circumstances of justice are conditions that create conflicts of interest in the distribution of power over resources.[19] As such, they make principles of justice both possible and necessary. The existence of moderate scarcity is one such condition. We don't face conflicts of interest over resources in abundant supply. Your enjoyment of the sunset doesn't diminish the quantity or quality of my enjoyment of it (unless, of course, we desire to enjoy the sunset from precisely the same vantage point). It would be a reason to treat official and unofficial processes differently if opportunities to influence the former were inherently scarce while opportunities to influence the latter were not. This appears to be Rawls's position on the matter. Focusing in particular on the election of officials, Rawls describes this process as "a public facility designed to serve a definite purpose."[20] This purpose is to "control the entry to positions of political authority." This public facility, moreover, "has limited space"—there are only so many positions of political authority. Thus, the distribution of influence over the selection of these positions is a relevant moral concern. By implication, Rawls seems to think that other aspects of public life don't exhibit this necessary justice-triggering feature.

At first glance, Rawls's remarks seem to highlight a critical difference between elections and other aspects of public life. While candidates for election compete for a fixed number of positions, there are no similar limitations on positions of power within civil society. For instance, when it comes to shaping the background public culture, the message space in which ideas vie for attention has multiple sites and porous boundaries. It may often be possible for alternative outlets to generate spontaneously. If one's view doesn't gain air time in a television broadcast, one can take to the streets, or to the press, or to the internet. Consequently, those with greater resources can't effectively silence the voices of the less well endowed. This is especially true in an era of internet communication, which erodes the barriers to entry endemic to more traditional methods of mass communication.

B. Scarcity of Cognitive Space

And yet, if scarcity weren't somehow a feature of the wider public sphere, it's difficult to explain why civil society groups typically adopt strategies of competition. Groups advocating particular positions generally seek to outperform one another in achieving public recognition of various kinds. Some seek to have their perspective triumph over rival perspectives. When there's no rival perspective, they seem to be competing among the universe of different causes for public attention. If scarcity weren't somehow a condition of civil society, what could explain this behavior?[21]

Building on developments in social psychology, Thomas Christiano argues that the conditions of modern citizenship include a "socially induced cognitive scarcity."[22] The idea is that most citizens, given their diverse other commitments, can reserve only a certain amount of cognitive space for considering public affairs. This need not be the regrettable result of apathy or disillusionment. Rather, a highly articulated division of labor and pressure from legitimate personal attachments leave citizens with little time to reflect on wider issues. Particularly under these circumstances, different propositions compete with another for access to our cognitive space and priority within it. One way of understanding the competitive nature of advocacy efforts, therefore, is to take these groups as competing with each other over access to our cognitive space. This would also indicate that we have reason to take concern with the way in which propositions gain access to this space. If we object to parceling out discrete positions of power on the basis of wealth, we should object similarly to parceling out access to our attention on the basis of wealth.

Admittedly, even when the most readily available sources of information reflect the perspectives of wealthy elites, attention remains something over which we can maintain some control. With some effort, we can avoid giving in to the dominant sources of information and take steps to seek out alternatives. Cognitive space and political office are disanalagous in this way. When someone controls the machinery of state, we can't simply avoid their authority. The fact that positions of official power come along with coercive enforcement suggests that we should take special concern with access to those positions. But it doesn't imply that we should therefore take no concern with inequalities in opportunities to influence the background culture.

Indeed, the fact that background influence lacks coercive authority makes it troubling in a special way. Background influence doesn't confront us head-on and directly invade our will in the way that coercive laws often do. It operates more insidiously, seeping into our assumptions often without our realizing it. Under modern conditions, expecting all citizens to adopt a disposition of constant vigilance toward the sources of their beliefs may not be reasonable.

In sum, the fact that political office is a scarce and valuable resource doesn't justify limitations on the scope of political equality, even if it does show the special significance of regulating elections by egalitarian procedures. But there may yet be a strong reason for limiting the scope of equality to formal electoral and administrative procedures, and to this we now turn.

C. The Workability Dilemma

One virtue of official proceduralism is that strategies for applying a principle of political equality to official procedures aren't difficult to conceive. As mentioned previously, official procedures are focal points of the political process. They have relatively distinct boundaries. The access points to these boundaries are readily apparent. There's nothing terribly mysterious about campaign finance reform or measures to insulate the government from lobbyists. By contrast, what it would mean to assure equal opportunity for wider public influence is unclear, as the mechanisms through which influence flows outside formal channels are nebulous and largely unobservable. As Cohen puts it, the way in which influence manifests outside of formal arenas is "not at all well defined and bounded: it extends throughout life, spreads through all its spheres, and the processes involved are not at all well understood."[23] This characterization rings true when one considers some of the different mechanisms that bear on the formation of public opinion: connections of kinship and friendship, formal education, commercial advertising, cultural media, government communication, and online social networks, to name just a few.

Faced with the apparent intractability of influential processes beyond the official political facilities, one might think that assuring equal availability of public influence exposes us to a dilemma. Taking the first horn would involve endorsing a radical extension of state control, permitting the state to set boundaries and monitor access points to an increasing number of arenas of social interaction. To see the challenges with this option, consider the demands it could make on our intimate relationships, within which we develop certain intellectual capacities and substantive convictions. The specter of a state that monitors and limits how much parents read to their children suggests some of the limitations of this strategy. Such a strategy threatens to undermine the value of privacy in numerous domains of social life. Moreover, it probably couldn't succeed without also granting the state broad powers that would be difficult to confine to particular domains.

Taking the second horn of the dilemma would commit us not to state monitoring and regulation of the processes of public influence, but rather to a radically egalitarian distribution of resources. When no one enjoys differential advantages to convert into additional influence in the first place, the need for egalitarian political procedures evaporates. While few commentators are prepared to seriously defend the first option, some egalitarian thinkers embrace this second option with more open arms.[24]

Two considerations counsel against following in this direction, however. In the first place, the radical egalitarian position prescribes a very blunt instrument for a problem that might be amenable to a surgical solution. Although many forms of economic inequality are objectionable, others may be either innocuous or beneficial. Before considering a radical treatment option, we should make sure we have exhausted localized alternatives. In the second place, the radical egalitarian position essentially folds political equality into a theory of distributive justice, such that the case for one stands and falls with the case for the other. While this position may be correct that the fullest achievement of the democratic ideal is only possible in a thoroughly just society, yoking the two ideals together too tightly fails to appreciate certain political realities. A primary purpose of democratic political procedures is to provide fair ways of resolving disagreements about justice itself. Agreement on the demands of political equality is often easier to reach than agreement on justice in other domains. Furthermore, democratic reform has historically served as precipitant to broader economic and social reforms—as the expansion of suffrage to the propertyless, women, and racial minorities then gave the formerly disenfranchised the power to demand substantive reforms. Sensitivity to these features of political conflict tell in favor of a more incremental approach.[25]

IV. Beyond Political Spending

A. Associational Proceduralism

In what follows, I defend a strategy for resolving the dilemma just posed: a position that at once avoids the repugnance of the totalitarian option and respects the distinction between political equality and distributive justice. I call this position *associational proceduralism*. Associational proceduralism holds that the subject of political equality extends to certain mechanisms that mediate political influence beyond the official processes of elections and administrative decision-making. It accepts that some aspects of the process of public opinion formation remain difficult to comprehend, challenging to control, or morally costly to regulate. It denies that all processes of public opinion formation necessarily possess one or more of these features. It proposes, furthermore, that the extension of political egalitarianism to unofficial processes doesn't need to encompass all such processes in order to be meaningful.

The official proceduralist position would be especially compelling if the landscape of associational life lacked any obvious formal basis: if civil society was composed of fleeting and loosely organized assemblages of people. This is an inaccurate depiction of modern conditions, in which the vast majority of activity within civil society is conducted by formally incorporated and professionally managed organizations.[26] The formal organization of civil society can be helpfully understood as a response to the same problem that electoral representation attempts to solve. Whereas electoral representation allows citizens to delegate the task of governing, civil society organizations allow citizens to delegate the task of public deliberation, by authorizing organizations to conduct research and advocacy on their behalf. Communicating through a variety of media, these organizational agents articulate interests, propose policies, debate one another's positions, and contest the conduct of the state. Some of these groups represent general ideologies; others advocate on particular issues. Unlike public officials, these groups don't directly control the coercive apparatus of the state. However, it would be a mistake to presume that such groups don't thereby play a significant political role.

The groups in question endeavor to shape a society's background political culture, its background political agenda, and its background public political opinion. Adding the modifier "background" to these familiar terms signifies that they represent phenomena operating at further remove from electoral politics.[27] One might define a political culture in terms of a society's repository of institutional traditions, constitutional doctrines, and historic texts. By contrast, its *background* political culture, as I mean it, furnishes and constrains the concepts that a society uses to make binding decisions. It contains the language, historical narratives, and commonsense epistemic and evaluative standards that citizens use to communicate about their interests.[28] Likewise, while the political agenda includes the docket of candidates contending for election and the bills proposed in legislatures, the *background* political agenda includes the pool of issues from which candidates and legislators draw. Similarly, while public opinion might be taken to refer to citizens' preferences for candidates and their approval of legislation, *background* public opinion refers to what citizens tend to believe about more general propositions: whether low taxes produce economic growth, whether capital punishment is morally permissible, or what kind of duties we have toward animals. Background public opinion serves to inform citizens' more specific opinions about candidates and policies.

In the contemporary American context, this functional description would apply to a wide swath of the nonprofit sector, covering "public education organizations," think tanks, NGOs, and any

other 501(c)(3) public charity that engages in a substantial degree of public expression.[29] All of these associations can be seen as
representing citizens in a process of public deliberation.

Such groups operate on a society's political common sense in
ways that can be difficult to appreciate. Yet their ultimate influence
on citizens' beliefs can be quite considerable. Think, for instance, of
the major social movements in recent American history: the "rights
revolutions" that began with the civil rights movement, the envi-
ronmentalist movement, the conservative legal movement, and
the ascendancy of right-wing populism. Each of these movements
evolved over several decades, in many cases flying under the radar
before earning recognition as a movement. In some cases, the success of these efforts lies less in their direct targeting of legislation
than in their reshaping of background assumptions in public discourse (which then conditioned official political decisions). What's
more, the emergence of such movements owes less to the spontaneous assemblage of individual citizens than it does to the coordinated efforts of well-funded organizations.[30]

But if these associations are sustained by donation, and
opportunities to make donations are differentially distributed, we
seem to run into a familiar conundrum. These organizations will
be initiated by, or more responsive to, the perspectives of those
with the deepest pockets.[31] And those organizations that raise the
most funds will enjoy significant advantages in getting their views
considered. Under conditions of economic inequality, the free flow
of gratuitous transfers to expressive associations distorts equal
opportunities to participate in public deliberation much in the same
way that the free flow of campaign donations undermines equal
opportunities to influence the election of candidates. Note that this
is very much an independent problem from the one of fairness in
campaign finance. Even in a society that publicly funds campaigns
for elected office, donations to expressive associations can also
serve as an important vehicle for inequalities in opportunities for
influence.

B. Voucher Schemes

What would it mean to apply a principle of political equality to the process of public deliberation? I believe we can make progress toward resolving this dilemma by considering some proposals submitted for slightly different purposes.

Some of the most sophisticated discussion of the political morality of philanthropy in recent years occurs in the work of Rob Reich and Ryan Pevnick. Each has emphasized how the scope and scale of the contemporary practice of philanthropy owe much to the policies that states use to support it. These authors also single out a particular feature of this policy as irreconcilable with the value of democracy.[32] Public finance regimes in many contemporary societies allow charitable contributions to be deducted from income tax assessments.[33] (The deduction applies to ordinary contributions as well as to contributions to foundations.) As commonly understood, a charitable deduction constitutes an implicit or indirect state subsidy to charitable enterprise. In effect, it allows qualifying taxpayers to allocate a portion of state expenditure to objects of their own choosing. Yet, how much citizens are able to donate and deduct depends on their level of income. Moreover, the policy requires that citizens contribute a certain amount in donations before they can be applied toward reductions in their income tax payments. Citizens who owe nothing in income tax can't take advantage of the subsidy at all. To Reich and Pevnick, this policy constitutes a formal political injustice. Under this policy, wealthier citizens are entitled by law to allocate a greater portion of state expenditure than less wealthy citizens are. Arguably, this provision violates democratic legitimacy on an even more basic level than I've been discussing. Even the least demanding understanding of democracy's equality constraint requires that citizens enjoy equal formal chances to influence public decisions.

However, as the foregoing discussion has now made clear, it would be a mistake to presume that the only, or the primary, conflict between philanthropy and democracy is entirely an artifact of the tax privileges that states afford charitable enterprise.[34] Even if the state offered no subsidies to the practice of philanthropy, or applied these subsidies in a more egalitarian spirit, we would still have grounds to question the compatibility of the practice with political equality.[35] Tax reform removes a way in which the state amplifies the voices of the rich. But it doesn't address the volume of those voices that need no amplification in the first place.[36] Thus, fixing on the deduction leaves us unable to assess whether differences in donative means are justified *apart from* any amplification they receive from the state.

Nevertheless, some of the proposals designed to redress this injustice in the tax code point us toward strategies for restraining inequalities in the means of donation more generally. Pevnick proposes replacing the charitable deduction in the United States with a system of indirect government grants.[37] On an annual basis, each citizen of voting age would receive an equally weighted voucher to contribute to the qualifying charitable organization of their choice. The effect of this proposal would be to prevent wealthier citizens from enjoying greater say over government expenditure, while also creating a baseline of equality in the means of philanthropic donation. Notably, however, in Pevnick's version of the proposal, individuals would be permitted to make additional cash donations in excess of their voucher allotment. This would leave in place considerable inequalities in the means of donation.

One might reply that this *equally weighted voucher scheme* succeeds in eliminating the worst forms of inequality. What's most objectionable isn't so much that citizens lack equal opportunities to influence state expenditure, but that some citizens are excluded from the practice altogether. Additionally, prohibiting citizens from making further contributions beyond their voucher allotment would be seriously undesirable in other ways. A distinctive feature of philanthropy is that donors may choose not only *whether* and *where* to direct funds, but also *how much*. Permitting donors to determine on their own how much of their property to donate to particular causes is valuable in at least two ways. First, it respects an important liberty interest. We derive satisfaction from determining how much a particular cause is worth our support, and how our distinctive judgment can make a unique contribution to the cause's success. Some citizens may wish to save extra income, or pursue more remunerative careers, precisely in order to donate more toward their conception of the common good. Insisting on strict equality of donative influence would be prejudicial to these citizens. Second, the liberty to determine the amount of one's donations helps to promote the efficient allocation of donative capital, not entirely unlike the for-profit financial market. Arguably, the more discretion that donors have, the greater are their incentives to weigh their donative decisions carefully.[38] Likewise, affording donors greater discretion can have a disciplining effect on potential intermediary organizations, who must demonstrate their efficiencies in order to compete successfully for additional funds.[39] These considerations indicate why an equally weighted voucher scheme would be ill-advised to prohibit citizens from making cash donations in addition to their voucher allotment. But they also point toward an alternative scheme that does a better job of balancing these various considerations.

Estlund has developed an alternative voucher proposal for the case of campaign finance that imposes greater limitations on the range of donative inequalities while at the same time protecting specific interests in liberty and efficiency.[40] In his version, each citizen initially receives an equally weighted voucher (at a nominal cost to the citizen). Citizens aren't permitted to make cash donations in excess of their voucher allotment, however. Rather, those who wish to make additional donations must purchase additional vouchers. The cost of these vouchers increases the more vouchers one purchases—while their redemption value remains the same. What's more, Estlund shows that the proceeds of the voucher sales can be used to fortify the value of the baseline voucher. This proposal has the effect of not only constraining the range of inequalities in input but also maximizing the opportunities available to ordinary citizens. Estlund believes that this "epistemic difference principle" suffices to render the remaining inequalities in input justifiable to less well-off citizens. Because they possess greater opportunities for influence under conditions of (moderated) inequality than they otherwise would, it's unreasonable for them to insist on strict equality. Furthermore, this *progressive voucher scheme* might be thought to preserve the liberty interest that citizens have in determining the amount of their contributions and the presumed returns to efficiency that come along with it.

Certain modifications of this proposal would make it more appropriate for philanthropic donations. In the case of philanthropy, it might be better to make the baseline voucher divisible (or a packet of many vouchers) so that citizens aren't limited to supporting a single entity. Besides offering citizens more choice, this modification allows citizens to register the intensity of their preferences. Additionally, to further incentivize donations overall in light of the arguments of Chapter 3, the redemption value of any voucher should be higher than its purchase price—with the state covering the difference. This maintains the goal of providing public support for charitable contributions.

Applying a version of the progressive voucher scheme to this setting indicates a possible strategy toward reconciling philanthropy with political equality. It could limit the extent to which wealthier citizens can convert property into dominance over a society's public culture. And it could furnish ordinary citizens with the resources to contribute meaningfully to the determination of these aspects of civil society. However, applying this progressive voucher scheme faces some remaining obstacles.

Although the equally weighted voucher scheme targets charitable donations of all kinds, the argument for the progressive voucher scheme recommends a more limited focus. I suggested that a particular reason for taking concern with the means of donation owes to the way that certain donations work to influence political decisions through changes in background political discourse. However, altering the background political discourse is neither the primary intention nor an equally obvious effect of all philanthropic donations. The primary purpose of many donative organizations isn't to participate in public deliberation, but rather to provide public goods or services. Donations to a neighborhood choir program and donations to a public interest group exhibit some notable differences in this respect. The latter can be expected to contribute significantly more influence on public affairs than the former.

Some may think that egalitarian worries apply equally to the finance of expressive and productive organizations. Indeed, it seems intuitively objectionable that wealthier citizens should enjoy greater opportunities to determine which public goods and services prevail in a society. We all have an interest in shaping the shared features of our social world, and there seems to be no good reason why one's economic position should grant one greater or lesser say in these matters. Perhaps further reflection will reveal a justification for regulating these financial opportunities as well. However, the logic of such an argument would likely depart significantly from what I've presented here. Recall that my question has been whether the demands of political equality, as a component of democratic legitimacy, extend beyond the traditional focus of electoral politics. As we have seen, the case for political equality is especially strong when it applies to decision-making processes that lead to coercively binding outcomes. Inequalities in opportunities to engage in public deliberation are especially objectionable because they affect a society's fundamental and nonvoluntary features. While inequalities in opportunities to finance discretionary public goods may indeed be objectionable, they are generally so in a different and lesser way. Furthermore, as we have seen, to extend the demands of political equality further may fail to preserve the distinctive purpose of this value. A broader conception of political equality in terms of equal opportunity for *social* influence is far more controversial in its foundations and more radical in its implications. The distribution of social and economic power more generally, I have maintained, is best addressed in the context of a theory of distributive justice and decided through democratic processes.

Limiting the application of the progressive voucher scheme to address the specific concerns of this chapter would likely require some modification to the way societies draw legal distinctions between targets of charitable donation. (Note that this proposal is meant to supplement commonsense regulations on narrowly "political" spending on campaigns, political parties, and political action committees.)[41] Namely, it would require donative organizations to account separately for expressive and productive income and expenditure.[42] While citizens would be permitted to contribute their baseline voucher for either purpose, additional cash donations would only be permissibly directed at productive activities. Further support for expressive purposes would require purchases of additional vouchers, at increasing cost to the donor. Certainly, policymakers would have many details to work out regarding which activities fall into these categories, how to ensure the integrity of the scheme,[43] and the effects of different regulatory strategies on behavioral incentives. A particular challenge here concerns balancing the aim of subsidizing support for philanthropic donation, along the lines suggested in Chapter 3, with the aim of curbing inequalities in opportunities for influence. A voucher scheme, particularly when applied selectively, can have the unintended consequence of disincentivizing donations in favor of other expenditures or incentivizing certain kinds of donations over others. While I am optimistic that further work may resolve these issues, the severity

of these challenges may ultimately push us back to the more conservative proposals mentioned earlier or to more creative solutions
for balancing the competing considerations.

V. Conclusion

To recap, we have been exploring one way in which philanthropy
might challenge democratic legitimacy. A number of scholars converge on the view that democracy's central requirement is that
the determination of collective decisions issue from a process in
which citizens enjoy equal opportunities for influence. Those who
have considered the place of donations in this mix have tended to
limit their concern to the finance of electoral campaigns and other
formal targets of political advocacy. I've questioned whether this
limited focus is ultimately justifiable.

Donations to campaigns aren't the only source of distortion of
the fairness in control over a society's common affairs. I suggested
that unregulated philanthropic donations can also undermine fair
opportunities to influence the shared features of a social environment. I then sketched a solution to this problem that accommodates
the interests in liberty and efficiency which help to explain the
attractions of laissez-faire systems.

Some may still worry that the problems I've described constitute
mere symptoms of background economic injustice. A society that
distributes the benefits and burdens of social interaction as inadequately as most actual societies do places tremendous advantages
in the hands of a small proportion of the population. Among these
advantages are opportunities to exert disproportionate control over
social outcomes. One might suspect that under conditions where
the distribution of property is less unequal this problem simply
dissolves. This would be a false conclusion to draw. While it's true
that under ideal conditions the extent of these problems may significantly diminish, none of them disappears altogether. This is

true at least if we view ideal theory through a lens that sees certain inequalities in a neutral or positive light.[44] An exploration of philanthropy brings into focus certain objectionable inequalities in power that this lens occludes. In this way, the problems with which philanthropy confronts us aren't merely symptoms of a failure to meet the demands of political morality as we know them. Rather, taking these problems seriously requires that we refine our understanding of what it is that political morality demands.

5

In Usufruct to the Living

A century has now passed since the death of Andrew Carnegie.[1] While the last chapter examined how the unlimited giftability of property might defy democratic ideals, public criticism of philanthropy more often takes aim at a particular device that Carnegie helped pioneer: the private charitable foundation. Citizens and scholars of various stripes have questioned the compatibility of this elite form of philanthropy with liberal-democratic principles. While some regard elite philanthropy as an unexceptional exercise of economic liberty,[2] others charge that it depends on, and serves to reinforce, objectionable disparities in wealth.[3] Some look to foundations to solve entrenched social problems;[4] others challenge the asymmetries in power that come along with foundation-driven experiments in social policy.[5] But whatever verdict awaits an overall assessment of foundations, one distinctive dimension of this practice hasn't generated significant scrutiny. This is the temporal dimension. A striking, albeit little noticed, fact is that although Carnegie and his peers are no longer living citizens, they are nonetheless still empowered to restrict the use of property and project influence over social conditions.[6] Dead donors enjoy these powers because contemporary societies recognize "intergenerational charitable transfers" (ICTs), legal devices that allow members of one generation to mark off property for charitable purposes in future generations.[7] The most prominent form of ICT is the *private charitable foundation*, typically designed as a perpetual endowment that makes grants for enumerated charitable purposes—a form that Carnegie himself helped to put on the map. Other forms include the ordinary *charitable bequest*, which allows a person to dedicate their estate to a charitable cause upon their death, and the *restricted charitable gift*, a donation made to a charity for the sake of perpetually endowing a specific activity.

Recent attention to these phenomena has considered how a society should regulate intergenerational charitable transfers, or how individual philanthropists should make the best use of these tools.[8] This chapter begins with a question that is in a sense more fundamental, even if its practical relevance may at first seem obscure. That is, do intergenerational charitable transfers have a legitimate place in a democratic society? Is there a convincing justification for permitting such transfers at all? If ICTs are ultimately impermissible, then questions about how to regulate them or how to make the best use of them take on a much different character. The chapter reaches the conclusion that ICTs do indeed have a place in a well-ordered democracy, but it's a role that comes with noteworthy limitations. In turn, I show how this exploration of the justification of ICTs helps us to answer pertinent questions of public policy.

The argument unfolds in five parts. To ground the philosophical discussion that follows, I proceed in the next section by describing the key features and prevalence of intergenerational charitable giving, particularly as it manifests in the contemporary United States. Drawing on the poignant remarks of Thomas Jefferson, Section II develops a skeptical challenge to the justification of intergenerational charitable transfers. Jefferson prompts us to see that ICTs are a form of "dead-hand control," a way by which the past restricts the liberty of the living and unborn. But, in Jefferson's view, the dead have no right to control the living. This casts the case for ICTs into doubt. Section III examines recent attempts by political theorists to justify ICTs. Although these views contribute essential foundations to a response to the Jeffersonian challenge, I show that the arguments behind them fall short of justifying dead-hand control. Section IV fills in the gap. It contends, *pace* Jefferson, that in the case of philanthropy, dead-hand control isn't categorically objectionable. Rather, dead-hand control is objectionable to the extent that past persons lack the capacity to make sound judgments about temporally distant conditions. Part V concludes that the resulting policy challenge becomes how to prevent the past from curtailing actions in the future on the basis of demonstrably false beliefs. Recent policy trends toward *cy-près* reform appear to be a step in the right direction, but they are not sufficient.

I. The Practical Context

Instead of automatically relinquishing property to named heirs or remitting it to the state, testation empowers a decedent to decide what shall happen with their property after they're no longer around to manage it. Donating property to a charitable purpose is a popular use of this power. A substantial portion of the resources committed to charitable causes comes from gifts at death (bequests) and gifts that continue to pay out after death (trusts).

Bequests on their own provide only a small portion of the funding for organized charitable endeavors today. In the United States, the proportion of charitable dollars from living individuals (69 percent) now dwarfs that of bequests (10 percent) by sevenfold.[9] But the declining status of bequests has been offset by the rising significance of perpetual charitable trusts. A charitable trust—whether established during one's life or through a bequest—allows a property owner to create a perpetual endowment by appointing agents (trustees) to invest and spend the entrusted property in a way that preserves its principal. Although the settlor of a charitable trust can opt to limit the trust's lifetime, perpetuity is the default. Barring gross mismanagement by trustees, national economic crisis, or changes in the law, a charitable trust can be expected to persist indefinitely.

Charitable trusts that are funded by a small number of people are called private foundations. Private foundations typically make grants to other charitable organizations rather than engaging directly in charitable work.[10] Despite some prominent exceptions, most private foundations are structured to exist in perpetuity.[11] The number and size of these entities have grown astronomically over the past few decades. According to estimates of the Internal Revenue Service, between 1985 and 2011 the number of American foundations tripled (from 31,171 to 92,990), and the value of assets held by foundations grew by six-fold (from $95 billion to $641 billion, in inflation-adjusted dollars).[12] In turn, the nonprofit sector has come to depend more heavily on foundations over time, with the proportion of funding that charitable endeavors draw from foundations rising from 5 percent in the 1980s to 17 percent in recent years.[13]

Restricted charitable gifts provide another possible example of perpetual philanthropy. Restricted charitable gifts are donations to charities for the purpose of supporting particular programs, typically on a perpetual basis. The receiving entity is bound to administer the gift according to the terms set out by the donor, which can be more or less specific. Restricted gifts, in other words, are charitable trusts under the trusteeship of individual charities. No statistical agency currently tracks the prevalence or extent of restricted gifts. However, some evidence suggests that the vast majority of "major gifts"—typically exceeding $1 million—possess this quality.[14]

To be sure, bequests, foundations, and restricted gifts raise many interesting issues apart from their relationship to time. However, as will become clear in what follows, philanthropy's temporal aspects are rarely examined, poorly understood, and tremendously important. Finding a legitimate place for intergenerational charitable transfers runs into a host of challenges.

II. The Jeffersonian Challenge

Though it hasn't exercised many contemporary theorists, the power of dead persons to restrict how property can be used in the future was particularly disturbing to many commentators in the past.[15] Thomas Jefferson was one of the most caustic critics. In his 1789 letter to James Madison, he considers it "self evident 'that the earth belongs in usufruct to the living'; that the dead have neither powers nor rights over it."[16] (To own something "in usufruct" is to enjoy rights to its use and fruits without rights to diminish or destroy it.)[17] Invoking the authority of nature, Jefferson points out that no "law of nature" entitles persons to control property after death. Although positive laws often recognize rights of bequest and inheritance, these legal rights shouldn't be conflated with moral rights. A legal right of testation is merely a social convention designed to solve the problem of property's succession: what should happen to property after its owner dies. Jefferson isn't entirely clear on what he wants his reader to draw from this observation. One strong possibility is that since dead persons have no natural right to control property beyond their lifetimes, succeeding generations shouldn't be in any way constrained by their wishes. In turn, a society ought to organize its laws of succession to prioritize the interests of the living and unborn.

Jefferson's remarks thus suggest one reason for preliminary discomfort with idea of intergenerational philanthropy: the fact that it restricts the way in which future persons may use property. A society has multiple alternatives at its disposal for organizing the succession of property and the finance of charitable enterprise. Some of these options would afford greater say to future generations. For instance, property could transfer to future generations without any restrictions on its use, leaving future generations entirely free to choose how much to devote to charitable purposes, as well as which purposes to pursue. Alternatively, a society could permit persons to dedicate property for future charitable purposes while leaving the choice of those purposes entirely up to future persons. Or, a society could license ICTs, but restrict their duration or subject them to the possibility of amendment. Given that the succession of charitable resources could be organized in different ways that afford greater control to future generations, we have reason to question whether the status quo is defensible.

Jefferson's remarks also furnish us with an additional source of skepticism about ICTs. He appears to believe that coexisting members of a political community stand in a much different relationship to each other than they do to past or future members of the same community. The letter continues, "We seem not to have perceived that, by the law of nature, one generation is to another as one independant nation to another [sic]." Jefferson appears to believe that coexisting in time and space is a necessary condition of membership in political community. Only through membership in such a community do we acquire claims against other members of that community, including a say in community affairs. Just as each nation is entitled to sovereignty, to exclude other nations from control over its own internal affairs, so too is a generation entitled to sovereignty, to exclude past generations from control over the affairs of living persons.[18] If we follow this analogy to its end, we reach the implication that instances of dead-hand control are tantamount to colonialism, an implication that should be even more unsettling to us today than it would have been to Jefferson's contemporaries.

Even if we could overcome the obstacle that dead persons have no natural right to testation, these remarks indicate that justifying intergenerational charitable transfers faces an additional challenge. The challenge emerges in light of a crucial difference between charitable and noncharitable gift-giving. The practice of interpersonal gift-giving is primarily a private affair. Its immediate effects are limited to the giver and the receiver. By contrast, charitable giving aims to affect wider civic conditions. Its point isn't to benefit a friend or family member, but to promote one's particular conception of the common good. In a liberal democracy, however, what constitutes the common good and how to promote it are inherently contested questions. Opinions differ considerably about the proper size of the charitable sector within a society's broader political economy, and about the relative merits of different potential charitable causes.

This distinction between interpersonal and charitable giving interacts with the passage of time in a normatively significant way. Arguably, part of the justification for respecting the charitable choices of our contemporaneous fellow citizens, even when we find them misguided, is the fact that our contemporaries are equally susceptible to our own such choices. We have reason to tolerate their philanthropic choices insofar as they respect ours. This isn't to say that the reciprocal liberty to make philanthropic gifts is all that matters in the justification of philanthropy within a single generation. For instance, vast inequalities in wealth that make philanthropy the province of a tiny elite might pose a serious challenge to this justification. Nonetheless, the very possibility of this kind of mutual toleration is absent in the case of intergenerational philanthropy. ICTs unilaterally impose past persons' conceptions of the public benefit on future generations. Because time moves in one direction, future generations enjoy no reciprocal opportunity to influence civic conditions in the past.[19] From the future's perspective, the expectation to honor the philanthropic directives of the past may seem like an unwarranted invasion. Why ought we allow former citizens a say in our common affairs?

Thus, Jefferson's letter gives rise to two related but distinct worries about intergenerational philanthropy. The first concern is that intergenerational philanthropy depends on recognizing a right of testation as a solution to the succession of property. This solution appears to be prejudicial to future persons, who have an interest in receiving property unrestricted. The second concern is that intergenerational philanthropy allows past persons to influence civic conditions in future generations, encroaching on the sovereignty of future generations to determine social conditions for themselves.

III. Recent Justifications for Intergenerational Philanthropy

A. A Right of Testation?

As we saw earlier, part of the Jeffersonian challenge to intergenerational philanthropy is the absence of a natural right to testation. Jefferson makes plain that he regards this as a "self-evident" proposition needing no elaboration or defense. But we should try to flesh out this idea in some greater detail. Theories of natural rights typically hold that rights derive from a fundamental entitlement to individual self-ownership, an entitlement that preexists and constrains political institutions. According to Steiner and Vallentyne, such theories diverge on the question of which sorts of agents have these rights.[20] On one view, agents are eligible for natural rights if they are capable of making *choices*. If some class of agents possesses the capacity for choosing between alternative options, that class of agents is a bearer of natural rights. On another view, agents are eligible for rights if they are the sorts of being that have *interests*—regardless of whether they are able to make choices of their own. Important for our purposes is that both views tend to converge on the conclusion that the dead have no rights. Clearly enough, dead persons are incapable of making *choices*, so they can't be rights-bearers on the choice-making conception of natural rights. To have an *interest* in something, meanwhile, is precisely to be in a position to derive benefits from its success and harm from its failure. A person is incapable of suffering setbacks or enjoying achievements once she has died.[21] Thus, the interest-holding conception of natural rights has little to offer to the dead either. If recognizing a right to testation depends on ascribing rights to dead persons, the case for testation is in peril.

Testation would be ruled out from the start if government can't act legitimately except for the sake of protecting natural rights—as many libertarians believe. But Jefferson wasn't a thoroughgoing libertarian, and his letter leaves open the possibility that positive laws can derive legitimacy from sources other than natural law.[22] Might testation be justified on alternative grounds? Indeed, numerous scholars have recently observed that, even if persons have no natural right to testation, testation can nonetheless be valuable as a social practice.[23] A social practice of testation can be valuable, according to this view, not because it respects our posthumous rights as such, but because it increases the options available to us while alive and incentivizes greater social productivity.

One reason that testation is desirable is that it allows us to extend our plans and projects beyond our mortal existence, thereby affording us opportunities to pursue more or better options *during life*.[24] Suppose you're a person of advancing age with a deep commitment to your local community theater. However, you also face declining health, and a concern about having sufficient funds to cover your medical expenses prevents you from making more than token donations to the theater company during annual fundraising drives. Without the power of testation, each donation to the theater company would be money not saved for medical expenses, increasing your risk of facing greater suffering. Things look different with the power of testation, however. With that power, you can forego the annual contributions and instead arrange things so that whatever property remains in your possession at death goes to the theater group. This removes the trade-off between promoting your conception of the common good and protecting your own basic interests. By extending the range of available options in this way, testation facilitates the formulation and execution of a rational life plan.

A secondary benefit of a practice of testation is that it provides incentives for productivity and social savings that are generally advantageous to a society.[25] Lacking the option to pass on property after death might make it harder for us to undertake difficult or long-term projects.[26] If I'm not permitted to pass on my furniture store to my children, why should I put myself through the thankless travail of starting and running a business? But, clearly enough, the health of a market economy significantly depends on individuals' willingness to take such long-term risks. Part of what make such risks worthwhile lies in the ability to pass on the successes of our endeavors to successors.

Besides these potential effects on productivity, a right of testation might also induce greater savings. If we couldn't pass on property beyond our lifetimes, we would face pressure to consume as much as possible before death. The opportunity to control property beyond our lifetimes thus provides an incentive to preserve resources for future persons, rather than consume it all ourselves.[27]

These considerations indicate that attempts to justify intergenerational transfers need not ascribe natural rights to the dead. Rather, they indicate that recognizing a practice of testation can be a way of facilitating the interests of a society's members in living richer lives. Other things equal, a society that refused to honor wishes of the dead would be impoverished in many respects. But the fact that testation can be valuable as a social practice doesn't prove that it's justified in any and every possible form. For instance, an unlimited right of testation may very well lead to objectionable social conditions in the succeeding generation. It could also deprive members of a previous generation of their fair share of resources, if testators chose to save too much for the future. As the next subsection details, two notable strands of thought in contemporary political theory have explored in some detail what forms of testation are ultimately consistent with justice. They converge on the conclusion that while justifying interpersonal transfers faces certain challenges, the case for recognizing charitable transfers remains fairly strong.

B. ICTs and Equality of Opportunity

Several recent scholars have challenged the traditional practice of testation on grounds that it leads to objectionable inequalities in resources among members of the succeeding generations.[28] An unfettered right of individuals to make unilateral transfers can conflict with a society's attempts to secure or maintain conditions of equality of opportunity. As it happens, those who make intergenerational transfers often tend to transfer their estates to kin. This promotes the accumulation of wealth within families and serves as a catalyst for socioeconomic stratification. Heirs of great fortunes receive opportunities unavailable to those who inherit less or nothing at all. Under regimes that recognize a right of testation, the success of one's life plans may depend more on the accident of being born into a particular family than on one's merit or one's status as an equal citizen. Furthermore, unless a society takes special measures to insulate public affairs from accumulations of wealth, inheritance also threatens the integrity of democratic processes. The beneficiaries of accumulated family wealth can come to serve as gatekeepers for political office, as recent empirical research on campaign finance suggests.[29] This undermines a sacred constituent of the ideal of democracy, that citizens are entitled to equal opportunities for political influence.

However, the same liberal-egalitarian theorists who rail against the effects of inheritance on equality of opportunity tend to acknowledge that intergenerational transfers of wealth aren't inherently unjust. In particular, these scholars typically treat charitable gifts as unmitigated exceptions to the problem of justice in property succession. Several explicitly encourage intergenerational charitable transfers and seek to protect them from the restrictions that they would impose on noncharitable transfers.[30] This is so for two main reasons. First, because ICTs are gifts for purposes, rather than gifts to persons, their benefits tend to be widely distributed and, in turn, less prejudicial to distributive fairness. A bequest to a nature preserve, for example, benefits all who choose to visit the preserve, rather than any one heir. Encouraging charitable bequests and trusts helps to divert wealth from inequality-generating ends to ends that are inequality-neutral. A second reason for the liberal-egalitarian support of ICTs is that ICTs can work to combat the same objectionable inequalities that inherited wealth helps to create. This position reflects the thought that many charitable causes have as their aim the mitigation of poverty and inequality. For this reason, a practice of testation focused on charitable transfers might ultimately serve to reduce conditions of background injustice among members of succeeding generations.

These claims deserve some critical qualification. While it's true that ICTs don't pass on wealth to family members, they may in fact work against equality of opportunity in other ways. For instance, a testator might erect a family foundation and install their children as its trustees, allowing them to inherit the associated power and social status. Or, an ICT might be used to provide collective goods that predominantly benefit wealthy persons, either by concentrating its work in a wealthy suburb or by funding goods that predominantly appeal to richer people.[31] The liberal-egalitarian position can nonetheless respond that, odious as they are, the inequality-generating features of ICTs are only contingent possibilities, which we might manage through regulation or simply accept as lesser evils. This marks an important distinction between ICTs and intergenerational noncharitable transfers. For, whereas ICTs can contingently serve to perpetuate certain kinds of inequality, the transmission of dynastic privilege is a more inherent and inexorable function of noncharitable transfers of wealth.

Another challenge for this position is that the extent to which ICTs serve as instruments of poverty or inequality reduction depends on which purposes a society designates as charitable and how it structures the choice among different purposes.[32] In the contemporary United States, according to one recent estimate, less than 31 percent of donated dollars end up benefiting the disadvantaged.[33] Some believe that a society ought to provide greater incentives for charitable gifts aimed at reducing poverty and inequality.[34] Though Chapter 3 raised considerable doubts about the desirability of trying to combat poverty through charitable donation, for the sake of argument here I am willing to concede that the justification for ICTs would be strengthened if such transfers did indeed serve a genuinely redistributive function.

C. ICTs and Justice in Savings

Other scholars have made a more direct case for an affirmative policy toward ICTs, holding that ICTs are valuable not, or not only, because of their salutary effects on inequality *among* members of succeeding generations, but because of these salutary effects on inequality *between* generations. A significant aspect of the problem of justice between generations reflects the fact that each generation has a conflicting interest in consuming as much property as its members desire. Solving this problem requires determining what a present generation is obliged to save for the future, and what future persons can reasonably demand from their predecessors. John Rawls is often credited with helping to introduce this problem, as well as with offering a compelling general solution to it.[35] The "just savings principle," in Rawls's terms, directs generations to share the burden of developing and maintaining just institutions over time. Though rather vague in its particulars, the principle is distinct for holding that generations are neither to discount the interests of future persons (as economists often suggest), nor to engage in self-effacing sacrifice in the hope of delivering a future utopia. It's also distinct in holding that the aim of saving isn't to expand the economic pie continuously, but rather to establish stable, just institutions.

Cordelli and Reich argue that ICTs can serve as part of a strategy for satisfying Rawls's conception of justice in savings between generations.[36] In so doing, they draw attention to Rawls's overlooked remark that the savings required for this project may take various forms, including the conservation of natural resources, investment in buildings and technology, and the development of education and culture.[37] Building on this idea, Cordelli and Reich posit three elements—social capital, disaster preparedness, and social innovation—that are at once critical for securing just institutions over time and unavailable through public administration alone. Maintaining just institutions over time requires continuous investment in social capital, which provides indispensable support for the virtues of democratic citizenship. The reproduction of social capital requires a diverse, vibrant, and independent civil society, supported by voluntary donation. The stability of just institutions also requires research into, and instruments to mitigate, low-probability, high-magnitude catastrophes. Though the state might take certain steps to address general disaster scenarios, Cordelli and Reich believe that private supplementation of state efforts is necessary to hedge against obscure cataclysmic events. Finally, Cordelli and Reich contend that ICTs serve as a corrective to democratic "short-termism," the tendency of democratic processes to disregard the interests of future generations. Because of their insulation from electoral pressure and their extended time horizons, ICTs are especially suited to financing long-term projects whose discoveries contribute to just conditions in the future.

For these authors, a society can't develop and maintain a just basic structure without ongoing, affirmative measures to finance social capital, disaster preparedness, and technological innovation. Though they acknowledge that there might be other ways of investing in such goods, Cordelli and Reich hold that charitable bequests and trusts have much to recommend themselves in this respect.

IV. Reassessing the Jeffersonian Challenge

The foregoing section concluded that testation needn't presuppose that the dead have natural rights and can instead be justified by reference to its benefits to living and future persons. Testation in all its forms may not necessarily conform to the demands of justice, but there are good reasons to believe that recognizing charitable acts of testation can in fact satisfy certain compelling principles. Intergenerational charitable transfers may help to promote (or at least not necessarily undermine) equality of opportunity, and ICTs may also help to satisfy a principle of justice in savings between generations. These considerations go some way toward showing that devices of intergenerational philanthropy aren't nearly as prejudicial to the living and unborn as some have thought. But it isn't obvious that these considerations are sufficient to extinguish concerns about dead-hand control.

Recall that a constitutive feature of charitable bequests and trusts is that they impose the judgments of past generations onto future generations. In this way, such devices restrict the liberty of future generations to make their own economic decisions. Resources that might otherwise be theirs entirely, to allocate as they choose, must instead serve the purposes declared and specified by their forebears. In turn, because ICTs are public investments, designed to alter the nature and extent of collective goods within a society, these transfers restrict the degree of control that future generations may exert over the qualitative features of the social world they inhabit. Why ought future generations not enjoy sovereignty over these decisions?

A fixed point of political morality is that moral equals are entitled to a presumption of liberty. By default, each agent is entitled to govern their own affairs by their own lights. Your attempt to exercise practical authority over me—to substitute your judgment for mine over how I am to act—must be justifiable to me.

If a convincing justification isn't available, I am in turn justified in denying your authority and taking steps to resist it. One popular way to show how practical authority can be justified is to appeal to instrumental considerations.

Instrumental justifications of practical authority hold that an authority is legitimate if obeying its commands leaves subjects better off, in some relevant sense, than they would otherwise be.[38] To determine that future generations ought to abide by the directives of past generations, therefore, might involve showing that obeying the wills of the past makes future generations better off, in some relevant sense. In turn, a compelling reply to the Jeffersonian challenge could hold that obeying the wills of the past places future generations under conditions that are more beneficial and more just than they would be if future generations were to act independently. And it strikes me that each of the claims from the preceding section supplies an instrumental argument for the authority of the past over the future. That is, without intergenerational charitable transfers, future generations would be less able to advance their substantive aims, less able to maintain equality of opportunity, and less able to maintain various pillars of a just basic structure over time. To consider the foregoing justifications for ICTs as instrumentalist arguments for practical authority is also to open them up to pertinent objections, however.

A. Generational Sovereignty: An Intrinsic View

Obviously enough, some might reject instrumentalist justifications of authority out of hand. One might hold that, just as each nation is entitled to self-determination with respect to other nations, so each generation is entitled to self-determination with respect to other generations. It's generally wrong for one nation to colonize another on grounds that it has superior knowledge or capacity to promote justice, and it's equally wrong for past generations to "colonize" future generations in this way. If we reject colonial rule, must we also reject ICTs?

Answering this question requires that we consider positive arguments for collective self-determination, arguments that purport to show why it's distinctively valuable for a collectivity to control its own affairs. Such arguments hold that even if it were true that a benevolent despot, or advanced artificial intelligence, or a sacred text could more reliably track justice's demands, our lacking collective control over our laws and policies would be objectionable.[39] According to Zuehl, it would be objectionable because in some sense it would make our world not fully our own. We wouldn't be able to identify with, or see ourselves in, the decisions that affect our lives. We would feel like guests in a hotel room rather than residents of a home. The social world would confront us as other and alien.

One might think that ICTs undermine collective self-determination precisely in this way. These devices impose the judgments of the past on the future. They reflect the wills of past persons and not those of current cocitizens. I suspect, however, that ICTs can be made consistent with an appreciation of the value of collective self-determination.

For Zuehl, members of a collectivity can reasonably feel at home in their social world when their institutions are causally responsive to their will, as it's expressed through well-functioning representative democratic institutions. But members of a collectivity don't need to control each individual law and policy in order to be collectively self-determining in the relevant sense. Rather, Zuehl claims that a collectivity is self-determining when, by way of democratic decision-making, its "core institutions" intentionally reflect its "core values."[40] Thus, collective self-determination is undermined when the state isn't governed democratically, or when the state can't reliably regulate the society's core institutions in accordance with citizens' articulated values.[41] From this I believe we can also infer conditions for preserving collective self-determination in the face of external influences. Namely, a society suffers no objectionable setback to self-determination when such forces respect the collective's sovereignty over its core institutions or the conditions that core institutions are meant to regulate: fundamental rights, duties, and opportunities.[42]

Now we can begin to see how ICTs aren't morally equivalent to directives from a colonial administrator. A distinctive feature of colonial rule, and other forms of undemocratic authority, is that it involves domination of the society's core institutions and thereby deprives citizens of the opportunity to control their own affairs. But it's difficult to see ICTs as dominating in any meaningful sense. This is so for three reasons. First, even if ICTs require a future generation to pursue causes or implement strategies that it dislikes, ICTs are expected to supply only a portion of the funding for charitable pursuits. Future generations can still make their own charitable investments to counteract or supplement the investments of the past.[43] Second, given the wide range of charitable purposes, most ICTs bear only a tenuous relation to the distribution of fundamental rights, duties, and opportunities. It's difficult to see, for instance, how trusts for the preservation of historic architecture or bequests for advancing excellence in the performing arts bear on matters of basic justice. The value of collective self-determination might tell against the privatization of basic education and welfare provision, insofar as such measures inhibit citizens from effectively regulating the content and distribution of fundamental rights, duties, and opportunities. But offhand it seems that at least some degree of private provision can be consistent with living citizens holding the reins that establish basic liberties and entitlements to essential resources. Third, even if these first two conditions somehow failed to hold, ICTs don't prevent a well-functioning democratic state from asserting legislative supremacy over questions of basic justice. Legislation to nationalize health care, for instance, would instantly supersede ICTs designed to finance the provision of medical services.

At the very least, then, ICTs don't categorically prevent a generation from exercising control over its common affairs in the way that colonialism does to a society. I take these observations to show that although ICTs subject a society to control by alien forces, this control is reconcilable with one central reason we have for wanting freedom from that kind of control.[44]

B. Generational Sovereignty: An Epistemic View

As I have framed it, the challenge for the proponent of ICTs is to show that, although ICTs impose the judgments of the past onto the future, this imposition can be justified. It can be justified if it's true that obeying the wills of the past leaves future generations under conditions that are more beneficial and more just than they would be if future generations were to control property completely independently of the past. The immediately preceding subsection deflected a preliminary objection to this line of reasoning, that rule by the past would be impermissible even if it led to perfectly just outcomes. The present subsection considers a more direct challenge: that complying with the directives of past generations doesn't necessarily satisfy the instrumentalist justification at all. Complying with the directives of the past can often leave future generations in suboptimal conditions.

To see the force of this objection, consider some examples. When the Englishman Thomas Betton died in 1723, he ordered his estate placed into trust. His will declared that half of the trust's annual income be paid "forever to the redemption of British slaves in Turkey or Barbary."[45] Despite his good intentions, however, Betton failed to foresee that the white slave market would disappear in the 1830s, when France seized Ottoman territories and in short order rooted out the trafficking of human beings. Fidelity to Betton's stated wishes would require that the funds continue to accumulate unused should those markets somehow reappear. Also consider Bryan Mullanphy of St. Louis, Missouri. He died in 1851, but not before establishing a trust "to furnish relief to all poor immigrants and travelers coming to St. Louis on their way, bona fide, to settle the West."[46] Within a few decades, the West was mostly settled, and innovations in transportation made wagon stops in St. Louis obsolete. If Mullanphy had his way, his trust would still be idly accumulating funds, waiting perhaps for the Pacific Garbage Patch to become habitable.

The arguments in favor of ICTs that we considered earlier wouldn't necessarily rule out these kinds of troubling cases. Both cases appear consistent with the liberal-egalitarian perspective on inheritance, which approves of ICTs insofar as they are inequality-neutral or inequality-reducing. The succoring of weary immigrants and travelers, for instance, reduces a pertinent form of inequality. Each case also appears consistent with the justice-in-savings perspective on ICTs, which holds that ICTs are valuable as fonts of social capital, disaster preparedness, and technological innovation. Preserving Betton's slave-rescue fund would be a hedge against a kind of rare disaster. The slave rescue and repatriation organizations that it would fund could eventually contribute to the stock of social capital. The innovative methods that these organizations might develop could be adapted or scaled up by other organizations or by the state.

What we notice when we reflect on these cases is that although the donors in question appear to have been attempting to benefit future generations, the passage of time has called their judgment on this score into question. Clearly enough, Betton and Mullanphy respectively assumed that British slavery and waggoneer weariness would remain serious problems into the indefinite future. These judgments turned out to be false. Armed with new information, future generations charged with preserving these trusts might well believe that the risks of British slavery and weariness among St. Louis waggoneers are now too remote to warrant saving so much resources for them. They might think other causes more urgent or more cost-effective investments.

The challenge for ICTs is that although their putative justification depends on their resulting in significant benefits for future persons, past generations are entirely unreliable judges of what will be specifically useful to succeeding generations. Living persons are generally much better at gauging and satisfying the interests of their contemporaries. Partly this is because living donors have access to more intimate knowledge of the preferences of their potential beneficiaries. Being alive also enables them to update their judgments in response to new information. If I discover that no one is attending the museum that I have been supporting, I can change the direction of my donation (by funding some other cause) or change the strategy of my gift (say, by funding the museum's marketing efforts rather than its collection development). These features disappear with intergenerational philanthropy. For once I die, there is no guarantee that the judgments I formed while alive will satisfy the interests or preferences of any potential beneficiaries who survive me. The greater the separation of time, the worse the likely discrepancy between past judgments and future interests. Generally speaking, future generations may also be more reliable judges because of their privileged position in the historical sequence. Living later in time gives them access to improvements in technology and accumulations of historical data to draw more reliable causal inferences.

These initial considerations would appear to undercut the case for ICTs. If past generations are generally less wise about the interests of future persons and how to promote them, respecting directives from the past will not make future generations better off. In turn, future generations would then have no reason to regard these directives as binding. But this isn't the end of the story, as another example will help clarify.

Marie Robertson made a restricted gift to Princeton University in 1961.[47] The terms of the trust stated its purposes as "the education of men and women for government service." Particularly in the years after Robertson's death in 1981, Princeton started to interpret "government service" more loosely, using the gift to train students for careers in public service outside of formal government employment. The university believed a changing labor market for public service had rendered Robertson's intentions obsolete. The size of the federal bureaucracy had been shrinking while opportunities for jobs with private contractors and nonprofit organizations had become more numerous. Princeton's actions set off a rancorous dispute with Robertson's surviving family members, who believed that her gift was meant explicitly to train officials for the federal government.

For the sake of illustration, let us suppose that Robertson did intend her gift to express a specific commitment to government work as such. She might have believed, for instance, that official state agencies are more democratically accountable than private firms and nonprofits and thus more legitimate ways of administering public policy. Had she lived to observe them, Robertson might well have opposed recent trends toward outsourcing state functions and Princeton's willingness to follow suit. In this respect, the dispute didn't arise because Robertson failed to predict future circumstances accurately, but because of a principled disagreement between Robertson and her trustees. It would certainly not be unreasonable for someone to hold that a liberal democracy ought to rely more heavily on a well-trained official bureaucracy than on outsourcing, and that training students for official roles is an essential mission of schools of public administration.

I take this case to indicate something distinctive about the epistemic virtues of ICTs. Namely, not all disputes with dead donors come about as a result of the donors' lack of foresight. At least some disputes turn on matters of principle, where the past's judgment may ultimately be as wise as, or wiser than, the future's. Clearly, in cases where the judgments of the past are superior to the judgments of the future, deferring to the judgments of the dead would help the future better advance its own interests. With this in mind, suppose that Robertson's view about public service ultimately is the most reasonable position. If we were to think about the matter carefully and abstract further from the status quo, we would come to accept this position as uniquely correct. The case would then show that prohibiting ICTs risks depriving future persons of the superior wisdom of the past.

One might also think that a certain amount of deference to past judgments can be valuable even when their apparent wisdom is more controversial. Suppose we find, after due reflection, that Robertson's position provides a reasonable alternative to the status quo, but not an obviously superior alternative. Even so, we might agree that ICTs that are merely controversial, as opposed to those that depend on patently false beliefs, can still be useful to present and future persons, though in an indirect way. Obeying the reasonably controversial wills of the past can be useful because it forces the present and future to engage with conceptions of the common good that challenge the conventional wisdom of the moment. We don't need to endorse a thoroughgoing Burkean conservativism to appreciate that in some cases encountering judgments of the past exposes us to certain valuable advice that we wouldn't have otherwise considered.[48] At the very least, confronting the different practical judgments of past persons, as they manifest in the organizations of civil society, requires us to test the robustness of our assumptions. Thus, the fact that ICTs require a present generation to share the task of directing civil society with past persons can have certain educative effects on the present generation. Even when ICTs aren't altogether epistemically privileged, they can work in indirect ways to improve the present generation's ability to advance its aims consistent with the demands of justice.

Taken together, the observations of this section indicate that an instrumentalist justification for ICTs reaches mixed conclusions. Obeying the terms of ICTs that depend on patently false assessments would deeply undermine the ability of future generations to advance their interests. However, obeying the terms of ICTs that depend on assessments that are merely reasonably controversial might in fact leave future generations better off in relevantly valuable respects. Where does this leave us? If I am right, the resulting policy challenge that a society faces isn't the binary one of allowing ICTs or prohibiting them; it's one of fine-tuning the regulation of intergenerational transfers so as to screen out ICTs that become obsolete while protecting those that reflect merely controversial judgments. The final section offers some general thoughts on how different regulatory strategies might meet this challenge.

V. Policy Implications

One might think that a way of avoiding the possibility of obsolete ICTs is to restrict them to very general purposes. Restricting ICTs to general purposes would allow future trustees significant discretion over how to interpret and administer them. Future trustees would be able to make these decisions with reference to current understandings of empirical conditions. An immediate problem with this proposed solution, however, is that it squelches one of the main incentives for making ICTs in the first place. Arguably, a prime incentive for donors in making such transfers is the opportunity to give effect to their specific judgments about the public benefit. The pleasure in legacy giving is as much an expression of the donor's thoughtfulness and taste as it is an expression of their generosity. A scheme that significantly limits the degree of choice among potential objects of philanthropy might make ICTs much less attractive to most potential donors.[49] This would be an unfortunate implication in light of the hypothesis that ICTs are important instruments of justice.

Perhaps a more serious problem with confining ICTs to general purposes is that it would deprive ICTs of one of their chief virtues. As we have seen, one of the chief virtues of ICTs lies in their ability to preserve unique ideas from the past and counteract biases of the present. Confining trusts to general purposes would allow future generations to inherit the generosity of the past, but not its wisdom.[50] And, as we saw earlier, the promise of epistemic benefits is an integral component of a successful defense against the Jeffersonian challenge. If the past has no knowledge to offer the future, the future has fewer reasons to respect the past's attempts to meddle in future social conditions.

A second policy option is to prevent donors from making perpetual trusts. A one-time bequest, or a trust that spends down its assets after a limited number of years, stands a good chance of avoiding the tendency toward obsolescence. I think this strategy would also prove overinclusive, however. Certain types of initiatives take many years to get off the ground. Their benefits might not become apparent for many decades, if not centuries. Term limitations on ICTs would discourage the kinds of long-term thinking that some claim as one of their chief strengths.[51]

A third and more promising possibility is to take a permissive attitude to the terms of the ICT, allowing donors to select the narrowness of their aims and the duration of their purposes. This permission would be qualified, however, by periodic review. A proposal along these lines has enjoyed the support of some prominent figures. One is John Stuart Mill.[52] Mill argues that perpetual trusts pose a particular dilemma. On the one hand is the fact that even a "prudent man" lacks the foresight to predict what will be useful twenty or thirty years after his death. On the other hand is a danger in inviting the state to step in to revise the terms of a trust once that foresight proves faulty. Mill worries that public officials would be tempted to abuse this power, such as by reallocating trust funds to compensate for temporary budget shortfalls in other areas of public spending. He thus proposes to expose perpetual trusts to review after a fixed period of time (no longer than "the foresight of a prudent man may be presumed to reach"), but to limit the revisions that public officials may make. Public officials, he contends, may only resolve to amend a trust's terms if they have in fact become obsolete. And in revising obsolete terms, officials must seek, first, to deploy them toward efficient uses and, second, to select uses that are as close as possible to the trust's original purposes.[53]

Vestiges of Mill's proposal appear in ongoing efforts to reform the judicial doctrine of *cy-près*. In the United States and elsewhere, *cy-près* (from the archaic French *cy près comme possible*) permits public officials (typically judges) to revise a trust that has become obsolete. As it's traditionally practiced, officials are only allowed to revise the terms of the trust when those terms have become illegal by current standards or literally impossible to carry out. By protecting the intentions of the donor to the extent possible, the doctrine preserves the incentives that encourage making ICTs and devoting them to unique purposes. However, the doctrine has also been the object of considerable criticism, particularly since terms can prove objectionably impractical or wasteful despite remaining possible to implement.[54] It's *possible* to accumulate funds for the repatriation of British slaves or the relief of settlers passing through St. Louis. But is it worth saving millions or even billions of dollars for such rare causes?

In recent years, approximately half of American states have attempted to account for this kind of concern in their adoption of reformed guidelines for *cy-près*.[55] The Uniform Trust Code (UTC), a model law proposed by an independent commission of experts and adopted by numerous states, now contains a broadened understanding of *cy-près*.[56] The UTC allows a court to alter the terms of a trust when it judges that such terms have become impractical or wasteful, even if complying with the terms remains technically possible. From the perspective of the account I have offered in this essay, this is an encouraging development.

A noteworthy limitation of the UTC, however, is that it doesn't automatically subject perpetual trusts to periodic review. For a court to consider applying a *cy-près* remedy, an "interested person" must bring a challenge to the trust in question.[57] A predictable consequence of such a policy is that it exposes to scrutiny only a fraction of potentially obsolete trusts. But in view of Mill and Simes, *all* charitable trusts should come under review automatically after a fixed period of time. Only by subjecting all trusts to review can be we sure to address the problem thoroughly and fairly. (Lest this proposal appear to impose an unreasonably weighty administrative burden, imagine a process that reviews a pseudo-random sample of trusts—much like the Internal Revenue Service's current auditing procedures—with extra attention paid to trusts that control the largest endowments or operate within the most judgment-sensitive areas.)[58]

Another way of capturing the spirit of Mill and Simes's proposals is to build *cy-près* remedies into a trust's initial terms.[59] That is, donors could enumerate an ordered list of purposes to be pursued if or when the trust's initial purpose becomes obsolete. This proposal allows donors to protect themselves from having their intentions reinterpreted by public officials. It would also reduce the need for auditing by creating interested parties (contingent beneficiaries) who would then be empowered to challenge obsolete trusts in court.

Altogether, these observations point toward a particular regulative strategy. That is, a society ought to broadly recognize one-time bequests and limited-life trusts. Meanwhile, the price of adopting a longer time horizon is to expose one's endeavors to substantive audit and adjustment at successive intervals. Recent developments in American trust law go some way toward capturing the spirit of this regulatory ideal, but they also leave one significant aspect of the problem—the need for periodic review—unaddressed.

* * *

Intergenerational philanthropy involves a conflict over the desire of the past to benefit the future, and the desire of the future to govern itself by its own lights. This conflict is present in some form in any relationship of gift-giving and gift-receiving. But the public-facing nature of philanthropy and the passage of time conspire to make this conflict especially thorny. Attempts to find a place for intergenerational philanthropy in a liberal democracy have pointed to its potentially beneficial effects. I have argued that these attempts are incomplete.

To show that intergenerational charitable transfers are justifiable requires showing that such transfers are consistent with the value of generational sovereignty. Part of what makes generational sovereignty valuable, I contended, is the interest a generation has in control over matters of basic justice in its society. We have seen that ICTs don't ultimately pose a threat to the ability of living persons to exercise control over these fundamental questions. Another part of what makes generational sovereignty valuable is the superior knowledge that a generation is likely to have regarding its own interests. Living persons appear best positioned to understand their own interests and to take prudent steps to realize them. Dead-hand control appears to saddle a living generation with the well-meaning but obsolescent conjectures of the departed. I argued, however, that binding the living and unborn to obsolete notions is a dispensable feature of intergenerational philanthropy. Prudent regulation can cabin the tendency of ICTs to reflect obsolete ideas while also leveraging the unique wisdom of the past. The possibility of such regulation, and some encouraging steps currently being taken in its direction, supplies one strong response to the Jeffersonian challenge.

A striking upshot of the foregoing analysis is that it seems to vindicate the enduring influence of persons like Andrew Carnegie, whose general-purpose foundation shows no obvious signs of becoming obsolete. Those troubled by this implication may suspect that the analysis is mistaken. Perpetual philanthropy provides a way for donors who have accumulated wealth unjustly, or have accumulated an unjust amount of wealth, to further increase their power. How can this be democratically legitimate? To be clear, I see no reason why ICTs should be immune from confiscation or re-allocation if they are indeed founded on egregious wrongdoing. Additionally, while this chapter has defended the idea of intergenerational philanthropy as such, it has not defended any particular manifestation of this practice. Under conditions of irrepressible inequality, limitations on the privileges or scale of individual ICTs could certainly be consistent with the arguments offered here. But as the previous chapters have suggested, there are also other ways of mitigating the problems that perpetual philanthropy can sometimes exacerbate. Limits on economic inequality or the ways that wealth can purchase influence would preempt common criticisms of philanthropic foundations. Moreover, to regulate foundations without attending to the broader tensions between philanthropy and democracy would be short-sighted.[60] But intergenerational charitable transfers need not, and often do not, come from Robber Barons and plutocrats. They can and do come from ordinary people who want to leave something to the world after they depart it. This chapter has shown how, under the right conditions, such a practice could be a valuable contribution to a democratic polity.

6

The Effective Altruist's
Political Problem

The foregoing chapters have considered how the practice of philanthropy and some of its main dimensions might be justified. They have given us resources to reflect on how such a practice might be established, regulated, and reformed. Thinking about philanthropy as a social practice has helped us to move beyond the traditional focus of reflection on philanthropy, which interrogates the practice from the perspective of an individual participant. When laypersons and philosophers consider the ethics of philanthropy, they most frequently narrow their attention to the question of whether individuals have duties to donate and in what those duties might consist. These are certainly pivotal questions. But to think of philanthropy exclusively from the first-personal perspective is to overlook features of the larger practice that shape who may participate in it, for what purposes, and on what terms. The previous chapters have sought to reveal controversial choices behind these features and to show how they might be reappraised. The current chapter demonstrates how reflection on the politics of philanthropy also contributes essential and often neglected considerations to the practical ethics of giving itself.[1]

Debate about the practical ethics of giving principally concerns the choice of causes individuals might support and the level of contribution they might make. For instance, under what conditions is it permissible to support artistic and cultural organizations in a world marred by pervasive suffering and injustice? How should we choose between near and distant beneficiaries? How much, if anything, should one be expected to donate? These questions have been explored frequently and at great length by others, and giving them their due would take far more space than I can claim here.[2] The question I tackle presently in a sense lies further downstream. It concerns how donations might best respond to the particular challenge of severe poverty. This question addresses issues of immense importance, connects to an especially intense and interdisciplinary debate, and provides concrete illustration of how democratic considerations bear on individual conduct.

I. The Emergence of "Effective Altruism"

Almost no one denies that the affluent have duties to assist the poor in some way. What remains less clear are the bases of these duties and how best to discharge them. An important strand in the history of political thought discourages responding to poverty with donations to private charity. From Wollstonecraft, to Kant, to Marx, to Mill, to King, a long line of commentators has argued that almsgiving attends only to the symptoms of social disease.[3] Just as treating the symptoms of a disease can allow the disease to fester, treating the symptoms of poverty can overlook its institutional causes. Proponents of this *palliative critique* of charitable giving typically recommend that individuals in a position to help take a different approach: challenging and refashioning the institutions and policies that are responsible for systemic poverty and inequality in the first place.[4] While individuals might indeed have good reasons to make philanthropic donations for a variety of noble purposes, alleviating deprivation isn't one of them.

The emergence and surging popularity of the *effective altruism* movement presents an opportunity to test this critique. Effective altruism is at once a sophisticated ethical doctrine and a growing social movement that animates a growing number of think tanks,[5] meta-charities (charities that evaluate other charities),[6] philan-thropic foundations,[7] internet discussion groups,[8] and regional chapters.[9] Inspired partly by the ideas of philosopher Peter Singer, effective altruism urges people who are well-off in global terms to do the most good that they can for the world, and to do so on the basis of careful reasoning and reliable evidence.[10] Though its pur-view has broadened in recent years, a central focus of the move-ment remains the relief of severe poverty, particularly in the areas of the world where it is most concentrated. This reflects the judgment that global poverty is both one of the greatest sources of aggregate misery and also one of the most promising areas in which indi-vidual action can make a concrete difference. A variety of private charities have found successful, low-cost ways of reducing prema-ture death and improving quality of life for substantial numbers of people. Donating to these organizations offers one of the most reli-able ways for individuals to add value to the world. Thus, effective altruism has become most well-known for its attempts to change traditional attitudes toward organized philanthropy. Effective al-truist leaders have sought to identify and publicize the charitable initiatives that relieve poverty in the most cost-effective ways while heaping shame on charitable initiatives that pursue aims that they consider less valuable or strategies that they consider less scien-tific.[11] Cultural philanthropy and well-meaning but untested hu-manitarian efforts receive the harshest denunciations.

But effective altruism has also come in for sharp criticism from commentators who see its solutions as mere bandages for institu-tional pathologies (and its message as too congenial to those who benefit most from these pathologies).[12] These critics remind us that the prevalence of poverty isn't a natural disaster lying out-side of human control but the product of institutions that we can in fact control. Modern-day proponents of the palliative critique urge those with means to deploy their resources toward institu-tional reform and resistance, especially through forms of political advocacy. Effective altruism's leaders have responded by defending their commitment to service delivery while also exploring certain aspects of political engagement.

This chapter makes two main claims. The first is that the palliative critique is stronger than participants in this debate have realized. As I explain in the next section, recent work by political economists suggests that providing resources directly to disadvantaged populations isn't only ineffective but likely counterproductive to the larger aims of international development. Even when direct assistance doesn't undermine development, it is likely inefficient in comparison to institutional reform strategies. Meanwhile, as I detail in the third section, recent contributions to political philosophy suggest that assessments of efficacy in philanthropy must be qualified by how philanthropic initiatives exercise power. Unfortunately, the kinds of service delivery projects that effective altruists tend to recommend expose receiving communities to objectionable forms of control.

The chapter's other main claim is that proponents of the palliative critique should be careful what they wish for. As I explain in the fourth section, the evidence-based methodology that helps to define the effective altruist approach is likely to be inefficient when transposed to political engagement. Effective altruism's methodological proclivities bias it toward superficial policy reforms and away from the deeper institutional shifts that would satisfy its critics. Additionally, greater resource flows into advocacy from the relatively affluent can work to drown out less affluent voices, reintroducing concerns about objectionable exercises of power. As a result, a turn from assistance to advocacy risks succumbing to some of the very same challenges that it's meant to overcome. This is the effective altruist's political problem.

The chapter also explores some preliminary ways of solving the problem in the fifth section and suggests how future research might make further progress on these issues. My immediate aims are to dispel the myth that the relatively affluent can discharge their duties to strangers without sophisticated political analysis and the parallel myth that political advocacy is a morally unproblematic alternative. I explore these questions with particular reference to effective altruism, but, as I argue in the conclusion, their implications are clearly much broader. The trade-off between relief and reform is an enduring dilemma that confronts nearly every effort at social change. Greater sensitivity to the complexities of this conflict can help individuals navigate it more successfully.

II. The Palliative Critique: Positive Versions

Effective altruists have been especially vocal proponents of funding malaria nets and deworming initiatives, which consistently rank among the top-recommended causes of the charity evaluator GiveWell.[13] Malaria and intestinal parasites still run rampant in several areas of the world, particularly in sub-Saharan Africa. Malaria remains a primary cause of death among children, while intestinal parasites, though rarely fatal, reduce quality of life and can inhibit normal functioning and development. Antimalaria bed nets and parasite-killing drugs are cheap and effective interventions. A donor can be reasonably confident that a gift to these initiatives will indeed contribute to a long-term improvement in someone's life—a rare feat, given the uncertainty surrounding the effects of most charitable initiatives. Another top recommendation of effective altruism's leaders is a program that provides direct cash transfers to low-income individuals, particularly in sub-Saharan Africa. Evaluations of this program have found that recipients tend to spend their receipts on substantial improvements to their living conditions, such as by weather-proofing their dwellings.

One of the most frequent criticisms of effective altruism is that, seen as responses to global poverty, these kinds of programs only address the symptoms of deeper structural problems.[14] A growing consensus among scholars of international development is that the fundamental cause of widespread poverty is the absence of

decent and stable political institutions.[15] Institutions are the socially defined rules of the game that coordinate human interaction.
A special subset of institutions (what Rawls refers to as the "basic
structure") serves a critical function in determining a society's
major contours and its individual members' life prospects.[16] These
institutions include the political constitution and legal system, the
property regime and the design of markets, the system of public
finance, public health infrastructure, the education system, and social insurance schemes. They work together to define and distribute
fundamental rights, duties, and opportunities. The consolidation of
these critical institutions creates a social order in which individuals
can interact safely, profitably, and (perhaps, in time) fairly.

Examined through the institutional lens, the prevalence of malaria and intestinal parasites isn't merely an outcome of natural
forces but a remarkable failure of public policy. In some countries with similar climates but well-functioning institutions these
maladies don't register as epidemics.[17] Providing malaria nets
and deworming initiatives does little to address the dysfunctional
public health infrastructure that lies at the root of these epidemics.
Focusing on these initiatives distracts from the urgent but thorny
process of institution-building. And investing in these interventions
may even work to undermine the consolidation of functioning
institutions. The availability of free health services reduces pressure
on the state to finance and provide public goods on its own.[18] This
hinders the development of effective public administration and a
sustainable tax system. It lures competent professionals away from
public agencies and discourages the civic participation necessary
for holding the state accountable. Strikingly, GiveWell recognizes
some of these risks in its analyses of its top charities, but for reasons
that are unclear it fails to take them seriously.[19]

Similar things might be said about cash transfers, which offer
modest improvements in living standards but leave in place the
many systemic causes of income poverty in the developing world.
Cash transfers from abroad would appear to reduce pressure on

the state to regulate the economy in ways that serve its least advantaged citizens, to develop its own assistance programs, and to demand sacrifices from local economic elites. In other words, they short-circuit the local processes of distributive conflict negotiation, processes that are developmental foundations of a well-ordered society.

The fact that even the best foreign assistance projects may have these kinds of unintended negative consequences has led some observers to what Mathias Risse calls "the Authenticity Thesis."[20] This thesis claims that the conditions necessary for development cannot be successfully imported from abroad—they can only emerge organically from within. Risse affirms that the global affluent have demanding duties to assist the global poor. But he takes the authenticity thesis to limit the range of permissible assistance options to certain strategies of institutional development. "Often all external aid can contribute otherwise is analytical work, identification or training of internal reform champions, or technical assistance," he writes.[21] Risse acknowledges that the authenticity thesis can be suspended in certain cases, such as to provide assistance after natural disasters or as a temporary measure to foster conditions where strong public institutions can take root. But it puts the burden of proof on proponents of direct assistance to justify case-by-case exceptions to the rule of encouraging institutional development through modest means.

Proponents of an institutionalist approach to development do not limit their sights to domestic institutions. They also draw attention to the highly consequential international policies that restrain economic growth in developing regions. Among these are agricultural subsidies in affluent countries that disadvantage farmers in poor countries,[22] international resource-trading privileges that enrich dictators at the expense of their subjects,[23] and an international pharmaceutical regime that limits the accessibility of essential medicines to the global poor.[24] If certain assumptions hold, subtle shifts in international rules would result in far more sweeping distributional changes than even the most effective voluntary assistance project could expect to bring about.[25]

Altogether, these considerations form one face of what I call the *palliative critique*. Stated succinctly, it holds that the types of causes that effective altruism champions only address the most superficial symptoms of dysfunctional national and international institutions. This is objectionable, according to the line of thought that I've been exploring, because it directs resources away from, and serves to undermine, more consequential institutional reforms.

What has made effective altruism vulnerable to this kind of criticism? One explanation is that it has developed an unduly narrow conception of what constitutes scientific rigor, a conception that confuses rigor with statistical certainty.[26]

Effective altruism demands that donors make investments based on the best empirical evidence about the expected outcomes of different social interventions. Effective altruism's leaders often begin discussions of empirical rigor with the randomized controlled trial,[27] which is considered the best test of causal relationships in social science and medicine. Such trials attempt to isolate the effects of an intervention by assigning members of a population to treatment and control groups and monitoring differences in the ways that the two groups behave over time. If researchers observe a change in behavior among the treatment group, they can be extremely confident that the change is attributable to the treatment itself.

Randomized controlled trials have emerged as a controversial methodological tool in development studies.[28] Although such trials offer the most robust evidence about the effects of different social interventions, a significant limitation is that they are only practical in those rare situations where researchers have the power to control environmental conditions. Attempting to apply this method of analysis to large, complex institutional phenomena presents a host of administrative, methodological, and ethical challenges. A research team cannot randomly assign citizens to countries with different public health systems, nor can it assign a treatment population to a world with a different international trading regime. But a research team faces no such hurdles in randomly assigning antimalarial nets, deworming medicine, or cash transfers to different villages in a region, or to different households in a village. Studies that make use of randomized controlled trials thus tend to be small in scale, localized in their effects, and short in their time horizons. (Meanwhile, attempts to extract more general conclusions from such selective evidence alarm many development scholars.)[29] Studies of larger institutional phenomena must instead rely on other methods that yield less confident results. Imploring one's followers to rely on the best evidence, therefore, is effectively an invitation to limit one's options to narrowly targeted interventions that lie at the margins of more consequential sociological phenomena.[30]

It's true that compared to small-scale, neatly defined interventions by nongovernmental organizations, initiatives to spur institutional change have lower prospects of success. This is both because the methods of analyzing institutional change produce lower confidence in the strength of causal relationships and because institutional change involves thornier collective action problems. A privately organized, small-scale deworming program in a developing country only requires coordinating a small number of stakeholders. Most of these stakeholders also stand to gain from the intervention in some way, so getting them to go along takes little effort. By contrast, consider some of the institutional elements of parasite eradication: a publicly funded and monitored regime of sanitation regulations, vaccine distribution, health education, and access to health care. Outsiders might support internal reform initiatives to develop this infrastructure (and the background institutions necessary to sustain it) or campaign against international rules that restrain these developments. However, achieving the desired institutional changes clearly requires coordinating much larger numbers of stakeholders. Many of these stakeholders also stand to lose from changes in the rules, which may serve the interests of powerful minority groups—global pharmaceutical companies, foreign development professionals, and local economic and political elites. Convincing the rich and powerful to sacrifice their advantages can be extremely difficult, and such efforts take many years to gain traction. Thus, investing in institutional reform can often seem like a significant gamble.

It should be clear, however, that a high enough magnitude of potential gains can outweigh low prospects of success. In fact, it's often considered irrational to avoid gambles when their expected value is higher than sure-bet alternatives. And there are good reasons to think that the magnitude of the gains from institutional reform are so large that it would be foolish to spend one's energies on anything else. As an example, one can look to China's agricultural policy reforms, which involved radical administrative restructuring and redefinition of property rights but are now credited with lifting 800 million people out of poverty since the early 1980s.[31] Sometimes effective altruists acknowledge the expected value of institutional change.[32] But it doesn't occupy as central a place in their discussions as one might expect, particularly given effective altruism's other commitments.

Choosing to pursue long-term institutional change—which will primarily benefit future persons—is bad news for people who are currently needy. Some might hold that presently existing persons have especially weighty moral claims that limit our prerogative to act on behalf of future interests.[33] By contrast, effective altruists generally agree that we have no reason to value the lives of presently existing people any more than the lives of future persons.[34] If we can do more good overall by investing in the future, that's what we ought to do. With this in mind, consider that, as far as we currently know, there will be an indefinite number of future generations. Assume further that building strong institutions tends to be a self-reinforcing process. Once a society achieves a stable and reasonably just basic structure, the beneficial effects of these institutions tend to generate the conditions of their own reproduction. Hence, if donors were to consolidate all their present efforts into reforming dysfunctional and unjust institutions, they wouldn't merely be helping out the two billion or so people who compose the current global poor. Rather, they would be preventing many billions of future persons from being born into poverty. And, each time someone donates to relieve suffering in the present, they incur a substantial opportunity cost with respect to future persons. From an effective altruist perspective, benefiting a smaller number of persons at the cost of a larger number isn't just suboptimal; it's morally wrong. Even if the data on institutional change is weak and the prospects of success are relatively dim, the expected value of institutional change suggests that it should be effective altruism's dominant strategy.[35]

To be clear, the best understanding of the institutionalist position isn't that direct assistance is always inappropriate.[36] In some cases, for instance, providing health aid may be part of a sound strategy for laying foundations for institutional development. But to justify an intervention in developmental or emancipatory terms is very different from justifying it in terms of specific welfare improvements. These aims often pull in different directions.

III. The Palliative Critique: Normative Versions

While the first face of the palliative critique challenges effective altruism on the basis of its approach to empirical evaluation, the second face of this critique challenges effective altruism on the basis of its moral evaluation. Effective altruism's leaders insist that although the movement takes inspiration from utilitarian thinkers, it's not utilitarianism writ large.[37] Once considered the leading view in moral and political philosophy, utilitarianism has now been bruised by decades of trenchant criticism. Aligning effective altruism with utilitarianism would tie the fate of the movement to this controversial doctrine. Debate over effective altruism would become a proxy theater for reenacting the hackneyed quarrels between utilitarians and their critics. Whereas utilitarianism is heroically demanding in its drive to promote a single value, effective altruism acknowledges the legitimacy of individual personal prerogative and a plurality of values worthy of appreciation and pursuit. But the theoretical distance that effective altruism tries to place between itself and utilitarianism shrinks when it comes to practical application. Effective altruism's methodological orientation tends to push aside all values but those that are easily quantified, such as years of life unburdened by disease and rates of economic consumption. Its insistence on quantification thus calls into question the stated commitment to pluralism. Few would deny that a long and healthy life or a comfortable standard of living are significantly valuable, or that they can serve as useful instruments or approximations for other valuable conditions. But the emphasis on quantifiable metrics prevents effective altruism from appreciating less measurable elements of a valuable human life, especially conditions of freedom and equality. Recent work in political philosophy has done much to clarify the nature of these values and the demands they make on us.

A long tradition of thought has understood freedom simply as the absence of interference.[38] An agent counts as free when no one interferes with their actions. Recent developments in political thought have put this understanding of freedom as noninterference on the defensive. Consider a benevolent slaveowner who never lays a hand on his slaves, or the benevolent despot who allows her subjects considerable leeway in managing their own affairs, rarely if ever resorting to physical force. Because these slaves and subjects are not directly impeded, the proponent of freedom as noninterference must conclude that these individuals are free. But since one ordinarily takes slavery and despotism to be paradigmatic cases of oppression, this makes for an embarrassing theoretical implication.

Alternatively, neorepublicans and neo-Kantians have proposed that freedom and its absence are better understood as structural conditions: one is unfree when one falls under the power of others in some way.[39] For neorepublicans, unfreedom occurs when the options one has are conditioned by the arbitrary will of another agent.[40] To be free is to be undominated, that is, to live under circumstances where no agent has the opportunity to interfere with one's choices in discretionary ways—whether or not the agent actually does so.[41] For neo-Kantians, meanwhile, to be free is to be independent from the wills of private persons.[42] One can only enjoy this independence in a constitutional state that establishes reciprocal limits on private choices and public support for those who cannot support themselves. Both schools of thought maintain that one experiences unfreedom when access to vital resources unavoidably depends on the goodwill of a benefactor rather than one's own powers or legal guarantees.[43] Slavery and benevolent despotism are paradigm examples. The slave and the subject may be materially comfortable and rarely impeded, but each can only act in ways that their respective overlords permit.

Crucially for my purposes, these insights show that philanthropy can also pose a threat to freedom. Direct interventions allow donors and their agents to stand in relationships of domination to local residents by controlling the availability of important resources. Which resources are provided, to whom, how, and for how long are decisions that lie ultimately with private benefactors. Such resources can also be withdrawn at will if recipients display less than servile gratitude,[44] or in response to the latest findings on the relative effectiveness of alternative interventions.[45] These interventions place persons in need in a precarious state of dependency.

It's one thing to be dominated by other agents from one's own social group, and another thing entirely when those agents represent a privileged group of outsiders. To see this, one needs to think about what it means to treat someone as an equal, another question that recent contributions to political philosophy have helped to clarify. Until lately, the prevailing view held that treating people as equals means ensuring that they have equal access to resources of some kind.[46] Difficulties with this way of thinking in accounting for inequalities in power and status have now led many philosophers to endorse a relational or social conception of equality—a notion of equality that may certainly make demands on the distribution of resources but isn't reducible to resource distribution.[47] As I prefer to construe it, social equality refers to a way of relating to others in which no person is treated as inherently wiser or worthier than another. The contrast to a condition of social equality is one of arbitrary social hierarchy or subordination.[48] Subordination obtains when certain persons enjoy greater consideration or influence as a result of irrelevant characteristics or unfair advantages. Familiar examples of such traits are gender, caste, race, nationality, and class. There may often be good reasons to distribute resources or roles on a differential basis (such as between parents and children or managers and employees). But to have one's interests or judgment discounted on the basis of ascriptive or arbitrary characteristics is demeaning. Objectionable conditions of social inequality exist, for instance, when women receive lower salaries than men employed in the same job, when racial or ethnic minorities face informal discrimination in access to public education, and when the voices of poor persons are systematically excluded in political debate. Although the groups in question may enjoy the same formal liberties and be well off in other ways, these conditions indicate social practices that fail in some way to treat participants with equal respect and concern.

Private development assistance risks engaging in social subordination particularly when it adopts a technocratic orientation. At one end of the spectrum lie donors who merely make capital available for local communities to invest in the communities' own development projects.[49] At the other end lie those, like effective altruists, who provide funds only for projects that satisfy the donors' beliefs about value and cost-effectiveness.[50] Because local residents lack the bargaining power to contest these positions, the superior wealth of effective altruists allows them to impose their development priorities on local communities. Ordinarily, however, the fact that someone possesses superior wealth isn't a reason for granting them greater influence over social outcomes. Using one's financial power to push one's development preferences onto a community amounts to treating the members of that community as social inferiors, as people deserving pity but not respect. Subordinating behavior constitutes a distinctive kind of harm when the wealthy intervenors are not themselves members of the community and are conspicuously marked off by different demographic attributes. Effective altruism faces this problem acutely, since the effective altruist community is composed largely of white, Anglo-American, male millennials, with backgrounds in applied science, business, and analytic philosophy.[51]

Though most people will agree that freedom and equality are profoundly valuable, some may think that they represent mistaken priorities in development. Of what benefit is equal status to someone dying of malaria? Autonomy's great, some might say, but it's not something you can eat. These concerns are valid. Still, people often react to instances of domination and subordination in ways that involve greater emotional intensity than their responses to mere material deprivation. For many, freedom from certain forms of domination and subordination is worth the price of a shorter and less materially comfortable life, as shown by extensive surveys of persons living in extreme poverty. As Monique Deveaux reports, persons facing severe want tend not to point to physical pain or material discomfort as their chief concerns.[52] Rather, they describe overriding senses of powerlessness, shame, and humiliation, as well as resentment toward the arbitrary commands of local authorities. Precisely how these complaints map on to philosophical accounts of domination and social subordination isn't entirely clear. But the evidence suggests that philosophical worries about unjust power are not idle speculations: they resonate deeply with actual people and are worth taking seriously.

One might object that this argument fails to appreciate the sense in which the global poor are *already* subject to domination and subordination.[53] Indeed, some combination of domination and subordination might explain precisely what is objectionable about poverty in the first place. By combatting aspects of material deprivation, effective altruism might then be credited with working to disrupt these unjust relationships. This objection may be persuasive to the extent that effective altruists can justify their decisions on these grounds. But as I've discussed earlier, there is no direct line between material deprivation and subjection to the power of others. It would be surprising, for instance, if antimalaria nets and deworming pills turned out to be the most prudent strategies for increasing the relative power of poor persons. Perhaps more importantly, the fact that domination and subordination are deeply objectionable indicates that one should take avoiding these conditions as a constraint on how one helps others. In attempting to unseat these kinds of relationships, one should first try to avoid replacing them with similar forms of mistreatment. This isn't to say that a presumption against dominating and subordinating interventions can't be suspended in the absence of acceptable alternatives. In dire emergencies, for instance, one is sometimes willing to trade away some respect for better chances of survival. But if there are other ways of assisting members of the global poor that treat them with greater dignity, the onus is on effective altruists to explain to their beneficiaries why they should accept something less. I explore alternative assistance possibilities further in the penultimate section.

This section started from the hypothesis that effective altruism's preoccupation with material welfare to the exclusion of other important values might be a function of measurement bias. Another perspective holds that a failure to appreciate the specific risks of domination and subordination isn't so much the result of measurement bias, but rather an inevitable byproduct of a consequentialist understanding of beneficence. Consequentialism holds that we simply ought to promote good states of affairs, and that promoting good states of affairs needn't take account of why current states of affairs are bad. Our duties to others are no stronger in cases where we ourselves have caused their suffering than in cases where their suffering results from misfortune. An alternative view holds that the duties we have to make others' ends our own are weaker and less urgent than the duties we have to treat others fairly and to rectify circumstances when we fail to do this.[54] From this standpoint, our duties to distant others depend to a large extent on how we relate to those persons through institutions. We have particularly stringent obligations toward distant strangers when their disadvantages are consequences of practices in which everyone participates. We likewise have particular obligations toward distant persons when we have benefited from their historical oppression.

One might think that these justice-based considerations simply reinforce the strength of our duties to members of the global poor and thus serve as grist for the effective altruist's mill. Those who suffer from extreme poverty occupy positions at the bottom rung of a global division of labor that disproportionately benefits and is sustained by people in affluent countries. They also tend to reside in countries recovering from legacies of colonialism and foreign predations of other kinds. But while these considerations might amplify the strength of our duties toward the global poor, they also seem to alter the nature of these duties and require a different orientation than the one that effective altruism recommends.

When I'm fully entitled to property, it's mine to transfer in whatever manner and to whomever I wish, and to impose conditions on how others use it. But if the property has come into my possession because of injustice, I no longer have the right to exercise discretion over its transfer. My principal duty is to cease or reform the behavior that's responsible for my unjust enrichment and to compensate my victims. In such cases, the resources that I possess are neither gifts for me to give away to my chosen recipients nor investments for me to manage strategically: they are more like taxes or debts to be paid immediately and unconditionally.[55] And I'm not being altruistic by returning to others what is properly theirs. Thus, insofar as our duties to the global poor stem from our participation in institutional relationships, we are under a stringent obligation to reform the terms of these institutions and to provide unconditional recompense for their effects. Thinking of our duties to the global poor in terms of gift-giving or social engineering fundamentally mischaracterizes the nature of these relationships.

It's of course an open question just how much of the wealth that the global rich control can plausibly be described as unjust accumulation. Few thoughtful commentators would claim that all global resource inequalities are necessarily objectionable. Quite plausibly, *some* amount of wealth that the global rich control is rightly theirs and thus is fit to be consumed or transferred at the owner's discretion. Perhaps effective altruism could then be understood as a theory about how to think about our legitimate entitlements: resources that are conclusively our own and not already owed to anyone else.[56] And if this is so, the justice-based critique would seem to miss the point. But the critic will reply that one can't accurately think of most global wealth this way. When one reflects on the violent history of international development along with continuing institutional inequities, one is left to conclude that very little of what the global rich currently possess could rightly be described as unambiguously theirs.[57] One is left to think that preserving the philosophical coherence of effective altruism entails diminishing its practical relevance.[58]

Mistaking the bases of our duties toward the distant needy is an invitation for the creation of new relationships of domination and subordination. If I repay my debt to you unconditionally, I retain no power to interfere with your affairs and I implicitly recognize you as my social equal. However, if I impose conditions on repaying a debt (perhaps because I don't realize it's actually a debt), I may retain the power to withdraw the resource if I change my mind or I don't like the way you are managing it. In other words, I dominate you. Similarly, by imposing conditions on how you use the resource, I indicate that I don't respect your authority to use your property as you see fit—that my preferences on this question trump yours. In other words, I treat you as my social inferior.[59]

IV. From Effective Altruism to Effective Advocacy?

One reason why effective altruists may be skeptical of political engagement might be a narrow understanding of what it entails. Some construe institutional reform as a naïve and dangerous utopianism. In an important passage defending effective altruism's tendency to work within existing political arrangements, Singer praises modern capitalism's record on poverty reduction and warns of the dangers of alternative political experiments.[60] This response risks mischaracterizing alternative perspectives. Though their rhetoric sometimes indicates deep dissatisfaction with the status quo,[61] few if any critics of effective altruism have suggested the abolition of markets and private property. Rather, institutionalist critics are best understood as recommending improvements to existing institutions.[62]

It's also tempting to read calls for political engagement as apologies for complacency. For instance, Brian Berkey charges proponents of the institutionalist critique with combining ambitious accounts of institutional change with paltry demands on individual action.[63] If voting or writing one's representative—both low-impact and low-sacrifice activities—exhaust the demands on political engagement, one should regard appeals to systemic change as hopelessly ineffectual and self-indulgent. While some critics may certainly be guilty of Berkey's charge, they don't represent the best interpretation of the institutionalist position.[64]

The most compelling understanding of the call to political engagement is that individuals ought to deploy a wide range of ambitious tactics that operate within the confines of democratic norms. These tactics collectively fit under of the heading of "political advocacy," which here refers to using strategies of persuasion to change policies, social norms, or the distribution of power. It includes attempts to recruit and elect officials who will champion reform, to lobby and contest officials already elected, to research policy alternatives, and to join and coordinate social movements. The target need not be the state for an action to count as political advocacy. Labor and community activists trying to solve collective action problems among the disempowered, consumer activists who challenge industry practices, public-interest groups that lobby intergovernmental organizations, investigative journalists who chronicle and expose injustice, and individuals who take to social media to call out forms of social discrimination in everyday life are all engaged in political advocacy.

Under contemporary conditions, advocacy involves a highly articulated division of labor. Individuals can delegate much of their activism to professionalized organizations that identify issues, design strategies, and lead campaigns of various kinds. Ordinary individuals can support these organizations with donations and participate in calls to action, such as to attend protests, boycott practices, sign petitions, retweet, turn out to vote, and recruit their contacts to do the same.

One might suppose that advocacy offers a very promising avenue for effective altruism. Identifying what constitutes an effective campaign is a puzzle ripe for rigorous analysis. The world of social change is no less riddled with emotion-based reasoning and wishful thinking than the world of charity. Fortunately, some evidence suggests that effective altruism is becoming more sanguine about institutional reform, at least on a case-by-case basis. For instance, Singer himself now more openly embraces the reform proposals regarding sovereignty over natural resources.[65] William

MacAskill provides a framework for deciding whether to pursue a career in electoral politics.[66] The effective altruist charity evaluator GiveWell has spun off the Open Philanthropy Project in large part to study the prospects of advocacy for various causes within the United States.[67]

The voices behind the palliative critique are likely to see these as encouraging developments. Those who regard direct interventions as counterproductive or misconceived should welcome the increasing openness of effective altruism's leaders to institutional reform. Those who worry that direct interventions mistreat their intended beneficiaries should also be relieved to see efforts relocated to other settings. Indeed, some prominent critics who have been impressed with these developments now have become allies.[68] But there are also grounds for caution. Effective altruism's turn to advocacy risks running into some familiar traps.

The first risk is that the advocacy turn might fall prey to the very same measurability bias that it's in some sense attempting to correct. A preference for investments with predictable impacts limits effective altruists to strategies that are ill-suited to systemic change. The second risk reflects a concern with unequal opportunities to advocate. Rather than eliminate or sidestep objectionable exercises of power, the shift to advocacy might simply relocate them to a different setting.

Singer's main example of how effective altruists might consider advocacy concerns Oxfam's Oil for Agriculture campaign in Ghana.[69] Oil for Agriculture was a successful campaign to convince the government of Ghana to allocate profits from its oil reserves to support small farmers. Comparing Oxfam's campaign expenditures with the government's increase in outlays to agricultural investment, Singer estimates that Oxfam's one-year return on investment was 580 percent. The example aims to show that investing in this campaign would have been a worthwhile choice for effective altruists, and it's meant as a model for thinking about other advocacy opportunities. But even as the example serves to allay doubts about effective altruism's capacity to contribute to systemic change, it also raises new doubts about whether the movement's methodological orientation is well suited to the challenges that advocacy presents.

Steven Teles has distinguished between two general approaches to funding advocacy.[70] One attempts to secure specific measurable outcomes. This approach tends to confine investments to narrowly circumscribed issues with short time horizons and to enter the field at the final stages of the legislative process. The other approach focuses on building movements, by cultivating networks of innovative and well-run organizations. It tends to invest in organizations for the long haul, not specifically to achieve particular policy outcomes, but to shape public opinion and the political agenda which inform policy choices. In Teles's view, the latter approach is better suited to the nature of political competition. Maintaining a competitive advantage in politics requires the material and intellectual resources to adapt to circumstances that change rapidly and unfold in a nonlinear fashion. It also requires a willingness to make risky bets and accept some painful losses along the way. Teles contends that the capacity-building approach helps to explain both the emergence of the contemporary conservative movement in the United States and its relative dominance of the public agenda. Whereas liberal funders from the 1970s to 2000s became obsessed with measurement-based evaluation, conservative funders took a more hands-off approach that opted instead for developing organizational power. This strategy paid off in terms of a resilient and nimble movement, able to weather setbacks and adapt tactics to shifting circumstances.

These observations suggest that effective altruism's initial instincts about advocacy may not yield the benefits that both its leaders and its critics desire. Just as investing in individual development projects can undermine broader development goals, so too can investing in individual policy campaigns come at the expense of building viable reform movements. The Oil for Agriculture campaign attracts the interest of effective altruism because it exhibited a sizable measurable impact. But in my estimation, what allowed Oxfam to succeed in this particular case was the result of decades of work cultivating a global reputation, operational efficiency, seasoned expertise, and productive local partnerships, while learning from many costly mistakes along the way.[71] Oxfam couldn't have developed this organizational capacity if its donors had been fixated on quantifying the cost-benefit ratio of each campaign and each campaign tactic.

Fixating on the return on investment of particular campaigns fails to appreciate the supporting factors necessary for waging successful campaigns.[72] It also fails to appreciate the significance of protecting victories from future challenges and of using individual events to build momentum. A one-year, 580-percent return wouldn't be very impressive if the policy were to be reversed in the next budgeting cycle; a much more modest rate of return that stands up to countervailing pressure over time may ultimately prove more valuable. Likewise, even a negative return could be counted as a valuable investment, particularly if one is ultimately concerned with systemic change. A conspicuous and well-reported failure to alter the budget in Ghana might nevertheless have helped to solidify an international norm of popular sovereignty over natural resources, creating pressure on resource-rich countries to distribute resource wealth fairly.

Thus, one risk of effective altruism's turn to advocacy lies in a failure to adapt its metrics to the circumstances of the political setting. Because effective altruism is a movement predicated on evidence-based practical reasoning, it's poised to fall into the trap of investing in individual legislative victories at the cost of more robust institutional reforms. To be clear, nothing in the movement's official commitments prevents it from adapting its methods to new contexts. But as we've seen, the movement's leaders evince a predilection for methods that promise statistical certainty.

The second risk of effective altruism's advocacy turn is that, regardless of its ultimate efficacy, advocacy isn't altogether immune from moral costs. It can also subject others to objectionable treatment in the way in which it transmits inequalities in power.

Consider that many of the reforms that effective altruists might want to advocate are subject to considerable disagreement. People disagree about the moral basis for institutional reform, while those who agree on the moral basis may disagree on the best strategy. Many of these disagreements are reasonable. Thoughtful, well-motivated individuals with access to the same information reach wildly different conclusions. Now consider that effective altruists are likely in many cases to enjoy greater resources for advocating their positions than their opponents do. This is true even within affluent countries, where supporters of effective altruism are not only usually drawn from wealthy circles but also often encouraged to earn as much income as possible for the sake of maximizing their philanthropic potential. Hence, effective altruists have the potential to drown out the voices of persons with opposing views who have fewer financial resources to publicize their positions.

The recent history of philanthropist-led interventions in policy change in the United States offers a cautionary tale. Those with concentrated wealth to support good intentions have shown themselves able and willing to overpower their opponents. Take the movement for reform of public education, a movement spearheaded by a consortium of large foundations that most prominently includes the Bill and Melinda Gates Foundation, the Eli and Edythe Broad Foundation, and the Walton Family Foundation.[73] In the late 1990s, leaders at these foundations reached similar conclusions about an agenda for education reform—an agenda calling for integrating features of contemporary business management such as choice, competition, and performance-based evaluation into public schooling. For nearly two decades, this consortium has been experimenting with ways to deploy concentrated wealth in the service of getting these initiatives adopted, through creating and coordinating advocacy groups, lobbying and electing sympathetic officials, making conditional grants to cash-strapped public schools, and creating parallel school systems that embody the reform agenda's aims.[74] Survey research continues to show that wealthy elites and the general public profess systematically different education policy priorities—with ordinary individuals much less likely to support market-oriented reforms.[75] Nonetheless, because those who oppose the elite reform agenda lack access to the same political finance and organizational infrastructure, their voices have been relatively muted in debates on public education.

Commonsense morality holds that treating someone fairly in a debate requires affording that person the same opportunities to make their position known as one affords oneself. A helpful way of understanding this, according to Daniel Viehoff, is a willingness to set aside certain arbitrary advantages one may have.[76] It would be wrong of someone with a loud voice to shout down his opponents in a town hall meeting. It would be wrong of someone to threaten her friend with a knife in the course of an argument about where to order takeout food. And it would be wrong for a spouse to claim authority over household decisions on the basis of their superior salary. A loud voice, a capacity to inflict bodily harm, and a high-paying job don't make one's opinions more credible or one's interests more valuable than those of others. To the extent that they can influence the outcomes of a debate, these properties count as arbitrary advantages. Using these features to one's benefit in a debate is to mistreat one's opponent—to treat one's opponent as an object to be overcome, rather than as an equal person to be reasoned with.

Viehoff's argument seeks to explain why democracy enjoys special authority as a form of collective decision-making. Obeying democratic procedures, in his view, prevents us from relying on these kinds of arbitrary advantages. But I think the argument also contains a general point about the ethics of advocacy. That is, under conditions of radical economic inequality, leveraging one's superior wealth for the sake of political influence can be a way of mistreating one's opponents. It attempts to win extra influence by relying on an arbitrary source of strength. In so doing, one objectionably subordinates one's opponents.

The problem of social subordination can seem even more troubling in transnational cases. Effective altruists from affluent countries may be especially inclined to advocate for the reform of international rules or institutional conditions in developing countries. As the history of popular resistance to the International Monetary Fund's structural adjustment program illustrates, residents of developing countries may not agree with all reform proposals from abroad.[77] And yet residents of developing countries are likely to have access to vastly fewer resources for making their voices heard. The transnational case is troubling not only because the differences in the means of expression may be greater, but also because the effects of such reforms weigh more heavily on the persons with fewer resources. This cuts against a common intuition that persons should enjoy power over outcomes in proportion to their susceptibility to those outcomes.[78] Although the perspectives of well-intentioned outsiders may sometimes be helpful, the advice of outsiders should generally not displace the voices of those who must grapple directly with the outcomes of the decisions in question. Effective altruists from affluent countries who engage in transnational advocacy risk running afoul of this principle.

These considerations allow us to appreciate more fully what I mean by "the effective altruist's political problem." Critics of effective altruism argue that direct assistance programs are at best inefficient and at worst harmful. They urge relatively affluent individuals to channel their resources into political advocacy. While some doubt whether effective altruism has the philosophical flexibility to support this shift, others are more optimistic about the movement's capacity to engage in politics.[79] But optimists fail to appreciate that, without a change in orientation, redeploying effective altruism's efforts toward policy change might be equally inefficient and not obviously less harmful.

V. Toward an Ethics of Political Philanthropy

There are a variety of ways of working out this problem, though none of them offers a completely satisfying resolution. One might insist that effective altruism's ability to identify successful but underfinanced programs of direct aid offers distinct advantages. If so, effective altruists could address elements of the palliative critique by treating these programs as temporary demonstrations. If the programs meet with a positive reception from affected parties in the regions in which they operate, effective altruists could work to transfer their control (and eventually their finance) to local authorities. The idea here may be familiar from Rob Reich's attempt to reconcile philanthropic foundations with democratic legitimacy.[80] Reich contends that foundations are legitimate insofar as they serve to pilot social programs that then apply for public approval. One may wish to add a stronger criterion that makes the public audition process more explicit and inclusive, a move suggested by Waheed Hussain's discussion of how the use of economic power for political ends can be legitimate.[81] Hussain argues that private initiatives to promote a social agenda can be permissible when they serve as "waiting rooms" for democracy, essentially by modeling democratic principles in their internal governance and preparing themselves for future incorporation into formal legislation.[82] In turn, if direct aid programs were to audition for the approval of, and incorporation by, their host publics, they would mitigate some of the risk that direct aid poses to local autonomy and institutional development.

Another option is for effective altruists to embrace the turn to advocacy, but to avoid the temptation to advocate for substantive issues. Instead, they could focus on strengthening the *voices* of the persons they aim to assist, so that those who have most to gain and lose are able to advocate for themselves. This is obviously not a new idea. It was particularly popular among an earlier generation of philanthropists who funded the civil rights and community organizing movements in the United States. It's also a controversial idea. Development scholars point out that external support for grassroots organizing can taint a movement's perceived legitimacy.[83] Belying the aim of empowering the poor, participatory initiatives are also susceptible to capture by local elites.[84] But there is now a wealth of information on different attempts to mobilize poor communities in the global South. (A recent report by the World Bank cites nearly 500 studies of development projects with a participatory element.)[85] And there is a growing collection of organizations committed to identifying community activists and movements and connecting them to resources.[86] Effective altruists could bring their analytical tools to bear on evaluating successful organizing tactics and projects.[87] However, doing this well would require accustoming themselves to longer time horizons and alternative ways of assessing progress.

A third option is to restrict substantive advocacy efforts to particular kinds of causes in order to avoid subordinating one's opponents. One way to do this is to engage in efforts to counteract the undue influence of other powerful forces.[88] The idea may be familiar from Michael Walzer's discussion of military intervention in civil wars.[89] Walzer holds that, as a general matter, foreign states are not permitted to intervene in a society divided by civil war. Resolving the conflict is an internal affair. However, a foreign state may permissibly intervene in order to counteract another foreign power's intervention. Similarly, one might think that effective altruists are not justified in meddling in a country's development disputes when they reflect real internal disagreement. Conversely, however, effective altruists *could* be justified in bringing resources to bear to counteract the meddling of other powerful forces, such as the marketing efforts of tobacco corporations in developing countries or the distorting influence of energy corporations on perceptions about climate change.[90]

VI. Conclusion: Beyond "Beyond Good Intentions"

Effective altruism deserves great credit for trying to infuse philanthropy with sophisticated moral reasoning and scientific evidence. It forces us to countenance that good intentions alone may not make acts of philanthropy justifiable. We ought to think carefully about our duties to others and appeal to evidence to discover how best to discharge them. Even those who find effective altruism's approach deficient should welcome its stimulation of greater reflection about, and energy toward, caring for the needs of others.

I've argued, however, that adding effectiveness to noble intentions isn't a sufficient corrective. When we attempt to assist the distant needy, we inevitably implicate ourselves in complex political phenomena. Failing to appreciate these complexities can at best blunt the impact of our assistance efforts; at worst it serves to further entrench poverty's causes. The illusion that philanthropy somehow operates outside of politics also blinds donors to the possibility that beneficent initiatives may expose recipients to objectionable exercises of power.

Those who have voiced versions of this palliative critique of private charity have often presumed that institutional reform efforts provide an obviously superior alternative. I've tried to complicate this story, particularly with respect to effective altruism. Though effective altruists might be well-advised to engage in political advocacy, doing this well may require them to abandon the methodology that makes their position unique. By relocating from policy to politics, they also risk reinscribing the objectionable power relationships that dog their approach.

I've also suggested some ways in which effective altruists might make progress on resolving these challenges. Integrating procedural values into their interventions, exploring grassroots advocacy strategies, and expanding the criteria on which they select causes would work to address some of the problems that I raised.[91]

In closing, I want to stress that although the foregoing arguments are directly concerned with effective altruism, the issues they raise have much wider relevance. The concerns behind the palliative critique are hardly specific to effective altruism. The objections that it raises recur again and again in the history of moral and political thought. Likewise, many commentators have thought that the obvious alternative to direct assistance is to try to change political institutions. Less frequently and less clearly have critics of almsgiving noted the ethical challenges that lie in attempts to fund institutional change.[92]

Examining effective altruism has also provided an opportunity to illustrate how political morality can apply to individual giving decisions. If the observations of this chapter generalize, rarely if ever can political morality supply us with determinate guidance about whether, where, and how much to give. What it does do, however, is help to structure the parameters of these decisions and supply essential ingredients to weigh in navigating these challenges. As the next chapter shows, these contributions become especially significant when applied to decisions by powerful agents like business corporations.

7

Milton Friedman's
Corporate Misanthropy

One of the most remarkable developments in the modern practice of philanthropy has been the embrace and rapid evolution of giving by commercial corporations. Once rarely practiced and widely disparaged, corporate philanthropy is now a nontrivial activity of nearly every large company and supported by strong social norms.[1] Corporations today donate an average of 1 percent of their gross revenue and supply 5 percent of all charitable donations in the United States.[2] Local community causes regularly top favored areas of support, followed by education, the arts, and the environment.[3] Direct donations form an integral pillar in a broader movement among firms to demonstrate "corporate social responsibility," which involves various attempts to incorporate principles of justice and beneficence into business practices. In addition to direct donations, many firms offer donation-matching for their employees, incentivize employee volunteering, and provide pro bono goods or services.[4] As I discuss further in what follows, firms are also moving beyond traditional donative tools, by embedding philanthropic concerns more directly into their business models and engaging in more direct forms of political activism.

These developments look promising from opposing vantage points. Clearly enough, perspectives that champion economic liberty and market-driven production are likely to welcome greater efforts by private firms to address social demands. From this angle, corporate philanthropy harnesses the virtues of voluntary exchange and strategic management to deliver efficient improvements to the supply of collective goods. Though egalitarians may not necessarily share these premises, many may find corporate philanthropy a vital tool for addressing persistent poverty and other forms of disadvantage under contemporary conditions of staggering inequality and rising corporate profits. Rather than line the pockets of their investors and executives, egalitarians may believe, corporations should use their outsized wealth and power to strengthen communities and assist the less fortunate.[5]

Writing in the early days of these developments, one noted libertarian economist was far less sanguine about their prospects. Milton Friedman's seminal 1970 essay, "The Social Responsibility of Business Is to Increase Profits," challenged the emerging consensus that business firms have duties to others besides their shareholders.[6] Friedman's view appears to defend the naked and unlimited pursuit of profit, and the repugnance of this position might explain why its influence hasn't endured. While scholars continue to debate the merits of different kinds of corporate philanthropy, hardly anyone entertains the possibility that corporate philanthropy might be categorically unjustifiable. For many people, the central challenge in business ethics is to convince firms to be more philanthropic, not less.

This chapter argues, however, that Friedman's position proves substantially more attractive than many may realize—when read as a democratic critique. Though several of Friedman's claims don't hold up to scrutiny, a close reading of Friedman's text reveals the pillars of a sophisticated understanding of the value of democracy and the distinct challenges of reconciling corporate philanthropy with democratic legitimacy.

Attention to these issues is long overdue. Philosophers and political theorists have recently shown renewed interest in philanthropy, plumbing its complex and often problematic relationships to justice, democracy, and human flourishing more broadly.[7] But the recent attention to the ethics of philanthropy has so far had almost nothing to say about philanthropy by corporations. This omission is unfortunate, given the massive impact of corporate beneficence and the unresolved controversies that surround it.

This chapter attempts to fill some of the gap. It proceeds in the following section by unpacking Friedman's argument. Friedman holds that corporate philanthropy involves imposing an unjustified tax on shareholders, who rightfully own the firm. Section II levels a number of sharp challenges at Friedman's view, disputing the premise that shareholders own the firm as well as the implication that shareholder ownership forbids corporate philanthropy. While these challenges might seem like decisive objections, the remainder of the chapter argues that Friedman's position nevertheless contains some prescient insights, insights that dovetail with concerns from the foregoing chapters. Section III rehearses what makes democracy valuable and how philanthropy by individuals can both bolster and threaten this value. Section IV then shows how Friedman's view helps to illuminate how philanthropy by firms alters this picture. A concluding section clarifies that the argument applies most directly to traditional corporate philanthropy, understood as the gratuitous transfer of firm assets to nonprofit organizations. Emerging alternative forms of corporate beneficence, such as impact investing and social enterprise, exceed the scope of this study and suggest an important avenue for future research.

I. "The Social Responsibility of Business"

For Milton Friedman, corporate philanthropy is objectionable because it imposes a cost on shareholders, a cost that can't be justified on either deontological or consequentialist grounds. The argument begins from the premise that the primary responsibility of a firm is to its shareholders, who are its owners. In turn, Friedman claims, anytime a firm manager engages in philanthropy, she is spending its owners' money. Shareholders could choose to spend their own money on whatever they want, including donating it to their preferred causes. But whenever the firm engages in philanthropy, it's essentially imposing a tax on its investors, by preventing them from reaping the full profit of its enterprise. For Friedman, not only is the firm imposing a tax, but it's also appropriating for itself the exclusive authority to determine how those taxes are spent. It's taking the choice of whether to be philanthropic, and how so, out of the hands of its owners.

Friedman contrasts corporate philanthropy with democratic government. Only a democratic government has the legitimate authority to impose taxes and select social objectives. This is because a government is authorized by a process of popular representation and its officials are presumptive experts in public administration.

Friedman adds that these objections can't be undercut or outweighed by the superior capacity of corporate philanthropists to achieve socially beneficial outcomes. Business managers lack the requisite expertise to make sound judgments about philanthropy. The core competency of business executives lies in running a business, not in solving social problems.

What if philanthropy actually does serve to maximize profits for a firm's shareholders? Philanthropy can improve the firm's image with the government or with potential customers, resulting in reduced taxes or greater sales. If and when corporate philanthropy does serve to maximize profits, it seems to comply with Friedman's principle of shareholder primacy. Friedman responds that although such behavior may seem to comply with his principle, it's also fundamentally deceptive, as its success depends on misleading the public about a firm's true intentions. Though such deception may or may not be intrinsically objectionable, Friedman emphasizes its costly downstream effects. Either the firm will face blowback when people discover its ulterior motives, or its behavior will in fact work to promote a culture of corporate philanthropy that inappropriately sacrifices shareholder interests.

Friedman also entertains the possibility that the problems that corporate philanthropy might address are too urgent to leave to the political process. Some might believe that corporate philan-thropy is a quicker and more effective remedy for many important issues. Friedman responds, "What [this argument] amounts to is an assertion that those who favor the taxes and expenditures in question have failed to persuade a majority of their fellow citi-zens to be of like mind and that they are seeking to attain by un-democratic procedures what they cannot attain by democratic procedures."[8] In other words, Friedman thinks achieving desir-able ends can't justify the use of any and all means. We ought to resolve conflicts through democratic procedures rather than work around them.

II. The Logical Limits
of Friedman's Misanthropy

Before elaborating what I take to be the most compelling suggestions in Friedman's view, I want to address some of its considerable challenges. Chief among them is the premise that shareholders own the firm. Friedman makes no attempt to justify his notion of shareholder primacy in this piece, but a natural place to start might be with the theory of property. In particular, share-holder primacy might follow rather straightforwardly from a uni-fied theory of ownership.[9] According to that theory, ownership of an object entails enjoying rights to all of the various ways in which agents might relate to that object (the so-called incidents of owner-ship). Although an owner might delegate certain incidents to other agents, the status of ownership lies only with the principal. For Friedman, the firm represents a system in which property owners (shareholders) delegate certain incidents of ownership to agents (managers) for specific purposes. A firm's managers serve merely as shareholders' fiduciaries, entrusted with the responsibility to maximize the satisfaction of shareholders' interests or preferences. Since corporate philanthropy diverts resources away from the satisfaction of shareholders' interests or preferences, it amounts to a theft of their property.

This view faces at least two major objections. The first involves granting the unified theory of ownership but disputing the assignment of ownership to shareholders. Instead of conceiving of a firm as a relationship where "capital recruits labor" to carry out shareholder aims, one could conceive of the relationship conversely as one where "labor recruits capital" to carry out the aims of the firm's workers. From this standpoint, workers, not shareholders, own the firm. Workers simply hire holders of capital to provide resources needed for achieving their goals. Whatever its merits as a normative theory, this "laborer primacy" view goes some way in explaining the behavior of numerous firms. Entrepreneurs seeking venture capital, start-ups crowdsourcing seed funding, and established nonprofit associations seeking donations (such as churches, symphonies, and advocacy organizations) represent functioning models in which labor appears to hold the reins. In these cases, the firm's managers enjoy broad discretion, with investors playing only a passive, supporting role. If we believe these forms of organization legitimate, then the shareholder primacy thesis is at best conditionally true: it applies to some firms, but not to all. Consequently, Friedman's argument would only invalidate corporate philanthropy in a subset of cases.

The second objection to the shareholder primacy thesis involves rejecting the unified theory of property on which it appears to rely. Over the past several decades, the shareholder primacy thesis has come under threat from a rival "stakeholder" theory. That theory lacks a dominant articulation,[10] but one way of construing it might begin by observing that ownership of an object can be split among various parties. For instance, one agent might enjoy the right to profit from the object without the right to manage it, and another agent might enjoy the right to manage the object without the right to profit from it. (This is precisely what happens when property is held "in trust.") The firm, on this view, is a nexus of ownership relations between a variety of stakeholders, each of whom has rights to specific incidents of ownership but none of whom is the exclusive, sole owner. A firm's managers, therefore, aren't required to maximize the satisfaction of shareholders' interests or preferences, because shareholders are merely one stakeholder among several.

Even if the stakeholder theory alternative fails to dislodge Friedman's shareholder primacy thesis, Friedman's view faces additional challenges. Settling the question of who owns the firm doesn't settle the question of what permissions and duties these owners have. To claim otherwise—that in virtue of ownership, a firm's owners and their agents may only act in ways that promote the owners' interests—begs the question. Namely, it begs the question for ethical egoism, the view that an action is right insofar as it benefits oneself. But if we reject ethical egoism, as virtually all philosophers do, we must consider whether a firm's owners might have other-regarding duties that impose limits on the pursuit of their own rational advantage. Like other moral persons, shareholders might very well have duties of justice and beneficence. Constraining the pursuit of profit, or more affirmatively engaging in philanthropic activity, might be prudent ways of satisfying these duties. In other words, corporate philanthropy might be a perfectly reasonable way of satisfying shareholders' moral duties.

Admittedly, whether this objection succeeds depends on deeper questions about the structure of morality. Friedman's defenders could insist that morality has a federated or compartmentalized structure, which enables different principles to apply in different domains of social life. For instance, virtue ethics might be true for interpersonal relationships, while republicanism properly governs political relationships, and ethical egoism provides the correct theory for commercial relations. Just because we reject ethical egoism in interpersonal relations doesn't permit us to reject it in every domain. But if Friedman's defenders are correct about the structure of morality, the account still lacks an argument for why ethical egoism—and not some other theory—prevails in commercial enterprise.

Let's suppose for a moment that we accept both the shareholder primacy premise *and* the ethical egoism premise. Shareholders own the firm, and a firm's managers ought to maximize the satisfaction of the shareholders' interests or preferences. Are these premises sufficient to nullify corporate philanthropy? It depends. The picture that Friedman seems to have in mind is the following (fictitious) scenario. Imagine that we have a long-established, publicly traded company like General Electric. One day, the Vice President of Operations wakes up and decides to send part of his budget to Operation Smile, an organization that provides cleft palate surgery to children in impoverished regions. Cleft palate surgery has nothing to do with G.E. operations and nothing to do with the vice president's expertise. Moreover, shareholders generally don't invest in G.E. with the expectation that G.E. may engage in this kind of activity. In this case, it's easy to see how the executive might be acting without legitimate authority, and Friedman's view commands some sway.

But now consider a company like No Limit, LLC, better known by its trademark Newman's Own and its slogan of "100% profits to charity." Newman's Own was founded by the late actor Paul Newman, noted philanthropist and salad dressing hobbyist. The company produces a range of preserved foods and condiments and transfers all of its profits to a corporate foundation that focuses, among other things, on promoting nutrition and food security. Any potential investor in Newman's Own would surely know of the company's philanthropic mission. Many would likely invest precisely because of that mission. In this case, the company's philanthropic work also bears some relation to its expertise. How, then, would Newman's Own's philanthropic initiatives count as wronging its shareholders? Cases like this one indicate that Friedman's view applies more narrowly to traditional corporations founded without a social mission, or to companies without expertise in the domains of society where they seek to intervene.

The argument is difficult to accept even in this narrower range of cases, however. Friedman wants to get a lot of mileage out of the analogy he draws to taxation. He thinks that because corporate philanthropy involves spending shareholder money on social objectives they may not approve, it's a form of arbitrary taxation and spending, a form of undemocratic governance. But there's a crucial difference between corporate philanthropy and government spending. One is voluntary, and the other isn't. If they don't like what the firm is doing with their investments, shareholders can sell their shares. They're not forced to invest or continue to invest in firms whose managerial strategies they condemn. Indeed, the capacity for participants to enter and exit transactional relationships at will is central to the justification of a market economy. Meanwhile, if I don't like how the government is spending my tax dollars, I still have to pay my taxes. Taxation is by definition nonvoluntary. And the fact that supporting a state is nonvoluntary is a leading reason for why we are entitled to participate in decisions about what the state does.

III. Philanthropy and Democracy

At this point it might seem like there's nothing left standing in Friedman's view to sustain it. I've claimed that Friedman's view rests on the unjustified assumptions that shareholders own the firm and that shareholder ownership rules out corporate philanthropy. Both premises face hefty objections. If corporate philanthropy isn't akin to arbitrary taxation, as Friedman tries to claim, could it still be objectionable nevertheless? In short, I think Friedman is right to observe that corporate philanthropy stands in tension with the value of democracy, even as he is wrong in his assessment of where that tension lies. To mount this case, we'll first need to review what makes democracy valuable and how philanthropy in general might support or threaten that value. We'll then be prepared to examine

how these concerns might apply to philanthropy by corporations—
the topic of the following section.

A. Democracy's Value

As we've seen, democracy refers to a process of collective decision-
making that treats members of the collective as equals in some
way. When suitably defined, the democratic ideal also provides
the dominant conception of political legitimacy, that is, a basis for
evaluating the normative standing of coercively imposed decisions.
Decisions that issue from democratic procedures enjoy a certain
moral authority that nondemocratic decisions lack. Democracy
gives subjects of coercive power strong reasons to abide by
the outcomes of decisions even when they disagree with those
outcomes.

Precisely what lends democratic decision-making this authority
provokes significant debate. But this debate typically homes in on
four values: collective self-determination, political equality, deliberative justification, and substantive reliability.[11] Other forms of
rule might exhibit one or more of these desirable features to some
extent, but only the democratic ideal can capture all of them at once.

Collective self-determination refers to the idea that the "makers"
and "matter" of the laws, the rulers and the ruled, are one and the
same. Democracy is valuable in part because it affords subjects of
authority a measure of control over their common affairs. Forms
of authoritarianism—dictatorships, oligarchies, epistocracies,
theocracies, and so on—serve as natural contrasts. Which aspects
of society must be democratically controlled in order for citizens
to enjoy collective self-determination remains undertheorized.
Drawing on respective work by Stilz and Zuehl,[12] I argued in
Chapter 2 that the value of collective self-determination entitles citizens to collectively control matters of basic justice, i.e., the nature
and scope of fundamental rights, liberties, and opportunities. But

the value of collective self-determination permits the private provision of discretionary public goods, as I elaborate in what follows.

Political equality refers to conditions that allow citizens to enjoy this collective control on equal terms. A foundational premise of political morality holds that adult human persons are entitled to equal respect and concern. Several recent prominent studies argue that democracy is the only decision-making procedure that fully respects subjects as equal moral persons.[13] Attempts to mark off some people as more qualified to rule than others must draw distinctions between the more competent and the less competent. But even if we could identify criteria for competence in the abstract, attempts to apply such criteria in practice require making discriminatory judgments or "invidious comparisons" in order to sort people into these categories.[14] Thus, any decision-making procedure that restricts authority to certain people fails to respect the equal moral status of all. Democracy, on the other hand, consecrates moral equality by refusing to draw these kinds of distinctions. Democratic procedures uniquely affirm the bedrock principle of equal respect for persons. A critical implication of this position is that citizens ought to enjoy equal opportunities to influence their common affairs. Equally weighted votes are an important mechanism for assuring this condition, though as I argued in Chapter 4, they're hardly sufficient.

Deliberative justification prevails when decisions follow an open process of reflective reason-giving rather than a simple tallying of exogenous preferences. Deliberation helps to protect against the possibility that outcomes will reflect ignorance or prejudice. That decisions can be defended with reference to sound arguments also enhances their justifiability to those who fall subject to them.

Finally, *substantive reliability* characterizes a system of government that consistently generates high-quality outcomes, outcomes that promote justice and the common good. Democratic governance is thought to conduce to just outcomes partly due to the epistemic properties of deliberation, which exposes ideas to scrutiny

and screens out those political positions that can't be broadly ac-
cepted.[15] Democracy also tends to generate high-quality outcomes
because of the ways that it aggregates the wisdom of the multitude,[16] appoints competent officials through institutions of representation,[17] and reproduces itself stably over time.[18]

Democracy's critics continually charge that democratic
processes are no guarantee against unjust outcomes; in many
cases, alternative forms of rule might yield better results. Indeed,
democratic majorities may choose to elect tyrants or violate the
human rights of minorities. But these observations don't undermine the democratic ideal. Rather, they indicate two possibilities.
One possibility is that democracy as such isn't an absolute value
(one that admits of no trade-offs). Democracy provides a *pro
tanto* standard of legitimacy that can be outweighed or undercut
when it conflicts with other paramount values like the rule of law
and human dignity. A more attractive possibility is that the democratic ideal contains built-in constraints and scope conditions.
Constitutional limitations on majority rule are consistent with the
value of democracy because they preserve the very foundations of
democratic governance. On this reading, democracy shouldn't be
conflated with unbridled majoritarianism. Similarly, according to
this perspective, democracy isn't a general value that we ought to
promote in all aspects of social life but one that has a more limited scope. Democratic legitimacy applies principally to the regulation of the basic structure of society, the set of institutions that
establish the ground rules for social interaction and determine
fundamental rights, duties, and opportunities. This entails that
democracy provides the appropriate standard of legitimacy for
the design, administration, and enforcement of laws. Democratic
legitimacy doesn't ordinarily apply to the internal governance of
private associations and personal relationships. To count as legitimate, firms, religious societies, and families needn't necessarily
run themselves by democratic procedures. But democratic legitimacy does require that private associations respect the scope and

foundations of democratic authority. As I explain in what follows, respecting the scope and foundations of democratic authority can prove challenging for philanthropic entities.

B. Philanthropy and Democracy

As this book has demonstrated, philanthropy and democracy enjoy a complicated relationship. In several respects, using private property to advance public purposes can facilitate or supplement democratic governance. But interventions by private agents into some areas can interfere with democratic authority. And even in the areas where philanthropy offers unique advantages, it can subvert democratic governance through its interaction with other forces.

To flesh out this relationship further, it's helpful to classify philanthropy roughly into two ideal types: *expressive* and *productive*. Expressive philanthropy involves using private property to finance expressive activity, namely in the form of organizations that publicly champion ideas. Productive philanthropy involves using private property to finance the production of public goods, goods whose economic characteristics prevent them from being supplied efficiently by traditional markets.

Arguably, at least some degree of private financing of expressive activity is critical to realizing the values of collective self-determination, deliberative justification, and substantive reliability. Set aside the question of whether political morality permits the private financing of political parties and electoral campaigns. Even if private donations for these purposes are morally dubious, citizens of a democratic society have vital interests in being able to create, join, and support other expressive associations with minimal restrictions. Doing so allows them to participate effectively in public deliberation and to influence collective decision-making. Expressive associations—like the NAACP, Greenpeace, Human Rights Watch, the Federalist Society, and the Christian

Coalition—help to formulate the political agenda and engage in the public exchange of reasons. They also serve as checks on state power, exposing harmful, wasteful, or oppressive policies or behavior. As such, they help to improve the substantive reliability of a democratic order. And while public financing might assist with supporting this activity, the freedom to donate allows citizens to indicate most effectively the direction and strength of their political convictions. At the same time, if citizens possess different amounts of donative resources, philanthropy can pose a significant threat to the value of political equality—as Chapter 4 made plain. That is, in the absence of sensitive regulation, the liberty to support social and political causes financially allows wealthier citizens greater opportunities for expressing their opinions, to the prejudice of poorer citizens. Policies that allow or encourage such unequal opportunities for political influence fail to treat citizens as equal persons and express disrespect. Private citizens or organizations that take further advantage of these regulatory oversights—by willfully using their economic power to drown out the voices of the less advantaged—are complicit in this political injustice.

Apart from its role in financing social and political expression, philanthropy can also serve a productive function by financing so-called public goods. Public goods are those that are widely desired or desirable but exhibit economic characteristics that prevent them from being produced adequately by ordinary market mechanisms. (See Chapter 2 for further elaboration and examples.) Consequently, these goods must be provided by taxation or donation if they are to be provided at all. Public goods can be further classified as *essential* or *discretionary*.[19] Essential public goods are those that are necessary to maintain conditions of basic distributive justice. They include external and internal security, public health protections, civic education, protections against poverty and disease, and basic infrastructure for communication and transportation, among others. Discretionary public goods, meanwhile, are those goods which justice doesn't necessarily require, but which may be broadly valuable nonetheless. They include goods like historical preservation, scientific innovation, artistic expression, and recreation. In Chapter 3, I argued that philanthropy enjoys special advantages in supplementing the provision of these discretionary public goods. However, Chapter 2 showed that efforts by private agents to supply essential public goods interfere with the value of collective self-determination. They prevent citizens from authorizing and monitoring critical features of their common lives and are for this reason objectionable (though not necessarily objectionable all-things-considered).

The philanthropic provision of essential public goods may also be objectionable for other reasons. This is especially the case with goods designed to redress poverty and disadvantage. The dominant view is that most conditions of poverty and disadvantage aren't merely misfortunate circumstances, which deserve our compassion, but products of unjust social institutions, which deserve political solutions.[20] When equal moral persons join together to pursue their mutual advantage while subjecting one another to coercively binding laws, each gains claims to a decent social minimum and a fair share of the social product, and each incurs a duty to contribute equitably to the satisfaction of these claims. If citizens are owed certain resources as a matter of justice, there is a strong presumption that these resources must be guaranteed by law. This is so for several reasons. As Chapter 3 showed, trying to satisfy people's rights with a patchwork of voluntary initiatives is inherently unreliable. Without centralized coordination, it's virtually impossible to ensure that everyone's needs will be effectively met.[21] Redistributive philanthropy also subjects recipients to arbitrary and unaccountable power.[22] Recipients of gifts lack sufficient opportunities to influence or contest the content or terms of those gifts. And they are constantly at risk of those gifts being withdrawn at the will of the donor. Redistributive philanthropy also creates relationships of social subordination. It expresses the message that the poor and disadvantaged are victims worthy of pity, rather than equal citizens entitled to their fair share of resources. Separately, it prevents citizens from contributing their fair share to the maintenance of just conditions, a concern we encountered in Chapter 2.[23]

Appreciating the urgency of poverty and inequality often drives the counterargument that, while a world that didn't need to rely on redistributive philanthropy might be ideal, that is not our current world, and it may never come to pass. We ought to encourage redistributive philanthropy as a second-best solution to suffering in the far-from-ideal circumstances in which we find ourselves. However, critics of redistributive philanthropy can respond that the urgency of these problems indicates precisely why it's so essential to devote significant efforts to organizing to address them politically. If a significant portion of the efforts currently being devoted to relief of symptoms were redeployed toward institutional reform, these problems might very well disappear altogether. Another response is that even if some redistributive philanthropy remains necessary, these considerations underscore why it must be designed with extreme care. Chiefly, direct interventions must be designed in ways that facilitate, or at least don't interfere with, institutional reform. And they must be designed in ways that mitigate the risks of domination and social subordination as far as possible, a theme that Chapter 6 explored.

IV. A Democratic Reconstruction of Friedman's Corporate Misanthropy

With a clearer sense of what makes democracy a worthy ideal and how philanthropy can both support and undermine it, we are now in a position to consider whether philanthropy by corporations raises distinctive concerns.

Let's turn first to *expressive* philanthropy. As I suggested earlier, some degree of private financing of expressive activity is critical to realizing the values of collective self-determination, deliberative justification, and substantive reliability. Citizens of a democratic society have a vital interest in being able to create, join, and support expressive associations, and the freedom to donate helps to secure this interest. But it's hard to see how these liberties could extend to corporations. As we have seen, political equality demands that each citizen enjoy equal opportunities for political influence. Each of us should have roughly the same opportunities to express our views about how our society should be organized. People shouldn't enjoy extra opportunities to advance their social and political agendas simply because they are wealthy. Now, this principle suffers routine violation today in most countries, where wealthy individuals enjoy considerable advantages in agenda-setting and the electoral process. But allowing corporations to enter into this sphere takes the problem to new heights. Corporations that attempt to advance a social or political agenda are taking undue advantage of their economic power. As Friedman notes, both shareholders and executives enjoy considerable liberty to promote social and political causes in their capacities as individual citizens. So, corporations that promote social and political causes are essentially providing additional amplification to the voices of their executives and investors, persons whose voices are often already amplified by their privileged economic status.

One might think this problem would soften if firms determined their advocacy positions through internally democratic procedures, procedures that gave their least advantaged employees as much say over advocacy as senior management and large shareholders. Though such a proposal might reduce intra-firm political inequality, it would preserve or increase inequalities across firms, as firms vary in their resources for advocacy. Why should the wealth of my employer determine the extent of my opportunities for voicing political opinions? Such a proposal would also preserve or increase inequalities between citizens who are stakeholders in firms and those who are neither employees nor investors. The self-employed, the unemployed, uncompensated caregivers, and those who don't invest in corporate securities, would all find the relative volume of their voices reduced. Unless all citizens enjoy the same opportunities to have their voices amplified by firms, corporate advocacy objectionably increases political inequality.

This skepticism about expressive philanthropy by corporations admits of some exceptions. Naturally, certain matters of public deliberation may bear directly on a corporation's interests or expertise. Business interests are relevant considerations for public deliberation, and businesses may also have unique insights into the consequences of political decisions on broader economic conditions. If a society is considering new regulations on the production of widgets, widget producers may be specially positioned to know and to express how the regulations may affect their incentives to expand or contract, and how these decisions will ripple out across suppliers, customers, and connected industries. This shows why trade groups and some forms of lobbying by firms may have an important role in democratic politics. But it doesn't show that firms have a right to express positions about social and political issues that have no connection to the firm's business interests. Nor does it show that firms have a right to unlimited sponsorship of industry think tanks and advocacy groups.

How might we balance these competing considerations? One way would be to apply the progressive voucher scheme that Chapter 4 proposed for regulating inequalities in political influence among individuals. Like individuals, all firms could receive a government voucher redeemable for cash donations to the advocacy groups of their choice. Both individuals and firms could then purchase additional vouchers at increasing cost, with the profits from these purchases then used to fortify the value of the baseline voucher. Advocacy groups would be prohibited from accepting cash donations. Such a scheme seeks to preserve the value of expressive liberty while constraining political inequality.

The proposal does not offer a comprehensive solution to this conflict, and it comes with several implementation challenges. For better or worse, the scheme covers only donation-based avenues of political expression. It would not prevent firms from hiring armies of lobbyists or purchasing advertising space to advocate causes or policies. What it offers, rather, is a way of limiting an especially corrosive form of political inequality. Moreover, the success of this proposal depends crucially on whether workable distinctions can be drawn between expressive and nonexpressive donations. The possibility that individuals might create an unlimited number of "shell corporations" in order to capture additional vouchers serves as a reminder of the many other challenges of implementation.

Implementation challenges notwithstanding, a particular virtue of applying the progressive voucher scheme to expressive corporate donations lies in its immunity to a potent source of philosophical objections.[24] The moral responsibility of business corporations has sparked significant debate in recent years, motivated in part by high-profile corporate misdeeds (such as the 2010 Deepwater Horizon oil spill) and prominent US Supreme Court cases (*Citizens United* and *Hobby Lobby*) that resulted in expansive recognition of firms' Constitutional rights.[25] When corporations commit crimes, ordinary moral and legal practice often assigns blame to the corporation itself, rather than to individuals who compose it. Treating corporations as responsible for wrongdoing makes sense at least when the moral failure can't be attributed to the decisions of any individual officer. A popular line of reasoning maintains that recognizing corporations as responsible for misdeeds requires a correlative recognition of corporate rights. Treating corporations as morally responsible presupposes an ontological judgment about their moral agency; in turn, recognizing corporations as moral agents entitles them to the moral rights enjoyed by natural persons, such as freedom of speech and religion. If this argument succeeds, there is no basis for treating philanthropy by corporations any differently from philanthropy by individuals. Insofar as individuals have interests in making philanthropic donations—for expressing political beliefs, advancing conceptions of the good, rectifying injustice, and so on—so, too, do corporations. An alternative argument holds that the rights of corporations can't be derived through ontological reasoning alone. Settling the question of corporate moral agency doesn't settle the question of what rights they should enjoy. There may be strong grounds to treat corporations differently from natural persons regardless of any agential qualities they may share. For instance, the fact that natural persons have the capacities to provide military and jury service might provide reasons to afford them certain privileges of citizenship that don't apply to corporations; the value of economic growth might supply a reason to grant the privilege of limited liability to firms and not to natural persons.[26]

Applying the progressive voucher scheme to corporate donations would allow us to sidestep much of this controversy. Since, at least as I've sketched it, the scheme is indifferent to whether voucher purchasers are natural or artificial persons, it should be acceptable to proponents of expansive corporate rights.[27] Since the scheme seeks to limit the influence of wealth on political debate, it should be attractive to critics of corporate political activity, to the extent that their concerns are related to the relative volume of corporate speech.

Might *productive* philanthropy by corporations deserve more undiluted encouragement than philanthropy for expressive purposes? It depends. In most cases, corporate philanthropy for essential public goods appears to exacerbate existing concerns about the legitimacy of private power. This is partly because the median corporation can be expected to control far greater amounts of concentrated wealth than the median individual citizen. By leveraging this superior wealth, a corporation that attempts to redress deficits in a particular area can come to enjoy a kind of domineering influence over the people it's attempting to help—and over others who might have different ideas about what kind of help is needed.

Additionally, Friedman's worry that corporations often lack the requisite expertise to engage in these highly sensitive areas is particularly well taken. Most corporations don't handle issues or operate in industries that endow them with expertise on matters of essential public concern like education, poverty, and inequality. Corporate executives generally lack the knowledge necessary to identify appropriate interventions or even to identify the relevant experts who could determine appropriate interventions. Their view of social problems and solutions is shaped by their experience dealing with business matters. While this experience surely affords numerous transferrable insights, traditional tools of business analysis are often inadequate or counterproductive when transposed to noncommercial settings. And, as Friedman observes, corporate philanthropy's connection to marketing reveals a conflict of interest that may leave beneficiaries ill-served. Because corporations can earn customers, investors, and employees from "virtue signaling," they face a conflict of interest between authentically tackling social problems and addressing these problems in whatever ways best burnish their reputation (i.e., superficially). Corporate philanthropists therefore lack the incentives to use resources effectively and to treat vulnerable populations with sufficient respect and concern.

The conflict of interest between profit-seeking and beneficence can also interfere with the development of just institutions. Take the case of the pharmaceutical industry, which routinely tops annual lists of the most charitable segments of the corporate world. Médecins sans Frontières (MSF) made headlines in October 2016 when it announced that it was rejecting an offer from Pfizer for free pneumonia vaccines.[28] MSF alleged that while donations of pharmaceuticals may help some people in the immediate term, they also help to sustain a system that dominates and excludes many of the global poor while rewarding drug companies with unjustified profit margins. Because donated drugs relieve pressure on pharmaceutical giants to make essential medicines more reliably accessible, these donations help to prop up a global pharmaceutical distribution regime that many regard as unjust. Thus, even when corporate philanthropy does respond well to the needs of its intended beneficiaries, it can exacerbate distributive injustice, particularly when profits hang in the balance.

Although these considerations caution against corporate contributions to systemic shortfalls in the provision of essential public goods, they also leave space for certain exceptions. One noteworthy exception involves conditions of acute emergencies, particularly when firms have vital assets to share. For instance, in the wake of a natural disaster, a logistics company might donate the use of its network to connect victims to essential supplies. Airlines might donate seats to refugees of violent conflict. A medical equipment company might sell its products at or below cost to medical teams responding to a pandemic. Because these situations involve acute emergencies rather than systemic injustices, they leave less space for donors to exercise enduring political influence. These situations also sidestep Friedman's concern that corporations lack the requisite knowledge to address social problems meaningfully, as they involve firms contributing proprietary materials or technical expertise that is essential to relief efforts. Furthermore, even if firms are motivated to carry out these activities in part by expected financial returns from virtue signaling, this ulterior motive is less likely to cause harm in these cases. This is so because these cases involve short-term, carefully tailored, surgical interventions—rather than arbitrary cash donations to feel-good causes. Whether or not there exists a "corporate duty to rescue," as some argue,[29] thoughtful responses from firms to acute emergencies are generally praiseworthy forms of corporate philanthropy.

Things may look different when we consider corporate philanthropy for discretionary public goods. Of course, some might think that corporate productive philanthropy is objectionable for the same reason that corporate social advocacy is objectionable: it gives powerful agents undue control over the composition of the cultural environment. That a society's cultural space might become dominated by corporate patrons is a frightening thought. What gives Pepsi and Bank of America the right to determine which works of art are exhibited or where museums are located?[30]

On the other hand, corporate sponsorship seems difficult to oppose under certain conditions. In 1999, the International Paper Company donated an aging factory in Beacon, New York, to the Dia Arts Foundation.[31] Several state and local government bodies helped to facilitate the transfer and conversion. In donating the factory, International Paper didn't crowd out any community initiative to build a museum building—we can reasonably assume that without this donation, no other entity would have endeavored to bring a museum to Beacon. Although the company could have used its bargaining position to dictate the terms of the donation—such as by making demands on curation choices or building accessibility— it instead deferred these questions to artistic experts and representatives of the local community. The Dia:Beacon art museum, which opened its doors in 2003, is now a source of local pride and credited with revitalizing the former Rust Belt town.

Consider also the product discounts that software companies increasingly offer to nonprofits. Conducting business in a modern economy is almost impossible without access to industry-standard software for word processing, document formatting, accounting, and other basic operations. But the market price of most essential software packages is beyond the reach of many nonprofit organizations, driven up by the spending power of commercial firms. Many software companies, such as Microsoft, Adobe, and Intuit, now offer their enterprise software to nonprofits at reduced rates.[32] They do so, moreover, on a neutral basis, without attempting to promote or impede any particular group or mission. Ordinarily, any organization designated as not-for-profit by its area's governing law may qualify for the discount.

These cases suggest that corporate philanthropy may be welcome under particular conditions, namely when the firm is uniquely qualified to provide the goods in question and it does so with respect for beneficiary autonomy and fairness.

V. Conclusion: Lingering Puzzles about Corporate Beneficence

The previous section provided several reasons to limit corporate philanthropy. Corporate philanthropy can amplify unjust political inequalities. Firms' lack of competence in matters of social policy, and the conflicts of interest they face between profit generation and beneficence, lead to or help sustain substantive injustice. In view of these limitations, corporate philanthropy often smacks of arbitrary, corrupt, and domineering power. In many cases, it would be best for for-profit firms to do what Milton Friedman believes they are designed to do, which is to seek profits by satisfying consumer preferences. A society has better mechanisms for financing political expression and producing essential public goods. Thus, we've found reasons to agree with Friedman's general conclusion, even if we disagree with some or most of his reasoning.

The argument has also identified certain ways in which philanthropy by firms can satisfy the requirements of a democratic political morality. I suggested that firms have a legitimate, albeit limited, interest in sponsoring expressive activity that communicates their business interests. Though I cautioned against a general role for firms in providing essential public goods, firms can provide crucial assistance during acute emergencies, so long as this assistance is designed in ways that mitigate threats to democratic institutions and beneficiary autonomy. And while miscellaneous patronage of discretionary public goods lacks a strong justification, firms can play a valuable philanthropic role by sharing their unique assets with communities that can't afford them. These initiatives are especially laudable when firms make these assets available on fair terms and welcome deliberation with recipients on how they are to be used.

Besides the progressive voucher scheme, proposed as a way of regulating donations to expressive causes, this account has remained intentionally vague on how exactly its principles are supposed to apply. Should objectionable forms of corporate philanthropy be discouraged or forbidden by law? Should innocuous or praiseworthy forms of corporate philanthropy enjoy public subsidies? Or does it fall to individual firms, voluntary licensing bodies, and social norms to choose the best courses of action within a legal framework that affords them wide discretion? What's clear at least is that the account on offer provides a baseline for justifying policies and guiding managerial decisions. But to say more than this presents considerable difficulties, especially given recent developments that challenge the very definition of corporate philanthropy.

As traditionally understood, corporate philanthropy refers to beneficent behavior that occurs in a business's postproduction phase. A firm first maximizes its pursuit of profit then later uses some of those profits for social purposes. Meanwhile, particularly in the last few decades, firms have begun to pioneer ways of introducing philanthropic considerations into earlier stages of the production process. "Social enterprises," for instance, seek to pursue social aims more directly, on the basis of earned income. Consider a firm that seeks to assist people with physical disabilities by hiring them as telemarketers or customer service representatives. Philanthropy is the motivation, not the afterthought, and it comes in through the firm's human resources policies rather than a strategy for donating profits. Another model—"socially responsible business"—seeks primarily to generate profit, but in a way that's constrained by other values, such as fairness and environmental sustainability. Consider an ice cream company like Ben & Jerry's that pays all its employees above-market wages with generous fringe benefits. Profits are still the primary aim, but for this model, "philanthropy" enters through a willingness to forego some profits to embody certain virtues. "Impact investing" is another technique for promoting a social mission through business activity. It involves investing in firms that produce socially beneficial products or cater to underserved populations. Consider, for instance, a firm that provides internet service to rural areas of developing countries but whose profit margins are too low to attract traditional investors. Investors who choose to support such a firm are thereby blending profit-seeking with philanthropic aims. These are just a few ways in which commercial and nonprofit activity might combine beyond traditional corporate philanthropy.

Precisely how the foregoing arguments apply to this behavior isn't entirely clear. Many of these entities aim to promote just conditions outside of the democratic process. By using economic power to influence social outcomes, these practices appear to menace core principles of democratic legitimacy. As with other forms of corporate philanthropy, these practices may also relieve pressure on the state to regulate the basic structure in accordance with the requirements of justice. Additionally, these forms of corporate beneficence share with traditional corporate philanthropy the challenge of navigating an inherent conflict of interest between a firm's acquisitive and altruistic aims. This conflict intensifies when firms work with vulnerable populations whose needs must be balanced against profit margins.

At the same time, these alternative forms of corporate beneficence also exhibit noteworthy virtues. Because many social enterprises work directly for and with their intended beneficiaries, they may possess the technical and moral expertise that traditional corporate philanthropy often lacks. Whereas corporate expressive philanthropy faces objections for leveraging arbitrary advantages for social and political influence, socially responsible businesses might be defended on grounds of moral integrity. The primary point of environmentally sustainable sourcing or paying employees a living wage is not to broadcast an ideological viewpoint, but to avoid complicity in egregious forms of injustice. By diversifying the range of economic forms, hybrid entities might also foster productive experimentation and provide more meaningful opportunities for labor and consumption. Finally, some suggest that emerging forms of corporate beneficence might help to cement, rather than erode, the foundations for just institutions. Microfinance initiatives may be objectionably narrow in their reach and objectionably exploitative in their effects, but they may nevertheless empower a critical mass of individuals who can then demand institutional reform.[33] Voluntary egalitarian workplace policies may be inadequate substitutes for institutional guarantees against exploitation, but they may also help to cultivate a sense of justice among workers and prepare the way for institutionalized alternatives.[34]

Milton Friedman's position that the social responsibility of business is to increase profits draws most strength when "business" is defined by the commercial joint-stock corporation. Innovations in business organization and management force us to reconsider not only what social responsibilities businesses have but also what business is and ought to be. Further exploration of new forms of corporate beneficence might imperil the justification of corporate philanthropy by undermining the model of social organization on which it appears to rely. This exploration offers a promising avenue for additional research.

8

Overthrowing the Tyranny
of Generosity

This book has sought to show how the value of democracy contributes crucial yet neglected considerations to the justification and appraisal of philanthropy. Here, I rehearse the main claims of the foregoing chapters, identify some of the questions they leave outstanding, and reflect on their implications for theory and practice alike.

Chapter 1 ("Looking the Gift Horse in the Mouth") began by defining philanthropy as a social practice, constituted by voluntary donations of private property for public purposes. Although altruism and gift-giving may be pre-institutional elements of human sociality, the practice of philanthropy is deeply embedded in political institutions. Political institutions necessarily enable, circumscribe, and structure any recognizable practice of philanthropy. Yet ethical assessment of philanthropy has tended to focus on questions of individual conduct to the exclusion of institutional configuration. Recent work by political theorists and philosophers has begun to explore the problems that philanthropy raises for political morality. This work has made great advances toward revealing how philanthropy might be conducted and regulated in light of principles of justice. The book has sought to show how deeper reflection on questions of legitimacy, conceived in democratic terms, qualifies this picture and provides distinctive guideposts for various aspects of the practice.

As there are various ways to exchange gifts and various ways to advance the common good, what is distinctively valuable about philanthropy? Chapter 2 ("Of Sovereignty and Saints") examined a common justification for this practice: that philanthropy supports the provision of public goods. Public goods are goods whose characteristics prevent their efficient provision by conventional markets. They must be supplied either by taxation or by donation if they are to be provided adequately. Common treatments of this topic presume that philanthropy is an equally if not superior mechanism for providing these goods. I contended that common arguments fail to appreciate how democratic principles regulate public goods provision. Democracy gives us strong grounds to reserve certain decisions for collective determination. Democracy, I argued, makes citizens sovereign over the legislation and administration of matters of basic justice. Our interests in democratic sovereignty supply a strong reason to maintain public control over public goods that are intimately linked to fundamental rights, duties, and opportunities. The argument implies skepticism about privately sponsored social assistance and basic education, while vindicating private philanthropy in the arts, culture, religion, advocacy, and advanced research, among other places. However, I insisted that precisely how to account for the value of democratic sovereignty often requires contextual judgment and is difficult to specify in the abstract. What is nonetheless clear is that this value provides an essential and often-neglected ingredient to weigh in practical deliberation.

While Chapter 2 concluded that a polity might have reason to limit philanthropy's reach, Chapter 3 ("A Farewell to Alms") held that, when operating within its legitimate remit, philanthropy deserves both public protection and public subsidy. Policies that subsidize philanthropic donations in some way are common to many contemporary societies. Most versions of this policy make subsidies available on a neutral basis, to the chagrin of numerous critics, who regard subsidies as justifiable only on redistributive grounds. The chapter challenged this charity-based justification for state support in favor of a democratic justification that backs a wider array of aims. Public support for citizens' varied philanthropic commitments, I argued, is valuable as a way of mediating the limitations of majority rule, correcting market failures, and securing the organizational foundations of democratic deliberation.

How should opportunities for donation be distributed? Laissez-faire treatment of the ability to convert wealth into voice allows wealthier citizens to augment their influence over public affairs, further marginalizing poorer citizens. Chapter 4 ("Donation and Deliberation") contended that this state of affairs is ultimately incompatible with the requirements of political equality. The reasons to regulate political spending, I argued, also apply to certain kinds of philanthropic donations. I explored various policy proposals for redressing this problem, including a Progressive Voucher Scheme that would replace cash donations for expressive activities with vouchers whose price increases the more vouchers one purchases. Such a proposal seeks to balance interests in liberty and efficiency with the demands of political equality.

Chapter 5 ("In Usufruct to the Living") explored an especially underappreciated problem in the ethics of philanthropy: that popular instruments of donation may objectionably bind future generations to respect the wills of past donors. The chapter drew on Thomas Jefferson to illustrate how donations meant to benefit future persons may also mistreat them by imposing conditions on their use of resources. Each generation, I argued, has an interest in sovereignty over its common affairs that qualifies how resources can be donated across time. Taking the value of sovereignty seriously doesn't forbid intergenerational philanthropy, but it does recommend certain restrictions on the duration that donors can expect to have their wills honored.

Chapter 6 ("The Effective Altruist's Political Problem") used the effective altruism movement as a foil to examine how democratic principles might inform the practical ethics of giving. A core component of effective altruism is the relief of poverty through targeted interventions in the developing world. Critics of using philanthropy to relieve the symptoms of poverty have frequently held up institutional reform as the superior object of donation. While the chapter reaffirmed the institutionalist critique, it also complicated the critics' proposed remedy. An unqualified recommendation for diverting more money into politics, I argued, falls into the trap of political injustice that I raised in Chapter 4. Chapter 6 explored some ways in which individual donors might overcome these challenges, such as by making assistance projects self-consciously transitional, investing in community organizing rather than direct policy change, and deploying donations to counteract antidemocratic forces. The value of democracy can't tell us where to give, I maintained, but it can tell us how to give more respectfully.

Chapter 7 ("Milton Friedman's Corporate Misanthropy") considered how the foregoing arguments might inform the ethics of corporate philanthropy. It also drew help from an unlikely ally, the libertarian economist Milton Friedman. Friedman remains notorious for his opposition to corporate philanthropy. Friedman's claim that a corporation's sole purpose and obligation is to maximize profits enjoys vanishingly little support today. However, Chapter 7 argued that this controversial claim can be anchored in a democratic critique of corporate power. Because a firm's shareholders, managers, and employees are already free to make donations in their individual capacities as citizens, allowing firms to donate in addition can objectionably multiply the public influence of their stakeholders. Citizens who can't call upon a firm to multiply the effects of their own donations have strong grounds for complaint. Furthermore, as firms typically command concentrated wealth, the freedom to deploy that wealth for social purposes can afford them domineering influence over receiving communities. Finally, I showed how the inherent conflict between a commercial firm's acquisitive and altruistic motives exposes vulnerable beneficiaries to high risk of mistreatment. The chapter revealed how certain kinds of corporate philanthropy can overcome this criticism. It also proposed that new developments in business that blend commercial and nonprofit aims invite further research. Through such activities as impact investing, social enterprise, socially responsible management, and corporate activism, businesses are increasingly pursuing social ends through means other than donation. Future work might show how the principles uncovered here might extend beyond donation to address broader challenges of private power.

This book has offered a selective rather than exhaustive treatment of the relationship between philanthropy and democracy. As I stressed in Chapter 1, the choice of coverage has more to do with fitting my particular contributions into a coherent plan than about the relative importance of different topics. Some topics have received only partial treatment. The justification of private foundations, for instance, is one topic I have addressed only obliquely, in connection with the question of intergenerational ethics in Chapter 5. While I defended certain aspects of intergenerational giving, the concerns about inequitable and domineering power developed throughout the book pose significant challenges for the justification of entities that are plutocratic almost by definition. I am largely unpersuaded by recent attempts to justify foundations on grounds that they offer unique epistemic benefits and contributions to pluralism.[1] Though I can't develop this point further here, I suspect that the functions foundations serve in discovering or piloting new programs could be better served by universities—with far less damage to democracy.[2] And as Chapter 2 suggested, expanding the range of options for public goods consumption is a feature that belongs to philanthropy generally and not to foundations specifically.

The practical ethics of giving is another topic I addressed only partially, despite its immense importance. Chapter 6 proposed certain guidelines for the goals and strategies that donors adopt when responding to severe poverty. It didn't directly engage the question of whether individuals have duties to donate, which causes might be morally superior to others, or how much individuals might be morally required to give. Besides the fact that these questions have already generated voluminous academic reflection, I set them aside because of a problem of indeterminacy.[3] Suppose we could agree, in theory, about the nature and scope of our duties to strangers. Whether or when these duties should be discharged through *philanthropy*, however, will often be indeterminate. There are innumerable ways in which individuals can advance justice, rectify injustice, benefit others, and reduce harm. Philanthropy is certainly one avenue, and an important one at that. But it's a grave and all-too-common mistake to presume that philanthropy is the only or primary method for discharging other-regarding duties. In many cases, political activism, career choices, volunteering of labor or bodily tissue, consumption choices, or business decisions may be more fundamental. Whether or how philanthropy fits into one's moral toolbox will depend to a great deal on one's historical context, past choices, inherited privileges and liabilities, expertise, and available resources. Although ethical theory can be tremendously helpful for disentangling the different considerations to be weighed in these decisions, the particularly wide variation in individual circumstances limits its ability to offer more than general guidance in this area.

We encountered a similar problem in Chapter 7's discussion of corporate philanthropy. Philanthropy might be one component of a broader strategy of corporate social responsibility. But there are numerous tactics besides philanthropy that firms might use to respect rights, promote well-being, transact virtuously, and so on. Making well-reasoned choices among these options requires a broader theory of business ethics.

While some topics received partial treatment, others received none at all. I have said nothing about donor-advised funds (DAFs), a new and controversial instrument of intertemporal giving. DAFs allow donors to contribute money to a pooled fund run by a financial service provider, to be paid out to a cause of the provider's choice at some future date. Critics allege that DAFs amount to little more than tax shelters.[4] I have also said little about the relationship between donors and intermediary organizations (variously called charities, nonprofits, and NGOs).[5] A particularly important question here is whether or when we should regard nonprofits as agents of their donors, and whether or when we should think the opposite. Throughout, I have largely assumed an individualist social ontology that treats donor-funded organizations as agents of their donors. Such a picture suggests that it's donors who enjoy the real power in this relationship and consequently invite the most scrutiny. However, I acknowledge that this might be a poor characterization of at least certain organizations. For instance, large NGOs like the Sierra Club, Amnesty International, and Habitat for Humanity that exist in perpetuity and raise funds from many different sources are able to achieve significant independence from their donors. Something similar happens with trusts, like the Ford Foundation, that become decoupled from the preferences of their settlors.[6] While these situations may sidestep certain concerns about the distribution and exercise of power among donors, they raise their own challenges of authorization and accountability.[7] What justifies the power of these organizations and their officers?

Throughout, we've seen how reflection on the value of democracy qualifies both common and academic wisdom about the ethics of philanthropy. Conventional perspectives urge scrutiny of philanthropy's motives, aims, and strategies. I have tried to show that even when philanthropy comes with noble intentions, just goals, and rigorous methods, it can objectionably privatize matters that all of us have equal interests in deciding, augment the power of the richer at the expense of the poorer, empower the dead at the expense of the living, and perpetuate structural inequalities between donors and recipients. Democracy's contribution to the ethics of philanthropy isn't merely critical, however. To overthrow the tyranny of generosity is not to vanquish it but to reorient it. Reflection on the value of democracy shows how philanthropy can be consistent with, and facilitative of, the democratic ideal. When sensitively regulated and conducted, philanthropy provides a valuable vehicle for individual liberty that complements and strengthens democratic institutions. By financing discretionary public goods, philanthropy can compensate for the inherent limitations of majority rule. By financing expressive associations, it can help foster a vibrant civil society that cultivates democratic virtues, nourishes public deliberation, and holds the state accountable. In cases where the state is crippled, corrupted, or nascent, philanthropy can be a vital force for securing the roots of democratic governance. For these reasons, a democratic order that thrives without philanthropy's support is exceedingly difficult to conceive.

The success of this claim depends, of course, on a particular view about the nature and value of democracy, a view that has come into focus in the course of this study. There certainly could be, and have been, nominally democratic orders that make no room for philanthropy. Investigating the practice of philanthropy has allowed us to reflect more carefully on what exactly makes democracy valuable and how that value should be institutionalized. On the view that has emerged, democracy is valuable when and because it affords subjects of fundamental social decisions fair opportunities for influence over those decisions. In turn, fair opportunities for influence are valuable because they enable subjects to share control over their social world and to stand in relationships of social equality with one another. Thoroughgoing legitimacy is impossible unless governance structures sufficiently institutionalize these features. This view suggests that free and fair elections may be a necessary requirement of democratic legitimacy, but they are far from sufficient. At the same time, the view also suggests that democracy's value is neither absolute nor unlimited. Unlimited popular control would be a perversion, rather than a fuller realization, of the democratic ideal. According to this view, democratic legitimacy is first and foremost a requirement of states. When states are democratic in this way, private agents are more or less free to govern their own affairs as they choose within the legally defined boundaries. But when states are less than fully democratic, requirements of democratic legitimacy can devolve onto private agents. The discretion that donors and other powerful agents might enjoy under democratic conditions shrinks when power is inequitably distributed.

One might protest that this elevation of democracy reflects a viewpoint whose relevance appears to diminish with each passing day. In the last few years, populism has disfigured democratic institutions, bulwarks of democratic stability have flirted dangerously with fascism, and authoritarian regimes that once teetered on the brink of collapse have tightened their grip on power. The apparent elusiveness of the democratic ideal might be taken to indicate that this ideal really isn't as valuable as it seems. Perhaps the failure of societies to embrace and perfect democratic institutions lies in the lackluster appeal of the democratic ideal itself. Or, this failure might be taken to indicate that such an ideal isn't realistically achievable. Difficulties in realizing the democratic ideal might suggest that we should set our sights on some less demanding alternative. Many are impressed with the rise of technocratic regimes, which frustrate democratic aspirations but deliver comfortable living standards and relative tranquility. Advances in technology also increasingly allow governance functions to be outsourced to artificial agents, which sidestep the challenges of collective human decision-making to offer dramatic improvements in efficiency.

These criticisms are serious. And in pessimistic moments, I sometimes wonder whether they contain some truth, particularly when I consider the aptitude of democratic institutions for confronting looming threats to human civilization. But I also see several causes for hope. Even as democratic institutions have quaked, in the last few years allegiance to democratic ideals has shown encouraging signs of strength. The world over, tolerance of social inequality is wearing thin, as racial and gender justice have inspired a vigorous global social movement. Resentment toward elites, though tragically often misdirected, has no shortage of supply. And arbitrary power continues to meet heroic popular resistance despite grave personal costs to protestors. Moreover, many of the technologies currently used to expand the control of elites and siphon power away from citizens can be harnessed for democratic ends.[8] Creative experiments in institutional design also breed new hope for democratic revival.[9]

Finally, and perhaps most importantly, a defense of democracy rests on the fact that no alternative ideal comes close to balancing the ingredients that matter when evaluating options for governing our common lives. The challenge for democracy's critics is to identify a viable alternative that respects the inherent freedom and equality of human persons. The apparent impossibility of this task indicates why democracy will continue to deserve our allegiance for the foreseeable future.

Notes

Chapter 1

1. Jeff Bezos, Twitter post, September 13, 2018, 5:00 p.m., https://twitter.com/JeffBezos/status/1040253796293795842.
2. Aaron Horvath and Walter W. Powell, "Contributory or Disruptive: Do New Forms of Philanthropy Erode Democracy?," in *Philanthropy in Democratic Societies: History, Institutions, Values*, ed. Rob Reich, Lucy Bernholz, and Chiara Cordelli (Chicago: University of Chicago Press, 2016), 87–112.
3. Donna Brazile, Twitter post, September 13, 2018, 5:53 p.m., https://twitter.com/donnabrazile/status/1040267354964471809.
4. Kelsey Piper, "The Problem with Jeff Bezos's $2 Billion Gift to Charity," *Vox*, September 18, 2018, https://www.vox.com/2018/9/21/17880000/jeff-bezos-amazon-philanthropy-gift-2-billion.
5. The 10 percent guideline is meant for middle-class residents of the Global North, based on the assumption that giving away such a percentage wouldn't prevent most people from continuing to enjoy a comfortable standard of living. This logic suggests that a much higher standard should apply to someone like Bezos, who could comfortably afford to give away at least 99 percent of his wealth. See Giving What We Can, http://www.givingwhatwecan.org.
6. Anand Giridharadas, "Why Jeff Bezos's Philanthropy Plan Is Well-Intentioned—and Misguided," *Time*, September 18, 2018, https://time.com/5398801/jeff-bezos-philanthropy/.
7. Vinod Khosla, Twitter post, September 16, 2018, 5:20 p.m., https://twitter.com/vkhosla/status/1041346033765179392.
8. This view is most famously associated with Andrew Carnegie. See Andrew Carnegie, "The Best Fields for Philanthropy," *North American Review* 149, no. 397 (1889): 682–99.
9. Darren Walker, *From Generosity to Justice: A New Gospel of Wealth* (New York: The Ford Foundation / Disruption Books, 2019).
10. Peter Singer, "Good Charity, Bad Charity," *New York Times*, August 10, 2013, sec. Opinion.

11. Patricia Illingworth, "An Ethicist Explains Why Philanthropy Is No License to Do Bad Stuff," *The Conversation*, December 19, 2019, https://theconversation.com/an-ethicist-explains-why-philanthropy-is-no-license-to-do-bad-stuff-127426.

12. Paul Brest, "The Outcomes Movement in Philanthropy and the Nonprofit Sector," in *The Nonprofit Sector: A Research Handbook*, ed. Walter W. Powell and Patricia Bromley, 3rd ed. (Stanford, CA: Stanford University Press, 2020), 381–408.

13. Karl Marx and Friedrich Engels, "Manifesto of the Communist Party," in *The Marx-Engels Reader*, ed. Robert C. Tucker, 2nd ed. (New York: Norton, 1978); Oscar Wilde, "The Soul of Man under Socialism," *Fortnightly Review* 49 (1891): 292–319.

14. Peter Dobkin Hall, "Philanthropy, the Nonprofit Sector and the Democratic Dilemma," *Daedalus* 142, no. 2 (April 1, 2013): 139–58; Gara LaMarche, "Democracy and the Donor Class," *Democracy Journal* 34 (2014): 48–59; David Callahan, *The Givers: Wealth, Power, and Philanthropy in a New Gilded Age* (New York: Alfred A. Knopf, 2017).

15. For a comprehensive study of the history of the term, see Marty Sulek's pair of papers, "On the Classical Meaning of Philanthrôpía," *Nonprofit and Voluntary Sector Quarterly* 39, no. 3 (2010): 385–408, and "On the Modern Meaning of Philanthropy," *Nonprofit and Voluntary Sector Quarterly* 39, no. 2 (2010): 193–212.

16. Robert A. Gross, "Giving in America: From Charity to Philanthropy," in *Charity, Philanthropy, and Civility in American History*, ed. Lawrence J. Friedman and Mark D. McGarvie (Cambridge, UK: Cambridge University Press, 2003), 29–48.

17. According to Giving USA, an annual report produced by the IUPUI Lilly Family School of Philanthropy, 31 percent of donations in 2017 went to religious congregations, while 14 percent went to education (primarily universities), 11 percent went to foundations, and 5 percent went to arts, culture, and the humanities. Even if we assume that foundation recipients spent some of these donations on addressing social problems or their symptoms, that still leaves more than half of all donations undefined. See IUPUI Lilly Family School of Philanthropy, "Giving USA 2018: The Annual Report on Philanthropy for the Year 2017" (Indianapolis: Lilly Family School of Philanthropy, 2018).

18. I explore the concept of a social practice at greater length in Theodore M. Lechterman, "The *Potestas* of Practice," *History of Political Thought* 42, no. 2 (2021): 240–51.

19. Stephen R. Munzer, *A Theory of Property* (Cambridge, UK: Cambridge University Press, 1990), 380ff.

20. My definition of philanthropy seeks to exclude traditional political spending, such as donations to electoral campaigns, political parties, and political action committees (PACs). As I understand it, narrowly political donations ordinarily seek to accomplish more particular goals; they are not necessarily directed at benefitting an indefinite number of people. More importantly, perhaps, the topic of political spending has already inspired a voluminous literature. For recent treatments of this topic, see Lawrence Lessig, *Republic Lost: The Corruption of Equality and the Steps to End It*, Rev. ed. (New York: Twelve, 2015); Robert Post, *Citizens Divided: Campaign Finance Reform and the Constitution* (Cambridge, MA: Harvard University Press, 2016); and Prithviraj Datta, *Why Campaign Finance Matters: Normatively Evaluating the American Electoral Spending Regime* (unpublished book manuscript, n.d.). I explore the boundaries between political spending and philanthropy in Chapter 4.

21. See, e.g., Francie Ostrower, *Why the Wealthy Give* (Princeton, NJ: Princeton University Press, 1995), 4.

22. Consider that "public" can mean "open to all" (in the way that a "pub" is open to any customer with the means to pay for a drink), "universal" (in the way that "public utilities" are meant to cover all residents of a region), as well as "collectively authorized," "collectively beneficial," and "governmental."

23. I assume that this definition also includes labor as a form of donatable property. Volunteer labor doesn't significantly implicate the main issues of this study, however. The concluding chapter considers alternative modes of philanthropy.

24. IUPUI Lilly Family School of Philanthropy, "Giving USA 2020: The Annual Report on Philanthropy for the Year 2019" (Indianapolis: Lilly Family School of Philanthropy, 2020).

25. David Bivin et al., "The Philanthropy Outlook 2020 & 2021" (Indianapolis: Indiana University Lilly Family School of Philanthropy, 2020), 11.

26. "Gross Domestic Philanthropy: An International Analysis of GDP, Tax and Giving" (Kent, UK: Charities Aid Foundation, January 2016).

27. "An Overview of Philanthropy in Europe" (L'Observatoire de la Fondation de France / CERPhi, 2015).

28. My calculations, drawing on data from Patti Chu and Olivia Yutong Wang, "Philanthropy in China" (Singapore: AVPN, 2018).

29. David Bivin et al., "The Philanthropy Outlook 2020 & 2021."

30. Maya Imberg and Maeen Shaban, "The New Normal: Trends in UHNW Giving 2019" (New York: Wealth-X, 2019).

31. One of the oldest studies on this question is Marcus Tullius Cicero, *On Duties*, ed. M. T. Griffin and E. M. Atkins (Cambridge, UK: Cambridge University Press, 1991).

32. See Paul Woodruff, ed., *The Ethics of Giving: Philosophers' Perspectives on Philanthropy* (Oxford: Oxford University Press, 2018).

33. See, e.g., William MacAskill, *Doing Good Better: How Effective Altruism Can Help You Make a Difference* (New York: Gotham Books, 2015); Peter Singer, *The Most Good You Can Do* (New Haven: Yale University Press, 2015).

34. For an overview, see, Jerome B. Schneewind, ed., *Giving: Western Ideas of Philanthropy* (Bloomington: Indiana University Press, 1996).

35. On the prevalence of gift-giving across cultures and time periods, see Marcel Mauss, *The Gift: The Form and Reason for Exchange in Archaic Societies* (London: Routledge, 2002).

36. One of Aristotle's primary objections to common ownership among the guardians in Plato's *Republic* is that it seems to preclude opportunities for beneficence. For critical discussion, see T. H. Irwin, "Generosity and Property in Aristotle's Politics," *Social Philosophy and Policy* 4, no. 2 (1987): 37–54.

37. On the possibility of philanthropy in socialist theory, see Michael Walzer, "Socialism and the Gift Relationship," *Dissent* 29 (January 1, 1982): 431–41.

38. Peter Dobkin Hall, *"Inventing the Nonprofit Sector" and Other Essays on Philanthropy, Voluntarism, and Nonprofit Organizations* (Baltimore: Johns Hopkins University Press, 1992).

39. Gopal Sreenivasan, *The Limits of Lockean Rights in Property* (New York: Oxford University Press, 1995), 110.

40. On the rise of for-profit higher education in Brazil and China, see Marcelo Knobel and Robert Verhine, "Brazil's For-Profit Higher Education Dilemma," *International Higher Education*, no. 89 (2017): 23–24.

41. Athenian "liturgies" were voluntary contributions for public goods commonly expected of wealthy individuals. Although not technically required by law, individuals who refused to contribute risked a variety of informal sanctions. See Josiah Ober, "Classical Athens," in *Fiscal Regimes and the Political Economy of Premodern States*, ed. Andrew Monson and Walter Scheidel (Cambridge, UK: Cambridge University Press, 2018), 492–522.

42. Rob Reich, *Just Giving: Why Philanthropy Is Failing Democracy and How It Can Do Better* (Princeton, NJ: Princeton University Press, 2018); Ryan Pevnick, "Democratizing the Nonprofit Sector," *Journal of Political Philosophy* 21, no. 3 (2013): 260–82; Nick Martin, "Liberal Neutrality and Charitable Purposes," *Political Studies* 60, no. 4 (2012): 936–52.
43. Reich, *Just Giving*; Emma Saunders-Hastings, "Plutocratic Philanthropy," *The Journal of Politics* 80, no. 1 (2017): 149–61.
44. Jennifer C. Rubenstein, *Between Samaritans and States: The Political Ethics of Humanitarian INGOs* (New York: Oxford University Press, 2015); Thomas Pogge, "How International Nongovernmental Organizations Should Act," in *Giving Well: The Ethics of Philanthropy*, ed. Patricia Illingworth, Thomas Pogge, and Leif Wenar (Oxford: Oxford University Press, 2011), 46–66; Chiara Cordelli, "The Institutional Division of Labor and the Egalitarian Obligations of Nonprofits," *Journal of Political Philosophy* 20, no. 2 (2012): 131–55.
45. Liam B. Murphy, *Moral Demands in Nonideal Theory* (Oxford: Oxford University Press, 2003); Chiara Cordelli, "Reparative Justice and the Moral Limits of Discretionary Philanthropy," in *Philanthropy in Democratic Societies: History, Institutions, Values*, ed. Rob Reich, Chiara Cordelli, and Lucy Bernholz (Chicago: University of Chicago Press, 2016), 244–66.
46. A. John Simmons, "Justification and Legitimacy," *Ethics* 109, no. 4 (1999): 739–71; Philip Pettit, *On the People's Terms* (Cambridge, UK: Cambridge University Press, 2012).
47. Jeremy Waldron, "Theoretical Foundations of Liberalism," *Philosophical Quarterly* 37, no. 147 (1987): 127–50.
48. See, e.g., Thomas Christiano, *The Rule of the Many: Fundamental Issues in Democratic Theory* (Boulder, CO: Westview Press, 1996); Joshua Cohen, "Money, Politics, and Political Equality," in *Fact and Value: Essays on Ethics and Metaphysics for Judith Jarvis Thomson*, ed. Alex Byrne, Robert Stalnaker, and Ralph Wedgwood (Cambridge, MA: MIT Press, 2001), 47–80; Elizabeth Anderson, "Democracy: Instrumental vs. Non-Instrumental Value," in *Contemporary Debates in Political Philosophy*, ed. Thomas Christiano and John Christman (Oxford, UK: Wiley-Blackwell, 2009), 213–27; Niko Kolodny, "Rule over None I: What Justifies Democracy?," *Philosophy and Public Affairs* 42, no. 3 (2014): 195–229; Daniel Viehoff, "Democratic Equality and Political Authority," *Philosophy and Public Affairs* 42, no. 4 (2014): 337–75.
49. One exception to this may be Chiara Cordelli, *The Privatized State* (Princeton, NJ: Princeton University Press, 2020).

Chapter 2

1. A. M. Honoré, "Ownership," in *Oxford Essays in Jurisprudence: A Collaborative Work*, ed. Anthony Gordon Guest (Oxford: Clarendon Press, 1961), 107–47.
2. The classic statement is Paul A. Samuelson, "The Pure Theory of Public Expenditure," *Review of Economics and Statistics* 36, no. 4 (1954): 387–89.
3. Thomas Hobbes, David Hume, Adam Smith, and John Stuart Mill could all more or less fit this description.
4. See, e.g., John Rawls, *A Theory of Justice*, rev. ed. (Cambridge, MA: Harvard University Press, 1999), 234–39; Robert Nozick, *Anarchy, State, and Utopia* (New York: Basic Books, 1974); George Klosko, "The Obligation to Contribute to Discretionary Public Goods," *Political Studies* 38, no. 2 (1990): 196–214; David Schmidtz, *The Limits of Government: An Essay on the Public Goods Argument* (Boulder: Westview Press, 1991); Brian Barry, *Justice as Impartiality: A Treatise on Social Justice*, Vol. 2 (Oxford: Oxford University Press, 1995); David Miller, "Justice, Democracy and Public Goods," in *Justice and Democracy: Essays for Brian Barry*, ed. Keith Dowding, Robert Goodin, and Carole Pateman (Cambridge, UK: Cambridge University Press, 2004), 127–49.
5. Nozick, *Anarchy*, 169.
6. For a forceful defense of this idea, see Arthur Ripstein, *Force and Freedom* (Cambridge, MA: Harvard University Press, 2009), 259–65.
7. See, respectively, John Rawls, *Political Liberalism* (New York: Columbia University Press, 1993), 166; Jeremy Waldron, "Welfare and the Images of Charity," *Philosophical Quarterly* 36, no. 145 (1986): 463–82; Henry Shue, *Basic Rights: Subsistence, Affluence, and U.S. Foreign Policy* (Princeton, NJ: Princeton University Press, 1996).
8. Klosko, "The Obligation to Contribute to Discretionary Public Goods."
9. For a forceful statement of this problem, see Alan Patten, "Liberal Neutrality: A Reinterpretation and Defense," *Journal of Political Philosophy* 20, no. 3 (2012): 249–72.
10. See Peter Dobkin Hall, *"Inventing the Nonprofit Sector" and Other Essays on Philanthropy, Voluntarism, and Nonprofit Organizations* (Baltimore: Johns Hopkins University Press, 1992).
11. See Chiara Cordelli, "Privatization without Profit," in *Political Legitimacy*, ed. Jack Knight and Melissa Schwartzberg, Nomos LXI (New York: New York University Press, 2019), 113–44.

12. Margaret H. Lemos and Guy-Uriel Charles, "Patriotic Philanthropy: Financing the State with Gifts to Government," *California Law Review* 106 (2018): 1129–93.

13. See Joanne Barkan, "Plutocrats at Work: How Big Philanthropy Undermines Democracy," *Social Research: An International Quarterly* 80, no. 2 (2013): 635–52.

14. One of the classic examples of a putatively pure public good is the lighthouse. No one can be prevented from enjoying its light once it has been provided; and no one's enjoyment of the light diminishes the enjoyment of anyone else. But these are not natural facts. An extremely crowded harbor could very well create conditions of rivalry. Likewise, new technology could make it possible for lighthouses to exclude nonpayers from viewing the light. (Suppose it broadcasts light at a specific wavelength that requires proprietary technology to view.)

15. Russell Hardin, *Collective Action* (Baltimore: Johns Hopkins University Press, 1982), 17–20; Richard Steinberg, "Economic Theories of Nonprofit Organizations," in *The Nonprofit Sector: A Research Handbook*, ed. Walter W. Powell and Richard Steinberg (New Haven: Yale University Press, 2006): 117–39, 121.

16. Eric Beerbohm, "The Free-Provider Problem: Private Provision of Public Responsibilities," in *Philanthropy and Democratic Societies*, ed. Rob Reich, Chiara Cordelli, and Lucy Bernholz (Chicago: Chicago University Press, 2016), 207–25.

17. See, e.g., Philip Pettit, *Republicanism: A Theory of Freedom and Government* (Oxford: Oxford University Press, 1997).

18. Philip Pettit, *On the People's Terms: A Republican Theory and Model of Democracy* (Cambridge, UK: Cambridge University Press, 2013), 113; Robert Taylor, "Donation without Domination," *Journal of Political Philosophy* 42 (2018): 441–62.

19. Bernardo Zacka, *When the State Meets the Street* (Cambridge, MA: Harvard University Press, 2017).

20. Michael Walzer, *Spheres of Justice* (New York: Basic Books, 1983).

21. Debra Satz argues that privatization of public services can lead to the corruption of the central purposes of those services. Her understanding of corruption doesn't appeal to contingent social meanings. Rather, she suggests that the incentives that attach to private provision can stand in tension with any reasonable view about the purpose of certain practices. Private prisons, for instance, create incentives to maximize the incarcerated population, which conflicts with any plausible conception of

criminal justice. However, Satz's focus is on the incentives that attach to profit-seeking, not philanthropy. It remains unclear whether this kind of argument extends to nonprofit settings. See Debra Satz, "Some (Largely) Ignored Problems with Privatization," in *Privatization*, ed. Jack Knight and Melissa Schwartzberg, Nomos LX (New York: New York University Press, 2019), 9–29.

22. Beerbohm, "Free-Provider Problem."

23. Christiano names the first three of these in Thomas Christiano, *The Rule of the Many: Fundamental Issues in Democratic Theory* (Boulder: Westview Press, 1996), 3; Beitz names the last three in Charles R. Beitz, *Political Equality: An Essay in Democratic Theory* (Princeton, NJ: Princeton University Press, 1989), ch. 5.

24. Joshua Cohen, "Procedure and Substance in Deliberative Democracy," in *Deliberative Democracy: Essays on Reason and Politics*, ed. James Bohman and William Rehg (Cambridge, MA: MIT Press, 1997), 407–37.

25. David Estlund, *Democratic Authority* (Princeton, NJ: Princeton University Press, 2008).

26. J. S. Mill, "Considerations on Representative Government," in *The Collected Works of John Stuart Mill, Volume XIX—Essays on Politics and Society Part II*, ed. John M. Robson (Toronto: University of Toronto Press, 1977).

27. Josiah Ober, *Demopolis* (Cambridge, UK: Cambridge University Press, 2017).

28. Niko Kolodny, "Rule over None I: What Justifies Democracy?" *Philosophy and Public Affairs* 42, no. 3 (2014): 195–229; Niko Kolodny, "Rule over None II: Social Equality and the Justification of Democracy," *Philosophy and Public Affairs* 42, no. 4 (2014): 287–336. For a similar view, see Daniel Viehoff, "Democratic Equality and Political Authority," *Philosophy and Public Affairs* 42, no. 4 (2014): 337–75.

29. Kolodny, "Rule over None II."

30. See, e.g., Anna Stilz, "The Value of Self-Determination," in *Oxford Studies in Political Philosophy*, Vol. 2, ed. David Sobel, Peter Vallentyne, and Steven Wall (Oxford: Oxford University Press, 2016): 98–127.

31. Jake Zuehl, "Collective Self-Determination" (PhD diss., Princeton University, 2016).

32. Anna Stilz proposes a less demanding account, according to which individuals enjoy collective self-determination when they "reasonably affirm" their participation in a joint enterprise. Although reasonable affirmation includes the ability to express oneself effectively, it does not require

that individuals enjoy causal control over that enterprise. This more minimal criterion helps to explain the wrong in imposing alien rule on nondemocratic societies. But unless our understanding of collective self-determination incorporates some element of causal agency, it's not clear to me how this value could be robustly secured. See Stilz, "The Value of Self-Determination."

33. The social meanings account I considered earlier helps to remind us of the different values that flow from different forms of public goods provision. Its mistake is to see these values as immanent in a public culture, rather than objects of social choice.

34. Rawls, *A Theory of Justice*, 7, 96.

35. Elizabeth Anderson, "What Is the Point of Equality?" *Ethics* 109, no. 2 (1999): 287–337.

36. Burton Weisbrod, "Toward a Theory of the Voluntary Nonprofit Sector in a Three-Sector Economy," in *Altruism, Morality, and Economic Theory*, ed. Edmund S. Phelps (New York: Russell Sage Foundation, 1975); Rob Reich, "Repugnant to the Whole Idea of Democracy? On the Role of Foundations in Democratic Societies," *PS: Political Science and Politics* 49, no. 3 (2016): 466–72.

37. Harry Brighouse, "Neutrality, Publicity, and State Funding for the Arts," *Philosophy and Public Affairs* 24, no. 1 (1995): 35–63.

38. A suggestion along these lines appears in Gerald Gaus, "Coercion, Ownership, and the Redistributive State: Justificatory Liberalism's Classical Tilt," *Social Philosophy and Policy* 27, no. 1 (2010): 233–75.

39. I thank an anonymous reviewer for pressing me on this point.

40. John Stuart Mill, "On Liberty," in *The Collected Works of John Stuart Mill, Volume XVIII: Essays on Politics and Society Part I*, ed. John M. Robson (Toronto: University of Toronto Press, 1977): 213–310, 299–300.

41. Emma Saunders-Hastings, "Benevolent Giving and Philanthropic Paternalism," in *Effective Altruism: Philosophical Issues*, ed. Hilary Greaves and Theron Pummer (Oxford: Oxford University Press, 2019), 115–36.

42. On the origins of this principle, see Peter Landau, "The Origin of the *Regula iuris 'quod omnes tangit'* in the Anglo-Norman School of Canon Law during the Twelfth Century," *Bulletin of Medieval Canon Law* 32, no. 1 (2015): 19–35.

43. This is a critically important philosophical conundrum. See Robert Goodin, "Enfranchising All Affected Interests, and Its Alternatives," *Philosophy and Public Affairs* 35, no. 1 (2007): 40–68.

44. Emma Saunders-Hastings and Rob Reich ("Philanthropy and the All-Affected Principle," Paper Presented at the American Political Science Association Annual Meeting, September 2017) propose another way of applying the AAI principle to philanthropy. They argue that philanthropists themselves ought to take the principle as a guideline in their grant-making decisions, such as by considering, or soliciting participation from, those who are affected by their grants. But unlike the view I propose, the Saunders-Hastings and Reich account doesn't limit the range of interests that might trigger claims for democratic voice. Furthermore, whereas their account focuses on the direct and indirect recipients of philanthropy, the democratic sovereignty argument applies to the wider community, irrespective of whether a member stands to benefit personally from the provision of a good.

45. Cf. Cordelli, "Privatization without Profit."

46. In "The Case against Privatization," *Philosophy and Public Affairs* 41, no. 1 (2013): 67–102, Avihay Dorfman and Alon Harel contend that certain "inherently public goods" must be not only supervised by the state but also administered directly by it, as certain goods are partly constituted by the way they express the will of the state. Namely, criminal punishment and national defense are by nature expressive: respectively, they express public condemnation of wrongdoing and public judgments about just war. These goods lose their communicative purposes if they are not administered directly by the state. But the problem with this view is that many public goods appear to have this expressive quality, and the account lacks an argument for identifying these "inherently public goods."

47. Satz, "Some (Largely) Ignored Problems with Privatization."

48. I thank an anonymous reviewer for posing this objection.

49. For similar conclusions about the context-dependence of collective self-determination's moral priority, see Stilz, "The Value of Self-Determination," 122–24.

Chapter 3

1. Though I focus on familiar Anglo-American contexts, the practice isn't exclusive to these contexts. For instance, Brazil, France, Hungary, and Portugal subsidize charitable activity in similar ways. For a comparison of several subsidy schemes, see Calum M. Carmichael, "Doing Good Better? The Differential Subsidization of Charitable Contributions," *Policy and Society* 29, no. 3 (2010): 201–17.

2. For discussion of these two elements of the definition, see, respectively, Kerry O'Halloran, Myles McGregor-Lowndes, and Karla W. Simon, *Charity Law and Social Policy* (New York: Springer, 2008), 296; Richard Steinberg and Walter W. Powell, "Introduction," in *The Nonprofit Sector: A Research Handbook*, ed. Walter W. Powell and Richard Steinberg (New Haven: Yale University Press, 2006), 1–10, 1.

3. See, e.g., Rob Reich, "Toward a Political Theory of Philanthropy," in *Giving Well: The Ethics of Philanthropy*, ed. Patricia Illingworth, Thomas Pogge, and Leif Wenar (Oxford: Oxford University Press, 2011): 177–92.

4. Canada Revenue Agency, "Gifts and Income Tax 2017," P113(E) Rev. 17, available at http://cra.gc.ca/E/pub/tg/p113; "Giving to Charity through Gift Aid," H. M. Revenue and Customs Web site, http://www.hmrc.gov.uk/individuals/giving/gift-aid.htm.

5. 38.1 million people in the United States in 2018, according to official estimates (and based on official standards). Jessica Semega et al., "Income and Poverty in the United States: 2018," *Current Population Reports* P60-266 (Washington, DC: U.S. Census Bureau, 2019).

6. "Patterns of Household Charitable Giving by Income Group, 2005," Indiana University Center on Philanthropy / Google, Inc. (Summer 2007), available at http://www.philanthropy.iupui.edu/files/research/giving_focused_on_meeting_needs_of_the_poor_july_2007.pdf. This study examines donations given to organizations that provide direct service or support to low-income individuals, whether as a primary or ancillary component of the organization's mission. One might wonder whether low-income individuals might benefit more from public charities on an indirect basis. However, econometric analyses of the indirect benefits of public charities find no overall redistributive effect. See Charles T. Clotfelter, *Who Benefits from the Nonprofit Sector?* (Chicago: University of Chicago Press, 1992), and Julian Wolpert, "The Redistributional Effects of America's Private Foundations," in *The Legitimacy of Philanthropic Foundations: United States and European Perspectives*, ed. Kenneth Prewitt, Mattei Dogan, Steven Heydemann, and Stefan Toepler (New York: Russell Sage Foundation, 2005), 123–49.

7. IUPUI Lilly Family School of Philanthropy, "Giving USA 2019 Highlights" (Indianapolis: Lilly Family School of Philanthropy, 2019). Note that these statistics consider religiously sponsored service-delivery entities separately from churches.

8. In *Independent Schools Council v. Charity Commission*, the High Court concluded that "a trust which excludes the poor from benefit cannot be a

charity. There is no case which decides that point, but we consider it is right as a matter of principle, given the underlying concept of charity from early times" (para. 178). *Independent Schools Council v. Charity Commission*, [2011] U.K.U.T. 421 (T.C.C.). The Court's decision has been incorporated in the Charity Commission's current guidelines. See U.K. Charity Commission, "Analysis of the Law Relating to Public Benefit," September 2013, available at http://www.charitycommission.gov.uk/media/94849/lawpb1208.pdf.

9. Liam Murphy and Thomas Nagel, *The Myth of Ownership* (New York: Oxford University Press, 2002), 127; Robert D. Cooter, "The Donation Registry," *Fordham Law Review* 72 (2004): 1981–89; Rob Reich, "A Failure of Philanthropy," *Stanford Social Innovation Review* (Winter 2005): 24–33; Rob Reich, "Philanthropy and Its Uneasy Relation to Equality," in *Taking Philanthropy Seriously: Beyond Noble Intentions to Responsible Giving*, ed. William Damon and Susan Verducci (Bloomington: Indiana University Press, 2006): 27–49; Miranda Perry Fleischer, "Theorizing the Charitable Tax Subsidies: The Role of Distributive Justice," *Washington University Law Review* 87 (2009–2010): 505–66; Calum M. Carmichael, "Sweet and Not-So-Sweet Charity: A Case for Subsidizing Contributions to Different Charities Differently," *Public Finance Review* 40, no. 4 (2012): 497–518.

10. Reich, "Philanthropy and Its Uneasy Relation to Equality," 27. While Reich's more recent work has moved away from this view, the position remains influential.

11. Reich, "A Failure of Philanthropy," 27.

12. Fleischer, "Theorizing the Charitable Tax Subsidies," 556–66.

13. Murphy and Nagel, *Myth of Ownership*, 127.

14. Ibid.

15. The authors leave open whether it might be justifiable on other grounds. But if it's justifiable on other grounds, they contend, "the argument would be very different, and 'charity' is hardly the right word." Ibid.

16. Kymlicka contends that arguments for voluntary redistribution often evince a "pre-modern" worldview. See Will Kymlicka, "Altruism in Philosophical and Ethical Traditions: Two Views," in *Between State and Market: Essays on Charities Law and Policy in Canada*, ed. Jim Phillips, Bruce Chapman, and David Stevens (Montreal: McGill-Queens University Press, 2001), 87–126, 115. Similarly, Schneewind notes that a principled commitment to voluntary redistribution presupposes either conditions of extreme scarcity or a lack of technological sophistication. J. B. Schneewind,

"Philosophical Ideas of Charity: Some Historical Reflections," in *Giving: Western Ideas of Philanthropy*, ed. J. B. Schneewind (Bloomington: Indiana University Press, 1996), 54–75, 68.

17. Peter Brown, *Through the Eye of a Needle: Wealth, the Fall of Rome, and the Making of Christianity in the West, 350–550 AD* (Princeton, NJ: Princeton University Press, 2012).

18. Fleischer, "Theorizing the Charitable Tax Subsidies," 556–66.

19. Rawls appeals to this idea in "Two Concepts of Rules," *Philosophical Review* 64, no. 1 (1955): 3–32. Perhaps more importantly, he also explicitly denies that the difference principle in his theory of justice as fairness is meant to apply to every policy individually. See John Rawls, *Justice as Fairness: A Restatement*, ed. Erin Kelly (Cambridge, MA: Harvard University Press, 2001), 161–62.

20. Murphy and Nagel, *Myth of Ownership*, 127.

21. For an overview, see Kymlicka, "Altruism in Philosophical and Ethical Traditions."

22. Robert Nozick, *Anarchy, State, and Utopia* (New York: Basic Books, 1974), 79, 265–68. Compare Michael Otsuka, *Libertarianism Without Inequality* (Oxford: Oxford University Press, 2003), 12–41.

23. Jeremy Waldron, "Welfare and the Images of Charity," *Philosophical Quarterly* 36, no. 145 (1986): 463–82.

24. John Rawls, *Political Liberalism* (New York: Columbia University Press, 1993), 166.

25. The locus classicus on the instrumental significance of subsistence rights is Henry Shue, *Basic Rights: Subsistence, Affluence, and U.S. Foreign Policy* (Princeton, NJ: Princeton University Press, 1996).

26. Elizabeth Anderson argues in favor of the former. See Elizabeth S. Anderson, "What Is the Point of Equality?" *Ethics* 109, no. 2 (1999): 287–337, 326.

27. Advocates of a universal basic income argue in the affirmative. See, e.g., Philippe van Parijs, *Real Freedom for All: What (if Anything) Can Justify Capitalism?* (Oxford: Oxford University Press, 1995).

28. This type of concern motivates a persistent criticism of Rawls's use of social primary goods as the currency of justice. See, e.g., Martha Nussbaum, *Frontiers of Justice* (Oxford: Oxford University Press, 2006).

29. See, e.g., Andrew Lister, "Justice as Fairness and Reciprocity," *Analyse und Kritik* 33, no. 1 (2011): 93–112, 108.

30. The distinction and the stadium example belong to Ronald Dworkin, *Sovereign Virtue* (Cambridge, MA: Harvard University Press, 2000), 204–5.

31. Though some use the terms "voluntary" and "discretionary" interchangeably, I intentionally keep them distinct. "Voluntary" here means that a contribution isn't coercively extracted. "Discretionary" means that the donor enjoys choice over the direction and currency of a contribution. In principle, a contribution can be voluntary without being discretionary, and vice versa.

32. As Bentham observes bluntly, private charity, as a response to misfortune, "will experience daily vicissitudes, like the fortune and the liberality of the individuals on whom it depends. Is it insufficient? Such junctures are marked by misery and death." Jeremy Bentham, *Theory of Legislation* (London: Kegan Paul, 1908), 130.

33. Anna Schrimpf, "The Politics of Empathy: A Study of INGO Attention and Neglect" (PhD diss., Princeton University, 2016).

34. Daniel Shapiro claims that voluntary poor relief in late-nineteenth-century America was in fact remarkably efficient and indicative of what might occur if contemporary governments withdrew from the business altogether. See Daniel Shapiro, "Egalitarianism and Welfare-State Distribution," *Social Philosophy and Policy* 19, no. 1 (2002): 1–35. Supposing this is true, however, invites us to consider the manner in which that relief took place and the kinds of relationships it created. A recent historical investigation of these practices describes them as "draconian" and "punitive," by relying on threats of starvation or institutionalization, intrusive scientific observation, and arbitrary personal judgments. Brent Ruswick, "Just Poor Enough: Gilded Age Charity Applicants Respond to Charity Investigators," *Journal of the Gilded Age and Progressive Era* 10, no. 3 (2011): 265–87. Emma Saunders-Hastings claims that sensitivity to these kinds of troubling features helps to explain John Stuart Mill's opposition to practices of voluntary charity in Victorian England. See Emma Saunders-Hastings, "No Better to Give Than to Receive: Charity and Women's Subjection in J.S. Mill," *Polity* 46, no. 2 (2014): 233–54.

35. See Philip Pettit, *On the People's Terms* (Cambridge, UK: Cambridge University Press, 2013), 113.

36. See Niko Kolodny, "Being under the Power of Others," in *Republicanism and the Future of Democracy*, ed. Yiftah Elazar and Geneviève Rousselière (Cambridge, UK: Cambridge University Press, 2019), 94–114.

37. This last aspect reflects part of Rawls's case against welfare-state capitalism more generally. See *Justice as Fairness*, 139–40.

38. Philip Pettit, *Republicanism: A Theory of Freedom and Government* (Oxford: Oxford University Press, 1997), 158–63.

39. The locus classicus is Paul A. Samuelson, "The Pure Theory of Public Expenditure," *Review of Economics and Statistics* 36, no. 4 (1954): 387–89.

40. The concept originates in Richard A. Musgrave, *The Theory of Public Finance* (New York: McGraw-Hill, 1959), 13–15.

41. Russell Hardin, *Collective Action* (Baltimore: Johns Hopkins University Press, 1982), 17–20, and Richard Steinberg, "Economic Theories of Nonprofit Organizations," in *The Nonprofit Sector: A Research Handbook*, ed. Walter W. Powell and Richard Steinberg (New Haven: Yale University Press, 2006), 117–39, 121.

42. For instance, Rawls reflects this ambiguity when he writes, "the provision of public goods must be arranged for through the political process and not through the market." John Rawls, *A Theory of Justice*, rev. ed. (Cambridge, MA: Harvard University Press, 1999), 236.

43. According to the "economist's theory of the state," the existence of a state is justified entirely as a function of its ability to solve market failures. See Geoffrey Brennan, "Economics," in *A Companion to Contemporary Political Philosophy*, ed. Robert E. Goodin, Philip Pettit, and Thomas W. Pogge (Oxford: Blackwell, 2007), 118–52.

44. Alan Patten makes this case particularly clearly in, "Liberal Neutrality: A Reinterpretation and Defense," *Journal of Political Philosophy* 20, no. 3 (2011): 249–72, 261–64.

45. Rawls, *Theory of Justice*, 250.

46. Ibid.

47. Ibid., 244.

48. Ronald Dworkin, "Can a Liberal State Support Art?" in *A Matter of Principle* (Cambridge, MA: Harvard University Press, 1985), 221–33.

49. Joseph Raz, *The Morality of Freedom* (Oxford: Oxford University Press, 1986), 144.

50. Ibid., 414.

51. Although Raz offers no concrete proposal, Dworkin proposes that the duty to expand a society's cultural language allows the state to engage directly in funding cultural projects. But, as Harry Brighouse charges, this proposal risks violating the doctrine of liberal neutrality, particularly as Dworkin himself defines it in his other work. Subsidizing donations appears to sidestep the thrust of Brighouse's critique. Compare Harry Brighouse, "Neutrality, Publicity, and State Funding for the Arts," *Philosophy and Public Affairs* 24, no. 1 (1995): 35–63.

52. Jürgen Habermas, *Between Facts and Norms*, trans. William Rehg (Cambridge, MA: MIT Press, 1996), 366–67.

53. Iris Marion Young, *Inclusion and Democracy* (New York: Oxford University Press, 2000), 158.

54. Habermas, *Between Facts and Norms*, 368.

55. Ibid., 369.

56. Ibid.

57. Pevnick reaches a similar conclusion. See Ryan Pevnick, "Democratizing the Nonprofit Sector," *Journal of Political Philosophy* 21, no. 3 (2013): 260–82, 266–68.

58. Though not referring to subsidies, Kymlicka suggests that voluntary responses to disadvantage might be "second-best" approaches to injustice. Kymlicka, "Altruism in Philosophical and Ethical Traditions," 94.

59. For an overview, see Laura Valentini, "Ideal vs. Non-Ideal Theory: A Conceptual Map," *Philosophy Compass* 7, no. 9 (2012): 654–64, and Enzo Rossi and Matt Sleat, "Realism in Normative Political Theory," *Philosophy Compass* 9, no. 10 (2014): 689–701.

60. A. John Simmons, "Ideal and Nonideal Theory," *Philosophy and Public Affairs* 38, no. 1 (2010): 5–36; Pablo Gilabert, "Justice and Feasibility: A Dynamic Approach," in *Political Utopias: Contemporary Debates*, ed. Kevin Vallier and Michael Weber (New York, NY: Oxford University Press, 2017), 95–126.

61. Simmons, "Ideal and Nonideal Theory," 22.

62. Kenneth Nelson, "Social Assistance and EU Poverty Thresholds 1990–2008: Are European Welfare Systems Providing Just and Fair Protection against Low Income?" *European Sociological Review* 29, no. 2 (2011): 386–401.

63. E.g., Olivier Zunz, *Philanthropy in America: A History* (Princeton, NJ: Princeton University Press, 2014).

64. Peter Dobkin Hall, *"Inventing the Nonprofit Sector" and Other Essays on Philanthropy, Voluntarism, and Nonprofit Organizations* (Baltimore: Johns Hopkins University Press, 1992).

65. These statistics refer to all charitable organizations and not specifically those engaged in social services provision. The most recent year for which this data is available is 2013. See Brice S. McKeever, "The Nonprofit Sector in Brief: Public Charities, Giving, and Volunteering, 2015," Washington, DC: The Urban Institute, 2015.

66. A long-standing critique of the nonprofit sector is that it props up capitalism by softening the impact of capitalism's excesses. For a canvassing of some versions of this critique, see Barry D. Karl and Stanley N. Katz, "Foundations and Ruling Class Elites," *Daedalus* 116, no. 1 (1987): 1–40.

67. Seth H. Werfel, "Does Charitable Giving Crowd Out Support for Government Spending?" *Economics Letters* 171 (2018): 83–86; Seth H. Werfel, "Household Behaviour Crowds Out Support for Climate Change Policy When Sufficient Progress Is Perceived," *Nature Climate Change* 7 (2017): 512.

68. Rob Reich, Lacey Dorn, and Stefanie Sutton, "Anything Goes: Approval of Nonprofit Status by the I.R.S." (Stanford: Stanford University Center on Philanthropy and Civil Society, 2009).

69. Nick Martin, "Liberal Neutrality and Charitable Purposes," *Political Studies* 60, no. 4 (2012): 936–52.

Chapter 4

1. See, e.g., Frank Walsh, "Perilous Philanthropy," *The Independent*, August 23, 1915, 262; Peter Dobkin Hall, "Philanthropy, the Nonprofit Sector, and the Democratic Dilemma," *Daedalus* 142, no. 2 (2013): 139–58; Joanne Barkan, "Plutocrats at Work: How Big Philanthropy Undermines Democracy," *Social Research* 80, no. 2 (2013): 635–52; Gara LaMarche, "Democracy and the Donor Class," *Democracy* (Fall 2014): 48–59.

2. See, e.g., Linsey McGoey, *No Such Thing as a Free Gift: The Gates Foundation and the Price of Philanthropy* (London: Verso, 2016), Anand Giridharadas, *Winners Take All: The Elite Charade of Changing the World* (New York: Knopf Doubleday Publishing Group, 2018), and Vanessa Williamson, "The Philanthropy Con," *Dissent Magazine*, Winter 2019, https://www.dissentmagazine.org/article/the-philanthropy-con.

3. For a critical analysis of philanthropy's influence on education, see Diane Ravitch, *The Death and Life of the Great American School System* (New York: Basic Books, 2011).

4. Defenders of this principle, in one form or another, include John Rawls, *Political Liberalism* (New York: Columbia University Press, 1993), 324–31; Harry Brighouse, "Egalitarianism and Equal Availability of Political Influence," *Journal of Political Philosophy* 4, no. 2 (1996): 118–41; Jack Knight and James Johnson, "What Sort of Political Equality Does Deliberative Democracy Require?" in *Deliberative Democracy: Essays on Reason and Politics*, ed. James Bohman and William Rehg (Cambridge, MA: MIT Press, 1997): 279–319; Joshua Cohen, "Money, Politics, and Political Equality," in *Fact and Value: Essays on Ethics and Metaphysics for Judith Jarvis Thomson*, ed. Alex Byrne, Robert Stalnaker, and Ralph Wedgwood (Cambridge, MA: MIT Press, 2001): 47–80; Niko Kolodny,

"Rule over None II: Social Equality and the Justification of Democracy," *Philosophy and Public Affairs* 42, no. 4 (2014): 287–336; Daniel Viehoff, "Democratic Equality and Political Authority," *Philosophy and Public Affairs* 42, no. 4 (2014): 337–75.

5. Some political egalitarians build in additional conditions to the criteria of legitimacy. Rawls, for instance, requires that the outcomes of decisions respect a constitution that's reasonably acceptable to those it governs. See Rawls, *Political Liberalism*, 137.

6. See especially Viehoff, "Democratic Equality and Political Authority," and Kolodny, "Rule over None II."

7. The distinction between impact and influence here takes inspiration from Ronald Dworkin, *Sovereign Virtue* (Cambridge, MA: Harvard University Press, 2000), 184–210.

8. See, e.g., James Bohman, "Deliberative Democracy and Effective Social Freedom," in *Deliberative Democracy: Essays on Reason and Politics*, ed. James Bohman and William Rehg (Cambridge, MA: MIT Press, 1997), 321–47.

9. Representation based on lottery might avoid this objection. But lottery-based representation also sacrifices certain purported gains of expertise. Space forecloses a thorough treatment of these issues here.

10. Cohen, "Money, Politics, and Political Equality," 50.

11. Ibid., 51.

12. The locus classicus on agenda-setting remains Steven Lukes, *Power: A Radical View*, 2nd ed. (London: Palgrave-Macmillan, 2005).

13. A point that Cohen readily acknowledges. "Money, Politics, and Political Equality," 54.

14. This seems to be one upshot of Rawls's remarks on the noninstrumental value of self-government. See John Rawls, *A Theory of Justice*, rev. ed. (Cambridge, MA: Harvard University Press, 1999), 205–6. That democratic citizens have a compelling interest in public recognition also figures in Charles R. Beitz, *Political Equality* (Princeton, NJ: Princeton University Press, 1989), 109–10.

15. Cohen, "Money, Politics, and Political Equality," 55.

16. Niko Kolodny, "Rule over None I: What Justifies Democracy?" *Philosophy and Public Affairs* 42, no. 3 (2014): 195–229, 221.

17. David Estlund, "Political Quality," *Social Philosophy and Policy* 17, no. 1 (2000): 127–60.

18. Viehoff, "Democratic Equality and Political Authority"; Kolodny, "Rule over None II." Viehoff and Kolodny inherit a tradition of thinking about

equality that counts Elizabeth Anderson and Samuel Scheffler as major contributors.

19. The classical account comes from Hume's *A Treatise of Human Nature*, bk. 3, pt. 2, sec. 2, and *An Enquiry Concerning the Principles of Morals*, sec. 3.1. See David Hume, *A Treatise of Human Nature*, ed. L. A. Selby-Bigge and P. H. Nidditch (Oxford: Oxford University Press, 1978), 486–9); David Hume, *An Enquiry Concerning the Principles of Morals*, ed. J. B. Schneewind (Indianapolis: Hackett, 1983), 20–3.

20. Rawls, *Political Liberalism*, 328.

21. One might reply that the scarce resource in question is none other than finance. Groups act competitively because they seek to maintain or increase their funding. Without a deeper exploration of the sociology of nonprofit organizations, we can note that this explanation fails two paradigm cases: endowed organizations, which have no need to raise additional funds, and volunteer-run organizations, which maintain small budgets. Despite having little financial motivation, both types of group still often adopt competitive strategies.

22. Thomas Christiano, "Money in Politics," in *The Oxford Handbook of Political Philosophy*, ed. David Estlund (Oxford: Oxford University Press, 2012), 241–58.

23. Cohen, "Money, Politics, and Political Equality," 55.

24. See, e.g., Bohman, "Deliberative Democracy and Effective Social Freedom."

25. Beitz, *Political Equality*, xvi.

26. See, e.g., Theda Skocpol, *Diminished Democracy: From Membership to Management in American Civic Life* (Norman: University of Oklahoma Press, 2003).

27. These concepts can also be seen as instantiations of Lukes's third dimension of power. See Lukes, *Power*.

28. This distinction isn't quite the same one that Rawls draws between a "public political culture" and what he calls the "background culture." He defines the latter in terms of "the culture of daily life," and includes among its constituents the activities of clubs and teams. What I describe here as the "background public political culture" is meant to be more narrowly confined. See Rawls, *Political Liberalism*, 13–14.

29. I discuss the challenge of distinguishing between expressive and nonexpressive nonprofit activity further in what follows.

30. For case studies on the funding of the civil rights movement, the conservative legal movement, and the rise of right-wing populism, see, respectively,

Oliver Zunz, *Philanthropy in America: A History* (Princeton, NJ: Princeton University Press, 2011), ch. 7; Steven M. Teles, *The Rise of the Conservative Legal Movement: The Battle for Control of the Law* (Princeton, NJ: Princeton University Press, 2012); Jane Mayer, *Dark Money: The Hidden History of the Billionaires behind the Rise of the Radical Right* (New York: Doubleday, 2016).

31. This is a main finding of Kay Lehman Schlozman, Sidney Verba, and Henry E. Brady, *The Unheavenly Chorus: Unequal Political Voice and the Broken Promise of American Democracy* (Princeton, NJ: Princeton University Press, 2012).

32. Rob Reich, "Toward a Political Theory of Philanthropy," in *Giving Well: The Ethics of Philanthropy*, ed. Patricia Illingworth, Thomas Pogge, and Leif Wenar (Oxford: Oxford University Press, 2011): 177–92; Ryan Pevnick, "Democratizing the Nonprofit Sector," *Journal of Political Philosophy* 21, no. 3 (2013): 260–82.

33. See Chapter 3 for further discussion of the mechanics of this policy and its variants.

34. Emma Saunders-Hastings reaches a similar judgment in her discussion of the influence of large foundations. Emma Saunders-Hastings, "Plutocratic Philanthropy," *Journal of Politics* 80, no. 1 (2018): 149–61.

35. It's worth noting that the amount of funds that the state contributes to charitable enterprise through the deduction is only a fraction of what citizens contribute on their own. In the United States, $45.1 billion dollars of federal revenue were foregone in 2019 as a result of the charitable deduction. This contrasts with $427.7 billion in charitable donations in 2018. See Jane G. Gravelle, Donald J. Marples, and Molly F. Sherlock, "Tax Issues Relating to Charitable Contributions and Organizations" (Washington, DC: Congressional Research Service, September 19, 2019).

36. One might think that the deduction has an incentive effect on amount that citizens donate. In the absence of the deduction, wealthier citizens simply wouldn't donate as much to charitable causes. While this may be true, the rich would still retain significant reserve power to shape outcomes by donation. Furthermore, it's worth pointing out that donations to the most controversial causes (such as education reform) probably don't depend much on tax incentives for their motivation.

37. Pevnick, "Democratizing the Nonprofit Sector," 278–80.

38. A point that Pevnick also makes in support of his own proposal. Pevnick, "Democratizing the Nonprofit Sector," 280.

39. However, this disciplining function can also have perverse implications, as when donors use their discretion to control the behavior of vulnerable beneficiaries.

40. Estlund, "Political Quality," 153–55.

41. Reform of philanthropic donations would likely be ineffective in a society that fails to adopt egalitarian regulation of more traditional political spending. In such a scenario, more regulated philanthropy could simply incentivize the diversion of more resources into campaigns, elections, and lobbying.

42. Note that many American organizations already do something like this. That is, advocacy organizations typically have both a 501(c)(3) arm and a 501(c)(4) arm that allows them to engage in more direct political activity. Both arms share the same set of officers, and the officers must clearly account for the resources they devote to each purpose. See John Simon et al., "The Federal Tax Treatment of Charitable Organizations," in *The Nonprofit Sector: A Research Handbook*, ed. Walter W. Powell and Richard Steinberg (New Haven: Yale University Press, 2006), 267–306, 285.

43. As an anonymous reviewer reminds me, without adequate safeguards, a black market could easily develop for individuals to trade their vouchers for cash. Measures for authenticating vouchers might benefit from applications of blockchain technology.

44. Some believe, for instance, that Rawls's difference principle positively requires wide inequalities in property ownership. Compare Samuel Freeman, "Property-Owning Democracy and the Difference Principle," *Analyse und Kritik* 1 (2013): 9–26, with Kevin Vallier, "A Moral and Economic Critique of the New Property-Owning Democrats: On Behalf of a Rawlsian Welfare State," *Philosophical Studies* 172, no. 2 (2015): 283–304.

Chapter 5

1. A version of this chapter appears as Theodore M. Lechterman, "'That the Earth Belongs in Usufruct to the Living': Intergenerational Philanthropy and the Problem of Dead-Hand Control," in *Giving in Time: Temporal Issues in Philanthropy*, ed. Benjamin Soskis and Ray D. Madoff (Lanham: Rowman & Littlefield, forthcoming).

2. See, e.g., Joanne Florino, "The Case for Philanthropic Freedom," *Alliance* 21, no. 3 (2016).

3. See, e.g., Anand Giridharadas, *Winners Take All: The Elite Charade of Changing the World* (New York: Knopf, 2018).

4. See, e.g., Judith Sealander, "Curing Evils at Their Source: The Arrival of Scientific Giving," in *Charity, Philanthropy, and Civility in American History*, ed. Lawrence J. Friedman and Mark D. McGarvie (Cambridge, UK: Cambridge University Press, 200), 217–39; Matthew Bishop and Michael Green, *Philanthrocapitalism: How Giving Can Save the World* (New York: Bloomsbury, 2010).

5. E.g., Emma Saunders-Hastings, "Plutocratic Philanthropy," *Journal of Politics* 80, no. 1 (2018): 149–61.

6. One exception is Ray D. Madoff, *Immortality and the Law: The Rising Power of the American Dead* (New Haven: Yale University Press, 2010).

7. In this terminological choice, I follow Chiara Cordelli and Rob Reich, "Philanthropy and Intergenerational Justice: How Philanthropic Institutions Can Serve Future Generations," in *Institutions for Future Generations*, ed. Axel Gosseries and Iñigo González (Oxford: Oxford University Press, 2016), 229–44.

8. See Benjamin Soskis and Ray D. Madoff, eds., *Giving in Time: Temporal Issues in Philanthropy* (Lanham, MD: Rowman & Littlefield, forthcoming).

9. IUPUI Lilly Family School of Philanthropy, "Giving USA 2020: The Annual Report on Philanthropy for the Year 2019" (Indianapolis: Lilly Family School of Philanthropy, 2020).

10. Private foundations that engage directly in charitable work are called private operating foundations.

11. One notable exception is the Bill and Melinda Gates Foundation, which is set to terminate fifty years after the death of the last to die of Bill and Melinda Gates and Warren Buffet.

12. Internal Revenue Service, Statistics of Income Division, "Historical Table 16: Nonprofit Charitable Organization and Domestic Private Foundation Information Returns, and Exempt Organization Business Income Tax Returns: Selected Financial Data, 1985–2011," October 2014.

13. Compare American Association of Fund-Raising Counsel, *Giving USA 1986* (New York: AAFRC Trust for Philanthropy, 1986) with IUPUI Lilly Family School of Philanthropy, "Giving USA 2020."

14. Iris J. Goodwin, "Ask Not What Your Charity Can Do for You: *Robertson v. Princeton* Provides Liberal-Democratic Insights onto the Dilemma of *Cy Pres* Reform," *Arizona Law Review* 51 (2009): 75–125, 97.

15. E.g., Plato, *Laws*, XI, 923a *et seq.*; William Godwin, *Enquiry Concerning Political Justice, and Its Influence on Morals and Happiness*, Vol. 2 (London: G. G. and J. Robinson, 1798), Bk. VIII, Ch. II, 444–48.

16. Thomas Jefferson, "Letter to James Madison," September 6, 1789, in *The Works of Thomas Jefferson*, Vol. 6., Federal ed. (New York and London: G.P. Putnam's Sons, 1904–1905).

17. In fact, Jefferson's famous sentence appears to contain a contradiction. If the rights of the living are only usufructory in nature, this doesn't prevent the dead from possessing certain property rights. However, the ordering of the words suggests that Jefferson is using "usufruct" in a more figurative sense to emphasize his view that the property claims of the living deserve more considerable weight.

18. Jefferson was also aware of the challenge of defining the concept of a generation. If we believe that generations of persons are possible subjects of moral claims, we will need some way of distinguishing one generation from the next. But on what basis shall we make this distinction? One could say that "my generation" consists only of the persons born on the same day or within the same year as me. Or my generation might include persons born decades before or after me. Jefferson's letter suggests a complicated mathematical formula for sorting persons into separate generations, a formula that Michael Otsuka has attempted to clarify and operationalize in his *Libertarianism without Inequality* (Oxford: Oxford University Press, 2003), 132–50.

19. A future generation may of course enjoy opportunities to influence social conditions in the generations that follow its own. But this isn't a reciprocal relationship. Nor are the opportunities necessarily equal: given the scarcity of resources, generations that come earlier in the historical sequence may enjoy significantly greater opportunities to shape social affairs in the future.

20. Hillel Steiner and Peter Vallentyne, "Libertarian Theories of Intergenerational Justice," in *Intergenerational Justice*, ed. Axel Gosseries and Lukas H. Meyer (Oxford: Oxford University Press, 2009), 50–75.

21. Although Joel Feinberg once famously tried to argue otherwise—that interests could persist posthumously—he later abandoned this position in his *Harm to Others* (Oxford: Oxford University Press, 1984). Thanks to Ray Madoff for this point.

22. Andrew Holowchak emphasizes the pluralistic origins of Jefferson's philosophical thought in his "Thomas Jefferson," *Stanford Encyclopedia of Philosophy*, ed. Edward N. Zalta, Winter 2016, https://plato.stanford.edu/archives/win2016/entries/jefferson/.

23. Those who defend views of this type include Janna Thompson, *Intergenerational Justice: Rights and Responsibilities in an Intergenerational Polity* (New York: Routledge, 2009), 60ff., and Rahul Kumar, "Wronging

Future People: A Contractualist Proposal," in *Intergenerational Justice*, ed. Axel Gosseries and Lukas H. Meyer (Oxford: Oxford University Press, 2009), 252–71.

24. Reeve holds that the role of bequest in helping to facilitate responsible planning explains the support it enjoys from J. S. Mill, T. H. Green, and John Rawls. See Andrew Reeve, *Property* (Houndsmills: Macmillan, 1986), 161.

25. See, e.g., Edward J. McCaffery, "The Political Liberal Case against the Estate Tax," *Philosophy and Public Affairs* 23, no. 4 (1994): 281–312, 295–96.

26. Samuel Scheffler, *Death and the Afterlife*, ed. Niko Kolodny (Oxford: Oxford University Press, 2013). Scheffler's argument is addressed to the broader importance of posterity to the motivations of present persons.

27. Galle wonders how strong these incentives really are in Brian Galle, "Pay It Forward: Law and the Problem of Restricted-Spending Philanthropy," *Washington University Law Review* 93 (2015): 1143–207, 1168–71.

28. See, e.g., D. W. Haslett, "Is Inheritance Justified?" *Philosophy and Public Affairs* 15, no. 2 (1986): 122–55; McCaffery, "The Political Liberal Case against the Estate Tax"; Eric Rakowski, "Transferring Wealth Liberally," *Tax Law Review* 51 (1995–1996): 419–72; Liam Murphy and Thomas Nagel, *The Myth of Ownership* (New York: Oxford University Press, 2002), ch. 7.

29. Martin Gilens, *Affluence and Influence* (Princeton, NJ: Princeton University Press, 2012).

30. This is true of Haslett, "Is Inheritance Justified?," McCaffery, "The Political Liberal Case against the Estate Tax," and Rakowski, "Transferring Wealth Liberally."

31. On the first point, see Rob Reich, "A Failure of Philanthropy," *Stanford Social Innovation Review* (Winter 2005): 24–33.

32. This isn't to say that these are the only conditions that govern whether ICTs are effective instruments of redistribution.

33. "Patterns of Household Charitable Giving by Income Group, 2005," Indiana University Center on Philanthropy / Google, Inc. (Summer 2007), available at http://www.philanthropy.iupui.edu/files/research/giving_focused_on_meeting_needs_of_the_poor_july_2007.pdf.

34. See, e.g., Liam Murphy and Thomas Nagel, *The Myth of Ownership*, 127; Robert D. Cooter, "The Donation Registry," *Fordham Law Review* 72 (2004): 1981–89; Rob Reich, "A Failure of Philanthropy"; Rob Reich, "Philanthropy and Its Uneasy Relation to Equality," in *Taking Philanthropy Seriously: Beyond Noble Intentions to Responsible Giving*, ed. William

Damon and Susan Verducci (Bloomington: Indiana University Press, 2006), 27–49.

35. John Rawls, *A Theory of Justice*, rev. ed. (Cambridge, MA: Harvard University Press, 1999), 251–62.

36. Cordelli and Reich, "Philanthropy and Intergenerational Justice."

37. Rawls, *A Theory of Justice*, 252.

38. Joseph Raz, *The Morality of Freedom* (Oxford: Clarendon Press, 1986), 53.

39. Anna Stilz, "The Value of Self-Determination," in *Oxford Studies in Political Philosophy*, Vol. 2, ed. David Sobel, Peter Vallentyne, and Steven Wall (Oxford: Oxford University Press, 2016), 98–127; Jake Zuehl, "Collective Self-Determination," PhD diss. (Princeton, NJ: Princeton University, 2016).

40. Zuehl, "Collective Self-Determination," 1.

41. Zuehl claims that collective self-determination also fails when citizens lack basic agreement on fundamental assumptions, such as the moral equality of persons (ibid., 68ff).

42. Though Zuehl provides no definition of "core institutions," the common illustrations that he offers (the civil and criminal justice systems and systems for distributing employment, healthcare, and education) seem to possess a unifying quality (ibid., 42–43). That is, a central unifying feature of such institutions is their role in assigning fundamental rights, duties, and opportunities—what we might otherwise call matters of basic distributive justice. I borrow this definition of "core institutions" from Rawls's comments about the "basic structure," to which Zuehl seems partially indebted. See Rawls, *Theory of Justice*, 7, 96.

43. Historically this wasn't always the case. When the primary form of wealth was land, there was a real worry that a society's material basis would someday come to be controlled entirely by dead persons. See Lewis M. Simes, *Public Policy and the Dead Hand* (Ann Arbor: University of Michigan Law School, 1955).

44. An interesting consequence of this view is that it casts doubt on the legitimacy of perpetual constitutions, insofar as they presuppose substantive conceptions of justice. Perpetual constitutions enjoy monopoly or dominating influence over future generations in a way that I've claimed doesn't hold in the case of ICTs.

45. Simes reports this case in *Public Policy and the Dead Hand*, 122.

46. Ibid., 127.

47. I take these facts from Goodwin, "Ask Not What Your Charity Can Do for You."

48. Edmund Burke, "Reflections on the Revolution in France," in *Select Works of Edmund Burke*, Vol. 2 (Indianapolis: Liberty Fund, 1999).

49. One might object here that the prevalence of general-purpose foundations challenges the idea that the permission to craft narrow terms serves as an important incentive. However, I think it's more accurate to think of general-purpose foundations as exceptions to this rule. Those who possess vast sums of wealth may get as much, or more, satisfaction from endowing a general-purpose institution that bears their name. This alternative incentive isn't available to persons of more ordinary means.

50. I'm grateful to Rob Reich for bringing this point to my attention.

51. Cordelli and Reich, "Philanthropy and Intergenerational Justice."

52. J. S. Mill, "Corporation and Church Property (1833)," in *Collected Works of John Stuart Mill, Volume IV: Essays on Economics and Society Part I*, ed. John M. Robson (Toronto: University of Toronto Press, 1967), 193–222.

53. The precise details of Mill's position are difficult to pin down. In revisiting the question in 1869, he restates a similar regulatory ideal but appears to suggest a different way of implementing it. Rather than revise the terms of obsolete trusts, he writes in passing that trusts should come under state control, where they can then be redeployed to more lasting public purposes. However, the context of this statement makes it ambiguous as to whether nationalizing trusts is truly what he intends to advocate, and whether this represents his considered position. See J. S. Mill, "Endowments (1869)," in *Collected Works of John Stuart Mill Volume V: Essays on Economics and Society Part II*, ed. John M. Robson (Toronto: University of Toronto Press, 1967), 615–29.

54. Simes, *Public Policy and the Dead Hand*, 139–40.

55. Thanks to Paul Brest for bringing this to my attention.

56. *Uniform Trust Code* (National Conference of Commissioners on Uniform State Laws, 2010), sec. 413, https://www.uniformlaws.org/HigherLogic/System/DownloadDocumentFile.ashx?DocumentFileKey=3d7d5428-dfc6-ac33-0a32-d5b65463c6e3.

57. Ibid., sec. 201.

58. An audit system can also mitigate the potential for abuse of power by trustees, who can be tempted to spend trust funds for personal advantage (as discussed in Madoff, *Immortality and the Law*, 102–4).

59. I thank an anonymous reviewer for this suggestion.

60. As we saw in Chapter 1, according to one recent analysis, ultra-high-net-worth individuals are behind 30 percent of the donations contributed annually by individuals, which in turn composed 69 percent of donated funds in 2019. This would mean that superrich individuals contributed

21 percent of all dollars donated in 2019, in contrast to foundations, which contributed 17 percent. See Maya Imberg and Maeen Shaban, "The New Normal: Trends in UHNW Giving 2019" (New York: Wealth-X, 2019); IUPUI Lilly Family School of Philanthropy, "Giving USA 2020."

Chapter 6

1. An earlier version of this chapter has been previously published as Theodore M. Lechterman, "The Effective Altruist's Political Problem," *Polity* 52, no. 1 (2020): 88–115.
2. For a recent treatment of these issues, see Paul Woodruff, ed., *The Ethics of Giving: Philosophers' Perspectives on Philanthropy* (Oxford: Oxford University Press, 2018).
3. Mary Wollstonecraft, *A Vindication of the Rights of Woman* (New York: A. J. Matsell, 1833), 76; Immanuel Kant, *Moralphilosophie Collins*, in his *Gesammelte Schriften* (Berlin: de Gruyter, 1974), 455–56, as cited by J. B. Schneewind, "Philosophical Ideas of Charity: Some Historical Reflections," in *Giving: Western Ideas of Philanthropy*, ed. J. B. Schneewind (Bloomington: Indiana University Press, 1996), 54–75, 55; Karl Marx and Friedrich Engels, "Manifesto of the Communist Party," in *The Marx-Engels Reader*, ed. Robert Tucker, 2nd ed. (New York: Norton, 1978), 496; John Stuart Mill, *Principles of Political Economy*, Vol. 2 (New York: D. Appleton, 1896), 580; Martin Luther King Jr., "Beyond Vietnam," Speech delivered at Riverside Church, New York, N.Y., April 4, 1967. For remarks in a similar spirit, see also Jeremy Bentham, *Theory of Legislation* (London: Kegan Paul, 1908), 130; and Oscar Wilde, "The Soul of Man under Socialism," *Fortnightly Review* 49 (1891): 292–319.
4. See, e.g., Will Kymlicka, "Altruism in Philosophical and Ethical Traditions: Two Views," in *Between State and Market: Essays on Charities Law and Policy in Canada*, ed. Jim Phillips et al. (Montreal: McGill-Queens University Press, 2001), 87–126, 94.
5. For example, 80,000 Hours (www.80000hours.org), the Centre for Effective Altruism (www.centreforeffectivealtruism.org), the Future of Humanity Institute (www.fhi.ox.ac.uk), the Effective Altruism Foundation (www.ea-foundation.org), and the Open Philanthropy Project (www.openphilanthropy.org).
6. For example, GiveWell (www.givewell.org), Animal Charity Evaluators (www.animalcharityevaluators.org), Giving What We Can (www.givingwhatwecan.org), and The Life You Can Save (www.thelifeyoucansave.org).

7. To date, Good Ventures is the only explicitly effective altruist private foundation. However, other "high-impact" foundations such as the Bill and Melinda Gates Foundation and the Mulago Foundation frequently adopt elements of effective altruist methods.

8. For example, the Effective Altruism Forum (www.effective-altruism.com).

9. These are loosely coordinated by the Effective Altruism Hub (www.eahub.org/groups).

10. For concordant definitional statements, see Peter Singer, *The Most Good You Can Do* (New Haven: Yale University Press, 2015), 4–5, and William MacAskill, *Doing Good Better: Effective Altruism and a Radical New Way to Make a Difference* (New York: Gotham, 2015), 11.

11. Peter Singer, "Good Charity, Bad Charity," *New York Times*, August 10, 2013, SR4.

12. See, for example, the responses by Daron Acemoglu, Angus Deaton, and Jennifer Rubenstein in "Forum: The Logic of Effective Altruism," *Boston Review*, July 1, 2015; Emily Clough, "Effective Altruism's Political Blind Spot," *Boston Review*, July 14, 2015; Amia Srinivasan, "Stop the Robot Apocalypse," *London Review of Books* 37 (2015); and Iason Gabriel, "Effective Altruism and Its Critics," *Journal of Applied Philosophy* 34 (2017): 457–73.

13. On deworming, see MacAskill, *Doing Good Better*, 9; on malaria nets, see Singer, *The Most Good You Can Do*, 6.

14. See the responses by Acemoglu, Deaton, and Rubenstein in "Forum: The Logic of Effective Altruism"; Clough, "Effective Altruism's Political Blind Spot"; Srinivasan, "Stop the Robot Apocalypse"; and Gabriel, "Effective Altruism and Its Critics."

15. E.g., Amartya Sen, *Poverty and Famines* (Oxford: Oxford University Press, 1983); Dani Rodrik, *One Economics, Many Recipes* (Princeton, NJ: Princeton University Press, 2007); Daron Acemoglu and James Robinson, *Why Nations Fail* (New York: Crown Publishers, 2012); Mathias Risse, *On Global Justice* (Princeton, NJ: Princeton University Press, 2012), 63–85.

16. John Rawls, *A Theory of Justice*, rev. ed. (Cambridge, MA: Harvard University Press, 1999), 6–7.

17. Japan's Yamanashi Prefecture, which had struggled with schistosomiasis infections for four hundred years, declared the disease officially eradicated in 1996, thanks to a concerted campaign by local governments. See Noriaki Kajihara and Kenji Hirayama, "The War against a Regional Disease in Japan: A History of the Eradication of *Schistosomiasis japonica*," *Tropical Medicine and Health* 39 (2011): 3–44. In June 2018, the

World Health Organization certified Paraguay as a malaria-free country and attributed the disease's elimination to successful government policies. See World Health Organization, "Update on the E-2020 Initiative of 21 Malaria-Eliminating Countries," June 2018, WHO/CDS/GMP/2018.10.

18. Larry S. Temkin, "Being Good in a World of Need: Some Empirical Worries and an Uncomfortable Philosophical Possibility," *Journal of Practical Ethics* 7, no. 1 (2019): 1–23; Leif Wenar, "Poverty Is No Pond," in *Giving Well: The Ethics of Philanthropy*, ed. Patricia Illingworth, Thomas Pogge, and Leif Wenar (Oxford: Oxford University Press, 2012), 105–31; Angus Deaton, *The Great Escape* (Princeton, NJ: Princeton University Press, 2013), 291–312; Clough, "Effective Altruism's Political Blind Spot."

19. When addressing the question of whether donations displace government health funding in the case of the top-rated Against Malaria Foundation, GiveWell's report suggests that the conflict may be more pronounced in some countries than others but that much about the issue remains unknown. See GiveWell, "Against Malaria Foundation," November 2019, http://www.givewell.org/charities/amf. Similarly, GiveWell's report on its second-highest rated charity, the Schistosomiasis Control Initiative, states, "We have limited information about whether governments would pay for the parts of the program paid for by SCI in its absence." GiveWell, "Schistosomiasis Control Initiative," March 2020, http://www.givewell.org/charities/sci-foundation.

20. Risse, *On Global Justice*, 65.

21. Ibid.

22. Ibid., 261–78.

23. Leif Wenar, "Clean Trade in Natural Resources," *Ethics and International Affairs* 25 (2011): 27–39.

24. Thomas Pogge, "The Health Impact Fund: Boosting Pharmaceutical Innovation without Obstructing Free Access," *Cambridge Quarterly of Healthcare Ethics* 18 (2009): 78–86.

25. For instance, Thomas Pogge points to several alterable features of global institutions that collectively deprive the global poor of nearly $1 trillion per year. See Thomas Pogge, "Are We Violating the Human Rights of the World's Poor?" *Yale Human Rights and Development Law Journal* 14 (2011): 1–33, 29–30. By contrast, the total flow of private philanthropic donations from OECD countries to developing countries amounted to $64 billion in 2014. See Carol Adelman, Bryan Schwartz, and Elias Riskin, *Index of Global Philanthropy and Remittances 2016* (Washington, DC: Hudson Institute, 2016).

26. For similar worries, see Gabriel, "Effective Altruism and Its Critics," 462–64, and Clough, "Effective Altruism's Political Blind Spot."

27. MacAskill, *Doing Good Better*, 5–9; Singer, *Most Good*, 14–15.

28. For an optimistic account, see Abhijit Banerjee and Esther Duflo, *Poor Economics: A Radical Rethinking of the Way to Fight Global Poverty* (New York: Public Affairs, 2011). Cf. Martin Ravallion, "Fighting Poverty One Experiment at a Time: *Poor Economics: A Radical Rethinking of the Way to Fight Global Poverty*: Review Essay," *Journal of Economic Literature* 50 (2012): 103–14.

29. As Clough notes, randomized controlled trials can't easily measure externalities or long-term effects, which in some cases might negate an experiment's positive effects. See Clough, "Effective Altruism's Political Blind Spot." Meanwhile, Ravallion worries about the temptation for researchers using such trials to overgeneralize the policy implications of their results: what works well in one Rajasthan town might be disastrous elsewhere. See Ravallion, "Fighting Poverty One Experiment at a Time," 111.

30. Leaders within the movement have acknowledged some of the limitations of randomized controlled trials. See, for instance, Holden Karnofsky, "How We Evaluate a Study," *The GiveWell Blog*, https://blog.givewell.org/2012/08/23/how-we-evaluate-a-study/ (updated September 2, 2016). It remains a striking fact, however, that as of 2020, each of GiveWell's top charity recommendations is based in large part on evidence from such trials.

31. Martin Ravallion, "A Comparative Perspective on Poverty Reduction in Brazil, China, and India," *World Bank Research Observer* 26 (February 2011): 71–104.

32. For example, see MacAskill, *Doing Good Better*, 94. Sometimes Singer also acknowledges that the expected value of long-range, uncertain options is significantly higher than the expected value of direct aid to victims of global poverty. However, he worries that most individuals can't be motivated to think clearly about these complexities. "We need to encourage more people to be effective altruists," he writes, "and causes like helping the global poor are more likely to draw people toward thinking and acting as effective altruists" (*Most Good*, 174). It's not clear why Singer believes that the logic of long-term and institutional strategies is more confusing than the logic behind the case for direct assistance—which involves counterfactual reasoning and marginal econometrics. This statement also raises the troubling possibility that the movement's leaders may adopt certain positions for marketing purposes rather than for their truth.

33. One might think, for instance, that we generally have weightier obligations to people with whom we share certain kinds of interactive relationships, which are attenuated or absent in the case of future persons.

34. Singer, *Most Good*, 170–74.

35. For a recent similar argument, see Alexander Dietz, "Effective Altruism and Collective Obligations," *Utilitas* 31, no. 1 (2019): 106–15. In a response, Brian Berkey acknowledges that there are indeed circumstances when reasoning from effective altruist commitments recommends pursuing institutional change. Though I agree with Berkey on this, what puzzles me is why effective altruists continue to give comparatively little attention to identifying and weighing discrete options for institutional change. See Brian Berkey, "Collective Obligations and the Institutional Critique of Effective Altruism: A Reply to Alexander Dietz," *Utilitas* 31, no. 3 (2019): 326–33.

36. I thank Minh Ly for pressing me on this point.

37. MacAskill, *Doing Good Better*, 215.

38. "Negative liberty," in Isaiah Berlin's famous account; See Berlin, "Two Concepts of Liberty," in his *Four Essays on Liberty* (London: Oxford University Press, 1969), 118–72.

39. Niko Kolodny proposes this way of synthesizing republican and Kantian positions in his "Being Under the Power of Others," in *Republicanism and Democracy*, ed. Yiftah Elizar and Geneviève Rousselière (Cambridge, UK: Cambridge University Press, 2019), 94–114.

40. See, e.g., Philip Pettit, "The Domination Complaint," *Nomos* 86 (2005): 87–117.

41. Although this definition still appeals to the notion of interference, it's distinct in two ways. First, where freedom as noninterference takes concern with actual instances of interference, freedom as nondomination is concerned with the opportunity to interfere, whether or not an agent actually exercises this opportunity. Second, republican freedom does not find interference objectionable as such: interfering with one another's choices is an ineliminable fact of political life. Rather, it objects to powers of interference that are unconstrained by law or strong norms.

42. For a systematic investigation of this idea, see Arthur Ripstein, *Force and Freedom* (Cambridge, MA: Harvard University Press, 2009).

43. In truth, Kantians and republicans disagree on whether legal entitlement is a necessary condition for individual freedom. Both accept that legal guarantees are not sufficient for individual freedom when the laws themselves are bad or their enforcement capricious. Republicans submit that while legal entitlement is often a reliable recipe for preventing domination,

domination can also be mitigated by having access to an array of private benefactors who are in some sense competing with each other. See Philip Pettit, *On the People's Terms* (Cambridge, UK: Cambridge University Press, 2012), 112–13. Meanwhile, for the Kantian, freedom categorically requires measures that liberate individuals from dependence on private wills. See Ripstein, *Force and Freedom*, 273–84.

44. Although the law typically treats donations as contracts, the prerogative to continue donating lies with the donor. See Evelyn Brody, "The Legal Framework of Nonprofit Organizations," in *The Nonprofit Sector: A Research Handbook*, ed. Walter W. Powell and Richard Steinberg (New Haven: Yale University Press, 2006), 243–66.

45. GiveWell releases new recommendations each year that revise the list of suggested organizations or their relative ranking. Sometimes GiveWell revises recommendations because a previously recommended organization or cause has already met its funding needs. But in other cases, shifting recommendations presumably result in budget shortfalls that may leave organizations and their beneficiaries scrambling.

46. Representative statements include Amartya Sen, "Equality of What?" Tanner Lecture on Human Values, Stanford University, May 22, 1979; G. A. Cohen, "On the Currency of Egalitarian Justice," *Ethics* 99 (1989): 906–44.

47. For a set of statements from major contributors to this movement, see Carina Fourie, Fabian Schuppert, and Ivo Wallimann-Helmer, eds., *Social Equality: On What It Means to Be Equals* (Oxford: Oxford University Press, 2015).

48. Kolodny, "Being Under the Power of Others." Kolodny sometimes argues that the value of freedom as nondomination is also better understood in terms of nonsubordination. At other times, he concedes that nondomination is in fact a distinct value, albeit one more narrowly circumscribed than its philosophical proponents acknowledge. It seems to me that nondomination properly captures a concern with liberty that's missing from the value of nonsubordination. That is, a society of equals could still be disposed to invade one another's choices in various ways. Thus, I find it useful to keep these two values distinct.

49. Of course, this approach comes with its own challenges, as I discuss further in what follows.

50. Cash transfers go only partway in meeting these concerns, as I discuss in n. 59.

51. For these and related reasons, some worry that effective altruism fails to sufficiently dissociate itself from practices of neocolonialism. See, for example, Cecelia Lynch, "Reconceptualizing Charity: The Problem with Philanthropy and 'Effective Altruism' by the World's Wealthiest People," Critical Investigations into Humanitarianism in Africa blog, January 11, 2016, http://www.cihablog.com/reconceptualizing-charity-the-problem-with-philanthropy-and-effective-altruism-by-the-worlds-wealthiest-people/.

52. Monique Deveaux, "The Global Poor as Agents of Justice," *Journal of Moral Philosophy* 12 (2015): 125–50, at 135–36. Deveaux is referring to the Voices of the Poor survey, which involved interviews with 60,000 individuals in fifty countries. See Deepa Narayan et al., *Voices of the Poor*, Vols. 1–2 (Oxford: Oxford University Press and World Bank, 2000 and 2002).

53. Thanks to Emma Saunders-Hastings and Brian Berkey for pressing me on this point.

54. See, for example, Barbara Herman, "The Scope of Moral Requirement," *Philosophy and Public Affairs* 30 (2001): 227–56; A. J. Julius, "Basic Structure and the Value of Equality," *Philosophy and Public Affairs* 31 (2003): 321–55; Thomas Pogge, "'Assisting' the Global Poor?" in *The Ethics of Assistance*, ed. Deen K. Chatterjee (Cambridge, UK: Cambridge University Press, 2004), 260–88.

55. Brian Barry pointed this out several decades ago in his "Humanity and Justice in Global Perspective," *Nomos* 24 (1982): 219–52.

56. I thank Désirée Lim and an anonymous reviewer for help with developing this point.

57. But what if one concluded that the global rich were legitimately entitled to a more substantial amount of the wealth they now possess? Would this not reopen the door for them to consider guidance from effective altruism? The nonconsequentialist critic might respond that their primary concern should be redressing the injustice that taints the remainder of their wealth. This is because duties of justice take priority over duties of beneficence: we ought to respect others and right our wrongs before we think about spending resources on other valuable projects.

58. In an important recent paper, Roger Crisp and Theron Pummer argue that effective altruism can indeed incorporate justice-based considerations, while those who believe that many of their duties to others are best understood in terms of justice can also incorporate aspects of effective altruism's methodology. In their view, agents who reason that they have a

justice-based duty to Φ ought to evaluate and select the most cost-effective options for Φ-ing. Yet, few if any deontologists would dispute that an agent faced with multiple options for discharging a duty of justice should select the one that is most cost-effective—if the options are equivalent in every other relevant respect. More troublingly, the view appears to regard the "all else equal" condition as a frequent characterization of many actual practical situations. Crisp and Pummer illustrate their view with examples of education and gender equality, arguing that an agent who finds justice-based reasons to support education reform or efforts to reduce gender disparities ought to consider the most cost-effective options, globally, for pursuing these goals. This advice surely applies to agents who believe they have "imperfect" or undirected duties to reduce injustice in these broad categories. But many duties of justice are in fact "perfect" or directed, requiring specific actions or specific targets. Initiative A may be less cost-effective, in some sense, than Initiative B, but justice may nevertheless guide me toward Initiative B because I am more responsible for the wrongs that B is attempting to right, or I have special obligations to the beneficiaries of B, or I believe that the depth of injustice to B's beneficiaries is more severe. See Roger Crisp and Theron Pummer, "Effective Justice," *Journal of Moral Philosophy* 17, no. 4 (2020): 398–415.

59. One might wonder whether the phenomenon I describe here is better understood as paternalism rather than subordination. I accept that these two phenomena can sometimes overlap. Often, what makes paternalism objectionable is the fact that it's subordinating. However, interventions can also be subordinating without being paternalistic. Cash transfers, for instance, are thought to be nonpaternalistic interventions. But when foreign philanthropists initiate a cash transfer program that circumvents democratic processes, they subordinate members of the local community.

60. Singer, *Most Good*, 50.

61. See, for example, Srinivasan, "Stop the Robot Apocalypse"; Pete Mills, Reply, "The Ethical Careers Debate," *Oxford Left Review* 7 (May 2012): 4–9.

62. See the responses by Acemoglu, Deaton, and Rubenstein in "Forum: The Logic of Effective Altruism"; Clough, "Effective Altruism's Political Blind Spot"; Srinivasan, "Stop the Robot Apocalypse"; and Gabriel, "Effective Altruism and Its Critics."

63. Brian Berkey, "The Institutional Critique of Effective Altruism," *Utilitas* 30 (2018): 143–71.

64. See the responses by Acemoglu, Deaton, and Rubenstein in "Forum: The Logic of Effective Altruism"; Clough, "Effective Altruism's Political Blind Spot"; Srinivasan, "Stop the Robot Apocalypse"; and Gabriel, "Effective Altruism and Its Critics."

65. Singer, *Most Good*, 161.

66. MacAskill, *Doing Good Better*, 89–93.

67. Open Philanthropy Project: www.openphilanthropy.org.

68. For instance, Thomas Pogge, who has been previously been sharply critical of Singer's views on global poverty, is now cited as a supporter of effective altruism; see Singer, *Most Good*, 187.

69. Singer, *Most Good*, 158–60.

70. Steven Teles, "Foundations, Organizational Maintenance, and Partisan Asymmetry," *PS: Political Science and Politics* 49 (2016): 455–60; Steven Teles and Mark Schmitt, "The Elusive Craft of Evaluating Advocacy," *Stanford Social Innovation* Review (Summer 2011): 39–43.

71. Somewhat ironically, the Life You Can Save, a meta-charity founded by Peter Singer himself, defends Oxfam's overall effectiveness on similar grounds. See "Oxfam," https://www.thelifeyoucansave.org/where-to-donate/oxfam (accessed July 11, 2019).

72. Gabriel, "Effective Altruism and Its Critics," 469.

73. For a critical overview of this movement, see Joanne Barkan, "Plutocrats at Work: How Big Philanthropy Undermines Democracy," *Social Research* 80 (2013): 635–52.

74. For a systematic overview of these strategies, see Sarah Reckhow, "More Than Patrons: How Foundations Fuel Policy Change and Backlash," *PS: Political Science and Politics* 49 (2016): 449–54.

75. See, e.g., Benjamin Page, Larry Bartels, and Jason Seawright, "Democracy and the Policy Preferences of Wealthy Americans," *Perspectives on Politics* 11 (2013): 51–73, 59–60.

76. Daniel Viehoff, "Democratic Equality and Political Authority," *Philosophy and Public Affairs* 42 (2014): 337–75.

77. See, for example, Paul D. Almeida, "Defensive Mobilization: Popular Movements against Economic Adjustment Policies in Latin America," *Latin American Perspectives* 34 (2007): 123–39.

78. Harry Brighouse and Marc Fleurbaey, "Democracy and Proportionality," *Journal of Political Philosophy* 18 (2010): 137–55.

79. Thoroughgoing skeptics include Acemoglu ("The Logic of Effective Altruism: Response"), Deaton ("The Logic of Effective Altruism: Response"), and Srinivasan ("Stop the Robot Apocalypse"). Critics who

encourage effective altruism to invest in political advocacy include Clough ("Effective Altruism's Political Blind Spot") and Gabriel ("Effective Altruism and Its Critics").

80. Rob Reich, "Repugnant to the Whole Idea of Democracy? On the Role of Foundations in Democratic Societies," *PS: Political Science and Politics* 49 (2016): 466–72.

81. Waheed Hussain, "Is Ethical Consumerism an Impermissible Form of Vigilantism?" *Philosophy and Public Affairs* 40 (2012): 111–43.

82. Ibid., 132.

83. Mick Moore, "Empowerment at Last?" *Journal of International Development* 13 (2001): 321–29, 325.

84. Susan Cotts Watkins, Ann Swidler, and Thomas Hannan, "Outsourcing Social Transformation: Development NGOs as Organizations," *Annual Review of Sociology* 38 (2012): 285–315, 296.

85. Ghazala Mansuri and Vijayendra Rao, "Localizing Development: Does Participation Work?" *World Bank Policy Research Report* (Washington, DC: World Bank, 2012). For critical discussion of subsequent research developments, see Stephen D. Krasner and Jeremy M. Weinstein, "Improving Governance from the Outside In," *Annual Review of Political Science* 17 (2014): 123–45, 140–41.

86. These include the Solidaire Network, Resource Generation, Grassroots International, Urgent Action Fund, Mama Cash, EDGE Funders Alliance, Human Rights Funders Network, Global Fund For Women, Oxfam, and UNICEF, among others.

87. An alternative approach, rooted in human rights theory, seeks to identify organizations that meet five criteria: "(1) utilizing intersectional analysis; (2) thinking about narrow issues with awareness of their cross-issue dimensions; (3) promoting the capacity for self-advocacy and other political skills of ourselves and of those throughout our web of partners and allies; (4) working against the complex forces that create obstacles to rights enjoyment by building community through connected activism; and (5) working in ways that enhance our learning." In its sensitivity to a broader range of important concerns, this approach provides a helpful counterbalance to effective altruism's more limited focus. Where it falls short, however, is in the limited role it allows for evidence and comparative evaluation. See Brooke A. Ackerly, *Just Responsibility: A Human Rights Theory of Global Justice* (New York: Oxford University Press, 2018), 185.

88. I thank Iason Gabriel for this idea.

89. Michael Walzer, "The Moral Standing of States: A Response to Four Critics," *Philosophy and Public Affairs* 9 (1980): 209–29, at 217.

90. On the latter, see, for example, Riley E. Dunlap and Aaron M. McCright, "Climate Change Denial: Sources, Actors, and Strategies," in *Routledge Handbook of Climate Change and Society*, ed. Constance Lever-Tracy (Abingdon, UK: Routledge, 2010), 240–59.

91. For some additional recommendations, see Jennifer Rubenstein, "The Lessons of Effective Altruism," *Ethics and International Affairs* 30 (2016): 511–26.

92. One important exception is Archon Fung, "Deliberation before the Revolution: Toward an Ethics of Deliberative Democracy in an Unjust World," *Political Theory* 33 (2005): 397–419. Another is INCITE!, *The Revolution Will Not Be Funded* (Durham: Duke University Press, 2017).

Chapter 7

1. Thomas W. Dunfee, "The Unfulfilled Promise of Corporate Philanthropy," in *Giving Well*, ed. Patricia Illingworth, Thomas Pogge, and Leif Wenar (Oxford, UK: Oxford University Press, 2011), 244–61; Arthur Gautier and Anne-Claire Pache, "Research on Corporate Philanthropy: A Review and Assessment," *Journal of Business Ethics* 126, no. 3 (2015): 343–69.

2. Megan O'Neil, Brian O'Leary, and Peter Olsen-Philips, "Corporate Cash Giving Rises 5%, Exclusive Chronicle Survey Shows," *Chronicle of Philanthropy*, September 5, 2018.

3. Ibid.

4. André Solórzano, "Giving in Numbers" (New York: Chief Executives for Corporate Purpose, 2019), http://cecp.co/home/resources/giving-in-numbers/.

5. See, e.g., Nien-hê Hsieh, "The Obligations of Transnational Corporations: Rawlsian Justice and the Duty of Assistance," *Business Ethics Quarterly* 14, no. 4 (2004): 643–61.

6. Milton Friedman, "The Social Responsibility of Business Is to Increase Profits," *New York Times Magazine*, September 13, 1970, 7–11.

7. See, e.g., Rob Reich, Lucy Bernholz, and Chiara Cordelli, eds., *Philanthropy in Democratic Societies: History, Institutions, Values* (Chicago: University of Chicago Press, 2016); Rob Reich, *Just Giving: Why Philanthropy Is Failing Democracy and How It Can Do Better* (Princeton, NJ: Princeton University Press, 2018); Emma Saunders-Hastings, "Plutocratic Philanthropy," *Journal of Politics* 80, no. 1 (2017): 149–61; Paul Woodruff, ed., *The Ethics of Giving: Philosophers' Perspectives on Philanthropy* (Oxford: Oxford University Press, 2018).

8. Friedman, "The Social Responsibility of Business," 10.

9. A. M. Honoré, "Ownership," in *Oxford Essays in Jurisprudence: A Collaborative Work*, ed. Anthony Gordon Guest (Oxford: Clarendon Press, 1961), 107–47.

10. Jeffrey Moriarty, "Business Ethics," in *The Stanford Encyclopedia of Philosophy*, ed. Edward N. Zalta, Fall 2017 (Stanford: Metaphysics Research Lab, Stanford University, 2017), https://plato.stanford.edu/archives/fall2017/entries/ethics-business/.

11. Christiano names the first three of these in Thomas Christiano, *The Rule of the Many: Fundamental Issues in Democratic Theory* (Boulder: Westview Press, 1996), 3; Beitz names the last three in Charles R. Beitz, *Political Equality: An Essay in Democratic Theory* (Princeton, NJ: Princeton University Press, 1989).

12. Anna Stilz, "The Value of Self-Determination," in *Oxford Studies in Political Philosophy*, ed. David Sobel, Peter Vallentyne, and Steven Wall, Vol. 2 (Oxford: Oxford University Press, 2016), 98–127; Jake Zuehl, "Collective Self-Determination" (Ph.D. diss., Princeton University, 2016).

13. David M. Estlund, *Democratic Authority: A Philosophical Framework* (Princeton, NJ: Princeton University Press, 2008); Elizabeth Anderson, "Democracy: Instrumental vs. Non-Instrumental Value," in *Contemporary Debates in Political Philosophy*, ed. Thomas Christiano and John Christman (Oxford, UK: Wiley-Blackwell, 2009), 213–27; Niko Kolodny, "Rule over None II: Social Equality and the Justification of Democracy," *Philosophy and Public Affairs* 42, no. 4 (2014): 287–336; Daniel Viehoff, "Democratic Equality and Political Authority," *Philosophy and Public Affairs* 42, no. 4 (2014): 337–75.

14. David M. Estlund, *Democratic Authority: A Philosophical Framework* (Princeton, NJ: Princeton University Press, 2008).

15. Joshua Cohen, "Procedure and Substance in Deliberative Democracy," in *Deliberative Democracy: Essays on Reason and Politics*, ed. James Bohman and William Rehg (Cambridge, MA: MIT Press, 1997), 407–37.

16. Estlund, *Democratic Authority*.

17. John Stuart Mill, "Considerations on Representative Government," in *The Collected Works of John Stuart Mill, Volume XIX: Essays on Politics and Society Part II*, ed. John M. Robson (Toronto: University of Toronto Press, 1977).

18. Josiah Ober, *Demopolis: Democracy before Liberalism in Theory and Practice* (New York: Cambridge University Press, 2017).

19. George Klosko, "The Obligation to Contribute to Discretionary Public Goods," *Political Studies* 38, no. 2 (1990): 196–214.

20. Will Kymlicka, "Altruism in Philosophical and Ethical Traditions: Two Views," in *Between State and Market: Essay on Charities Law and Policy in Canada*, ed. Jim Phillips, Bruce Chapman, and David Stevens (Montreal: McGill-Queen's University Press, 2001), 87–126.

21. Jeremy Bentham, *Theory of Legislation* (London: Kegan Paul, 1908), 130.

22. Philip Pettit, *Republicanism: A Theory of Freedom and Government* (Oxford: Oxford University Press, 1997); Philip Pettit, *On the People's Terms: A Republican Theory and Model of Democracy* (Cambridge, UK: Cambridge University Press, 2012).

23. Eric Beerbohm, "The Free-Provider Problem: Private Provision of Public Responsibilities," in *Philanthropy in Democratic Societies: History, Institutions, Values*, ed. Rob Reich, Lucy Bernholz, and Chiara Cordelli (Chicago: University of Chicago Press, 2016), 207–25.

24. I thank Lucia Rafanelli for discussion on these points.

25. For an overview of the debate, see Amy J. Sepinwall, "Corporate Moral Responsibility," *Philosophy Compass* 11, no. 1 (2016): 3–13. The relevant Supreme Court cases include *Citizens United v. Federal Election Commission*, 558 U.S. 310 (2010) and *Burwell v. Hobby Lobby*, 573 U.S. 682 (2014).

26. See, respectively, Amy J. Sepinwall, "Denying Corporate Rights and Punishing Corporate Wrongs," *Business Ethics Quarterly* 25, no. 4 (2015): 517–34; and Waheed Hussain and Joakim Sandberg, "Pluralistic Functionalism about Corporate Agency," in *The Moral Responsibility of Firms*, ed. Eric W. Orts and N. Craig Smith, 1st ed. (Oxford: Oxford University Press, 2017), 66–85.

27. Certainly, the Scheme will not be acceptable to those who endorse an absolutist view of expressive liberty. In *Citizens United*, the US Supreme Court upheld such a view in addition to an undifferentiated view of citizenship rights. While many commentators may in fact subscribe to both views simultaneously, they are theoretically separate.

28. Jason Cone, "There Is No Such Thing as 'Free' Vaccines: Why We Rejected Pfizer's Donation Offer of Pneumonia Vaccines," *Medium* (blog), October 10, 2016, https://medium.com/@MSF_access/there-is-no-such-thing-as-free-vaccines-why-we-rejected-pfizers-donation-offer-of-pneumonia-6a79c9d9f32f.

29. See, e.g., Thomas W. Dunfee, "Do Firms with Unique Competencies for Rescuing Victims of Human Catastrophes Have Special Obligations? Corporate Responsibility and the AIDS Catastrophe on Sub-Saharan Africa," *Business Ethics Quarterly* 16, no. 2 (2006): 185–210.

30. A. Deirdre Robson, "Industry: Art Angel? Pepsi-Cola's 'Portrait of America' Art Annual as an Early Instance of Corporate Art Sponsorship," *Journal of American Culture* 38, no. 4 (2015): 329–43; "Sponsorship Spending on the Arts to Total $1.03 Billion in 2018," *IEG Sponsorship Report*, March 12, 2018, https://www.sponsorship.com/Report/2018/03/12/Sponsorship-Spending-On-The-Arts-To-Total-$1-03-bi.aspx.

31. Carol Vogel, "An Old Box Factory Is a Haven for New Art," *New York Times*, April 23, 2003.

32. Software discount offers are collected and showcased by TechSoup, an organization that serves as an intermediary between nonprofits and technology companies. See https://www.techsoup.org/.

33. Miriam Ronzoni and Laura Valentini, "Microfinance, Poverty Relief, and Political Justice," in *Microfinance, Rights, and Global Justice*, ed. Tom Sorrell and Luis Cabrera (Cambridge, UK: Cambridge University Press, 2015), 84–104.

34. Abraham Singer, "Rawls Well That Ends Well: A Response to Welch And Ly," *Business Ethics Journal Review*, February 16, 2018, 11–17.

Chapter 8

1. Cf. Rob Reich, *Just Giving: Why Philanthropy Is Failing Democracy and How It Can Do Better* (Princeton, NJ: Princeton University Press, 2018).

2. Controversies regarding university donations and the financing of higher education more generally raise numerous specific issues that exceed the scope of this book.

3. For a recent treatment of these issues, see Paul Woodruff, ed., *The Ethics of Giving: Philosophers' Perspectives on Philanthropy* (Oxford: Oxford University Press, 2018). Cf. Theodore M. Lechterman, "Book Review: *The Ethics of Giving: Philosophers' Perspectives on Philanthropy* by Woodruff, P. (Ed.)," *Nonprofit and Voluntary Sector Quarterly* 48, no. 5 (2019): 1110–12.

4. See Ray D. Madoff, "When Is Philanthropy? How the Tax Code's Answer to This Question Has Given Rise to the Growth of Donor-Advised Funds and Why It's a Problem," in *Philanthropy in Democratic Societies: History, Institutions, Values*, ed. Rob Reich, Lucy Bernholz, and Chiara Cordelli (Chicago: University of Chicago Press, 2016), 158–77.

5. I discuss the role of nonprofits more directly in Theodore M. Lechterman and Rob Reich, "Political Theory and the Nonprofit Sector," in *The Nonprofit Sector: A Research Handbook*, ed. Walter W. Powell and Patricia Bromley, 3rd ed. (Stanford, CA: Stanford University Press, 2020), 171–91.

6. In 1948, Henry Ford II relinquished the Ford family's control over the foundation in protest of the foundation's increasing support for liberal causes. Over time, the foundation has drifted even further away from its founders' wishes. See Martin Morse Wooster, "On the Presidents of the Ford Foundation," *Philanthropy Daily*, June 27, 2016, https://www.philanthropydaily.com/on-the-presidents-of-the-ford-foundation/.

7. Similar issues troubled the English legal historian F. W. Maitland. See F. W. Maitland, *Maitland: State, Trust and Corporation*, ed. David Runciman (Cambridge, UK: Cambridge University Press, 2003).

8. Lucy Bernholz, Hélène Landemore, and Rob Reich, eds., *Digital Technology and Democratic Theory* (Chicago: University of Chicago Press, 2021); Johannes Himmelreich, "Democracy and Digital Technology: Should We Automate Democracy?" in *Oxford Handbook of Digital Ethics*, ed. Carissa Véliz (Oxford: Oxford University Press, forthcoming).

9. See, e.g., Hélène Landemore, *Open Democracy: Reinventing Popular Rule for the Twenty-First Century* (Princeton, NJ: Princeton University Press, 2020).

Bibliography

Acemoglu, Daron. "The Logic of Effective Altruism: Response." *Boston Review*, July 1, 2015. http://bostonreview.net/forum/peter-singer-logic-effective-altruism.

Acemoglu, Daron, and James A. Robinson. *Why Nations Fail: The Origins of Power, Prosperity and Poverty*. New York: Crown Publishers, 2012.

Ackerly, Brooke A. *Just Responsibility: A Human Rights Theory of Global Justice*. New York: Oxford University Press, 2018.

Adelman, Carol, Bryan Schwartz, and Elias Riskin. "Index of Global Philanthropy and Remittances 2016." Washington, DC: Hudson Institute, 2016.

Almeida, Paul D. "Defensive Mobilization: Popular Movements against Economic Adjustment Policies in Latin America." *Latin American Perspectives* 34, no. 3 (2007): 123–39.

American Association of Fund-Raising Counsel. "Giving USA, 1986." New York: AAFRC Trust for Philanthropy, 1986. http://ulib.iupuidigital.org/cdm/ref/collection/PRO/id/36068.

"An Overview of Philanthropy in Europe." L'Observatoire de la Fondation de France / CERPhi, 2015.

Anderson, Elizabeth S. "Democracy: Instrumental vs. Non-Instrumental Value." In *Contemporary Debates in Political Philosophy*, edited by Thomas Christiano and John Christman, 213–27. Oxford: Wiley-Blackwell, 2009.

Anderson, Elizabeth S. "What Is the Point of Equality?" *Ethics* 109, no. 2 (1999): 287–337.

Banerjee, Abhijit V., and Esther Duflo. *Poor Economics: A Radical Rethinking of the Way to Fight Global Poverty*. New York: Public Affairs, 2011.

Barkan, Joanne. "Plutocrats at Work: How Big Philanthropy Undermines Democracy." *Social Research: An International Quarterly* 80, no. 2 (2013): 635–52.

Barry, Brian. "Humanity and Justice in Global Perspective." *Nomos* 24 (1982): 219–52.

Barry, Brian. *Justice as Impartiality: A Treatise on Social Justice*. Vol. 2. Oxford: Oxford University Press, 1995.

Beerbohm, Eric. "The Free-Provider Problem: Private Provision of Public Responsibilities." In *Philanthropy in Democratic Societies: History, Institutions, Values*, edited by Rob Reich, Lucy Bernholz, and Chiara Cordelli, 207–25. Chicago: University of Chicago Press, 2016.

Beitz, Charles R. *Political Equality: An Essay in Democratic Theory*. Princeton, NJ: Princeton University Press, 1989.

Bentham, Jeremy. *Theory of Legislation*. London: Kegan Paul, 1908.

Berkey, Brian. "Collective Obligations and the Institutional Critique of Effective Altruism: A Reply to Alexander Dietz." *Utilitas* 31, no. 3 (2019): 326–33.

Berkey, Brian. "The Institutional Critique of Effective Altruism." *Utilitas* 30, no. 2 (2018): 143–71.

Berlin, Isaiah. *Four Essays on Liberty*. Oxford: Oxford University Press, 1969.

Bernholz, Lucy, Hélène Landemore, and Rob Reich, eds. *Digital Technology and Democratic Theory*. Chicago: University of Chicago Press, 2021.

Bishop, Matthew, and Michael Green. *Philanthrocapitalism: How Giving Can Save the World*. New York: Bloomsbury Publishing, 2010.

Bivin, David, Una Osili, Anna Pruitt, and Jonathan Bergdoll. "The Philanthropy Outlook 2020 and 2021." Indianapolis: Indiana University Lilly Family School of Philanthropy, 2020.

Bohman, James. "Deliberative Democracy and Effective Social Freedom." In *Deliberative Democracy: Essays on Reason and Politics*, edited by James Bohman and William Rehg, 321–47. Cambridge, MA: MIT Press, 1997.

Brennan, Geoffrey. "Economics." In *A Companion to Contemporary Political Philosophy*, edited by Robert E. Goodin, Philip Pettit, and Thomas Pogge, 2nd ed., 118–52. Blackwell Companions to Philosophy. Oxford: Blackwell, 2017.

Brest, Paul. "The Outcomes Movement in Philanthropy and the Nonprofit Sector." In *The Nonprofit Sector: A Research Handbook*, edited by Walter W. Powell and Patricia Bromley, 3rd ed., 381–408. Stanford: Stanford University Press, 2020.

Brighouse, Harry. "Egalitarianism and Equal Availability of Political Influence." *Journal of Political Philosophy* 4, no. 2 (1996): 118–41.

Brighouse, Harry. "Neutrality, Publicity, and State Funding of the Arts." *Philosophy and Public Affairs* 24, no. 1 (1995): 35–63.

Brighouse, Harry, and Marc Fleurbaey. "Democracy and Proportionality." *Journal of Political Philosophy* 18, no. 2 (2010): 137–55.

Brody, Evelyn. "The Legal Framework of Nonprofit Organizations." *In The Nonprofit Sector: A Research Handbook*, edited by Walter W. Powell and Richard Steinberg, 243–66. New Haven: Yale University Press, 2006.

Brown, Peter. *Through the Eye of a Needle: Wealth, the Fall of Rome, and the Making of Christianity in the West, 350–550 AD*. Princeton, NJ: Princeton University Press, 2012.

Burke, Edmund. "Reflections on the Revolution in France." In *Select Works of Edmund Burke. A New Imprint of the Payne Edition*, Vol. 2. Indianapolis: Liberty Fund, 1999.

Burton, Weisbrod. "Toward a Theory of the Voluntary Nonprofit Sector in a Three-Sector Economy." In *Altruism, Morality, and Economic Theory*, edited by Edmund S. Phelps. New York: Russell Sage Foundation, 1975.

Callahan, David. *The Givers: Wealth, Power, and Philanthropy in a New Gilded Age.*. 1st ed. New York: Alfred A. Knopf, 2017.

Canada Revenue Agency. "Gifts and Income Tax 2017, P113(E) Rev. 17." Ottawa: Canada Revenue Agency, 2017. https://www.canada.ca/content/dam/cra-arc/formspubs/pub/p113/p113-17e.pdf.

Carmichael, Calum M. "Doing Good Better? The Differential Subsidization of Charitable Contributions." *Policy and Society, Financing the Third Sector* 29, no. 3 (2010): 201–17.

Carmichael, Calum M. "Sweet and Not-So-Sweet Charity: A Case for Subsidizing Contributions to Different Charities Differently." *Public Finance Review* 40, no. 4 (2012): 497–518.

Carnegie, Andrew. "The Best Fields for Philanthropy." *North American Review* 149, no. 397 (1889): 682–99.

Center on Philanthropy, Indiana University, and Inc. Google. "Patterns of Household Charitable Giving by Income Group, 2005," 2007. https://philanthropy.iupui.edu/files/research/giving_focused_on_meeting_needs_of_the_poor_july_2007.pdf.

Christiano, Thomas. "Money in Politics." In *The Oxford Handbook of Political Philosophy*, edited by David Estlund, 241–58. Oxford: Oxford University Press, 2012.

Christiano, Thomas. *The Rule of the Many: Fundamental Issues in Democratic Theory*. Boulder: Westview Press, 1996.

Chu, Patti, and Olivia Yutong Wang. "Philanthropy in China." Singapore: AVPN, 2018.

Cicero, Marcus Tullius. *On Duties*. Edited by M. T. Griffin and E. M. Atkins. Cambridge, UK: Cambridge University Press, 1991.

Clough, Emily. "Effective Altruism's Political Blind Spot." *Boston Review*, July 14, 2015.

Cohen, G. A. "On the Currency of Egalitarian Justice." *Ethics* 99, no. 4 (1989): 906–44.

Cohen, Joshua. "Money, Politics, and Political Equality." In *Fact and Value: Essays on Ethics and Metaphysics for Judith Jarvis Thomson*, edited by Alex Byrne, Robert Stalnaker, and Ralph Wedgwood, 47–80. Cambridge, MA: MIT Press, 2001.

Cohen, Joshua. "Procedure and Substance in Deliberative Democracy." In *Deliberative Democracy: Essays on Reason and Politics*, edited by James Bohman and William Rehg, 407–37. Cambridge, MA: MIT Press, 1997.

Cone, Jason. "There Is No Such Thing as 'Free' Vaccines: Why We Rejected Pfizer's Donation Offer of Pneumonia Vaccines." *Medium* (blog), October 10, 2016. https://medium.com/@MSF_access/

there-is-no-such-thing-as-free-vaccines-why-we-rejected-pfizers-donation-offer-of-pneumonia-6a79c9d9f32f.

Cooter, Robert. "The Donation Registry." *Fordham Law Review* 72, no. 5 (2004): 1981–89.

Cordelli, Chiara. "The Institutional Division of Labor and the Egalitarian Obligations of Nonprofits." *Journal of Political Philosophy* 20, no. 2 (2012): 131–55.

Cordelli, Chiara. "Privatization without Profit." In *Political Legitimacy*, edited by Jack Knight and Melissa Schwartzberg, 113–44. Nomos LXI. New York: New York University Press, 2019.

Cordelli, Chiara. *The Privatized State*. Princeton, NJ: Princeton University Press, 2020.

Cordelli, Chiara. "Reparative Justice and the Moral Limits of Discretionary Philanthropy." In *Philanthropy in Democratic Societies: History, Institutions, Values*, edited by Rob Reich, Chiara Cordelli, and Lucy Bernholz, 244–66. Chicago: University of Chicago Press, 2016.

Cordelli, Chiara, and Rob Reich. "Philanthropy and Intergenerational Justice." In *Institutions for Future Generations*, edited by Iñigo González-Ricoy and Axel Gosseries, 229–44. Oxford: Oxford University Press, 2016.

Crisp, Roger, and Theron Pummer. "Effective Justice." *Journal of Moral Philosophy* 17, no. 4 (2020): 398–415.

Datta, Prithviraj. *Why Campaign Finance Matters: Normatively Evaluating the American Electoral Spending Regime*. Unpublished book manuscript, n.d.

Deaton, Angus. *The Great Escape: Health, Wealth, and the Origins of Inequality*. Princeton, NJ: Princeton University Press, 2015.

Deaton, Angus. "The Logic of Effective Altruism: Response." *Boston Review*, July 1, 2015. http://bostonreview.net/forum/peter-singer-logic-effective-altruism.

Deveaux, Monique. "The Global Poor as Agents of Justice." *Journal of Moral Philosophy* 12, no. 2 (2015): 125–50.

Dietz, Alexander. "Effective Altruism and Collective Obligations." *Utilitas* 31, no. 1 (2019): 106–15.

Dorfman, Avihay, and Alon Harel. "The Case against Privatization." *Philosophy and Public Affairs* 41, no. 1 (2013): 67–102.

Dowding, Keith, Robert Goodin, Carole Pateman, and David Miller, eds. "Justice, Democracy and Public Goods." In *Justice and Democracy: Essays for Brian Barry*, 127–49. Cambridge, UK: Cambridge University Press, 2004.

Dunfee, Thomas W. "The Unfulfilled Promise of Corporate Philanthropy." In *Giving Well*, edited by Patricia Illingworth, Thomas Pogge, and Leif Wenar, 244–61. Oxford: Oxford University Press, 2011.

Dunlap, Riley E., and Aaron M. McCright. "Climate Change Denial: Sources, Actors, and Strategies." In *Routledge Handbook of Climate Change and*

Society, edited by Constance Lever-Tracy, 240–59. Abingdon, UK: Routledge, 2010.

Dworkin, Ronald. "Can a Liberal State Support Art." In *A Matter of Principle,* 221–33. Cambridge, MA: Harvard University Press, 1985.

Dworkin, Ronald. *Sovereign Virtue: The Theory and Practice of Equality.* Cambridge, MA: Harvard University Press, 2002.

Estlund, David. *Democratic Authority: A Philosophical Framework.* Princeton, NJ: Princeton University Press, 2008.

Estlund, David. "Political Quality." *Social Philosophy and Policy* 17, no. 1 (2000): 127–60.

Feinberg, Joel. *Harm to Others.* Oxford: Oxford University Press, 1984.

Fleischer, Miranda Perry. "Theorizing the Charitable Tax Subsidies: The Role of Distributive Justice." *Washington University Law Review* 87, no. 3 (2010): 505–66.

Florino, Joanne. "The Case for Philanthropic Freedom." *Alliance Magazine,* September 6, 2016. https://www.alliancemagazine.org/feature/the-case-for-philanthropic-freedom/.

Fourie, Carina, Fabian Schuppert, and Ivo Wallimann-Helmer, eds. *Social Equality: On What It Means to Be Equals.* Oxford: Oxford University Press, 2015.

Freeman, Samuel. "Illiberal Libertarians: Why Libertarianism Is Not a Liberal View." *Philosophy and Public Affairs* 30, no. 2 (2001): 105–51.

Freeman, Samuel. "Property-Owning Democracy and the Difference Principle." *Analyse und Kritik,* no. 1 (2013): 9–36.

Friedman, Milton. "The Social Responsibility of Business Is to Increase Profits." *New York Times Magazine,* September 13, 1970, 7–11.

Fung, Archon. "Deliberation before the Revolution: Toward an Ethics of Deliberative Democracy in an Unjust World." *Political Theory* 33, no. 3 (2005): 397–419.

Gabriel, Iason. "Effective Altruism and Its Critics." *Journal of Applied Philosophy* 34, no. 4 (2017): 457–73.

Galle, Brian. "Pay It Forward: Law and the Problem of Restricted-Spending Philanthropy." *Washington University Law Review* 93, no. 5 (2016): 1143–207.

Gaus, Gerald. "Coercion, Ownership, and the Redistributive State: Justificatory Liberalism's Classical Tilt." *Social Philosophy and Policy* 27, no. 1 (2010): 233–75.

Gautier, Arthur, and Anne-Claire Pache. "Research on Corporate Philanthropy: A Review and Assessment." *Journal of Business Ethics* 126, no. 3 (2015): 343–69.

Gilabert, Pablo. "Justice and Feasibility: A Dynamic Approach." In *Political Utopias: Contemporary Debates,* edited by Kevin Vallier and Michael Weber, 95–126. New York: Oxford University Press, 2017.

Gilens, Martin. *Affluence and Influence: Economic Inequality and Political Power in America*. Princeton, NJ: Princeton University Press, 2012.

Giridharadas, Anand. *Winners Take All: The Elite Charade of Changing the World*. New York: Knopf Doubleday Publishing Group, 2018.

Giridharadas, Anand. "Why Jeff Bezos's Philanthropy Plan Is Well-Intentioned—and Misguided." *Time*, September 18, 2018. https://time.com/5398801/jeff-bezos-philanthropy/.

Godwin, William. *Enquiry Concerning Political Justice, and Its Influence on Morals and Happiness*. Vol. 2. London: G. G. and J. Robinson, 1798.

Goodin, Robert E. "Enfranchising All Affected Interests, and Its Alternatives." *Philosophy and Public Affairs* 35, no. 1 (2007): 40–68.

Goodwin, Iris J. "Ask Not What Your Charity Can Do for You: Robertson v. Princeton Provides Liberal-Democratic Insights onto the Dilemma of Cy Pres Reform." *Arizona Law Review* 51, no. 1 (2009): 75–125.

Gravelle, Jane G., Donald J. Marples, and Molly F. Sherlock. "Tax Issues Relating to Charitable Contributions and Organizations." Washington, DC: Congressional Research Service, September 19, 2019.

"Gross Domestic Philanthropy: An International Analysis of GDP, Tax and Giving." Kent, UK: Charities Aid Foundation, January 2016.

Gross, Robert A. "Giving in America: From Charity to Philanthropy." In *Charity, Philanthropy, and Civility in American History*, edited by Lawrence Jacob Friedman and Mark D. McGarvie, 29–48. Cambridge, UK: Cambridge University Press, 2003.

Habermas, Jürgen. *Between Facts and Norms*. Translated by William Rehg. Cambridge, MA: MIT Press, 1996.

Hall, Peter Dobkin. *"Inventing the Nonprofit Sector" and Other Essays on Philanthropy, Voluntarism, and Nonprofit Organizations*. Baltimore: Johns Hopkins University Press, 1992.

Hall, Peter Dobkin. "Philanthropy, the Nonprofit Sector and the Democratic Dilemma." *Daedalus* 142, no. 2 (2013): 139–58.

Hardin, Russell. *Collective Action*. Baltimore: Johns Hopkins University Press, 1982.

Haslett, D. W. "Is Inheritance Justified?" *Philosophy and Public Affairs* 15, no. 2 (1986): 122–55.

Hegel, Georg Wilhelm Friedrich. *Elements of the Philosophy of Right*. Edited by Allen W Wood. Translated by H. B. Nisbet. Cambridge, UK: Cambridge University Press, 1991.

Herman, Barbara. "The Scope of Moral Requirement." *Philosophy and Public Affairs* 30, no. 3 (2001): 227–56.

Hillel, Steiner, and Peter Vallentyne. "Libertarian Theories of Intergenerational Justice." In *Intergenerational Justice*, edited by Axel Gosseries and Lukas H. Meyer, 50–75. Oxford, New York: Oxford University Press, 2009.

Himmelreich, Johannes. "Democracy and Digital Technology: Should We Automate Democracy?" In *Oxford Handbook of Digital Ethics*, edited by Carissa Véliz. Oxford: Oxford University Press, forthcoming.

Holowchak, M. Andrew. "Thomas Jefferson." In *The Stanford Encyclopedia of Philosophy*, edited by Edward N. Zalta, Winter 2016. Stanford: Metaphysics Research Lab, Stanford University, 2015. https://plato.stanford.edu/archives/win2016/entries/jefferson/.

Honoré, A. M. "Ownership." In *Oxford Essays in Jurisprudence: A Collaborative Work*, edited by Anthony Gordon Guest, 107–47. Oxford: Clarendon Press, 1961.

Horvath, Aaron, and Walter W. Powell. "Contributory or Disruptive: Do New Forms of Philanthropy Erode Democracy?" In *Philanthropy in Democratic Societies: History, Institutions, Values*, edited by Rob Reich, Lucy Bernholz, and Chiara Cordelli, 87–112. Chicago: University of Chicago Press, 2016.

Hsieh, Nien-hê. "The Obligations of Transnational Corporations: Rawlsian Justice and the Duty of Assistance." *Business Ethics Quarterly* 14, no. 4 (2004): 643–61.

Hume, David. *A Treatise of Human Nature*. Edited by L. A. Selby-Bigge and P. H. Nidditch. Oxford: Oxford University Press, 1978.

Hume, David. *An Enquiry Concerning the Principles of Morals*. Edited by J. B Schneewind. Indianapolis: Hackett, 1983.

Hussain, Waheed. "Is Ethical Consumerism an Impermissible Form of Vigilantism?" *Philosophy and Public Affairs* 40, no. 2 (2012): 111–43.

Hussain, Waheed, and Joakim Sandberg. "Pluralistic Functionalism about Corporate Agency." In *The Moral Responsibility of Firms*, edited by Eric W. Orts and N. Craig Smith, 1st ed., 66–85. Oxford: Oxford University Press, 2017.

Illingworth, Patricia. "An Ethicist Explains Why Philanthropy Is No License to Do Bad Stuff." *The Conversation*, December 19, 2019. https://theconversation.com/an-ethicist-explains-why-philanthropy-is-no-license-to-do-bad-stuff-127426.

Imberg, Maya, and Maeen Shaban. "The New Normal: Trends in UHNW Giving 2019." New York: Wealth-X, 2019.

INCITE! *The Revolution Will Not Be Funded*. Durham, NC: Duke University Press, 2017.

Internal Revenue Service, Statistics of Income Division. "Historical Table 16: Nonprofit Charitable Organization and Domestic Private Foundation Information Returns, and Exempt Organization Business Income Tax Returns: Selected Financial Data, 1985–2011." October 2014.

Irwin, T. H. "Generosity and Property in Aristotle's Politics." *Social Philosophy and Policy* 4, no. 2 (1987): 37–54.

IUPUI Lilly Family School of Philanthropy, Indiana University. "Giving USA 2013 Highlights." Indianapolis: Lilly Family School of Philanthropy, 2013.

IUPUI Lilly Family School of Philanthropy, Indiana University. "Giving USA 2019 Highlights." Indianapolis: Lilly Family School of Philanthropy, 2019.

IUPUI Lilly Family School of Philanthropy, Indiana University. "Giving USA 2020 Highlights." Indianapolis: Lilly Family School of Philanthropy, 2020.

IUPUI Lilly Family School of Philanthropy, Indiana University, and Patrick Rooney. "Giving USA 2016: The Annual Report on Philanthropy for the Year 2015." Indianapolis: Lilly Family School of Philanthropy, 2016.

James, Aaron. "Political Constructivism." In *A Companion to Rawls*, edited by Jon Mandel and David A. Reidy, 251–64. New York: Wiley-Blackwell, 2013.

Jefferson, Thomas. "Letter to James Madison, September 6, 1789." In *The Works of Thomas Jefferson, (Correspondence 1789–1792)*, edited by Paul Leicester Ford. Federal ed. Vol. 6. New York and London: G.P. Putnam's Sons, 1904.

Julius, A. J. "Basic Structure and the Value of Equality." *Philosophy and Public Affairs* 31, no. 4 (2003): 321–55.

Kajihara, Noriaki, and Kenji Hirayama. "The War against a Regional Disease in Japan: A History of the Eradication of Schistosomiasis Japonica." *Tropical Medicine and Health* 39, no. 1 (2011): 3–44.

Kant, Immanuel. "Moralphilosophie Collins." In *Gesammelte Schriften*, 455–56. Berlin: de Gruyter, 1974.

Karl, Barry D., and Stanley N. Katz. "Foundations and Ruling Class Elites." *Daedalus* 116, no. 1 (1987): 1–40.

Karnofsky, Holden. "How We Evaluate a Study." The GiveWell Blog, September 2, 2016. https://blog.givewell.org/2012/08/23/how-we-evaluate-a-study/.

King, Martin Luther, Jr. "Beyond Vietnam." Presented at the Speech Delivered at Riverside Church, New York, April 4, 1967.

Klosko, George. "The Obligation to Contribute to Discretionary Public Goods." *Political Studies* 38, no. 2 (1990): 196–214.

Knight, Jack, and James Johnson. "What Sort of Political Equality Does Deliberative Democracy Require?" In *Deliberative Democracy: Essays on Reason and Politics*, edited by James Bohman and William Rehg, 279–319. Cambridge, MA: MIT Press, 1997.

Knobel, Marcelo, and Robert Verhine. "Brazil's For-Profit Higher Education Dilemma." *International Higher Education*, no. 89 (2017): 23–24.

Kolodny, Niko. "Being under the Power of Others." In *Republicanism and the Future of Democracy*, edited by Yiftah Elazar and Geneviève Rousselière, 94–114. Cambridge, UK: Cambridge University Press, 2019.

Kolodny, Niko. "Rule over None I: What Justifies Democracy?" *Philosophy and Public Affairs* 42, no. 3 (2014): 195–229.

Kolodny, Niko. "Rule over None II: Social Equality and the Justification of Democracy." *Philosophy and Public Affairs* 42, no. 4 (2014): 287–336.

Krasner, Stephen D., and Jeremy M. Weinstein. "Improving Governance from the Outside In." *Annual Review of Political Science* 17, no. 1 (2014): 123–45.

Kumar, Rahul. "Wronging Future People: A Contractualist Proposal." In *Intergenerational Justice*, edited by Axel Gosseries and Lukas H. Meyer, 252–71. New York: Oxford University Press, 2009.

Kymlicka, Will. "Altruism in Philosophical and Ethical Traditions: Two Views." *In Between State and Market: Essay on Charities Law and Policy in Canada*, edited by Jim Phillips, Bruce Chapman, and David Stevens, 87–126. Montreal: McGill-Queen's University Press, 2001.

LaMarche, Gara. "Democracy and the Donor Class." *Democracy Journal* 34, Fall (2014): 48–59.

Landau, Peter. "The Origin of the Regula Iuris 'quod omnes tangit' in the Anglo-Norman School of Canon Law during the Twelfth Century." *Bulletin of Medieval Canon Law* 32, no. 1 (2015): 19–35.

Landemore, Hélène. *Open Democracy: Reinventing Popular Rule for the Twenty-First Century*. Princeton, NJ: Princeton University Press, 2020.

Lechterman, Theodore M. "Book Review: *The Ethics of Giving: Philosophers' Perspectives on Philanthropy* by Woodruff, P. (Ed.)" *Nonprofit and Voluntary Sector Quarterly* 48, no. 5 (2019): 1110–12.

Lechterman, Theodore M. "The Effective Altruist's Political Problem." *Polity* 52, no. 1 (2020): 88–115.

Lechterman, Theodore M. "The *Potestas* of Practice." *History of Political Thought*. 42, no. 2 (2021): 240–51.

Lechterman, Theodore M. "'That the Earth Belongs in Usufruct to the Living': Intergenerational Philanthropy and the Problem of Dead-Hand Control." In *Giving in Time: Temporal Issues in Philanthropy*. Edited by Ray Madoff and Benjamin Soskis. Lanham: Rowman and Littlefield, forthcoming.

Lechterman, Theodore M., and Rob Reich. "Political Theory and the Nonprofit Sector." In *The Nonprofit Sector: A Research Handbook*, edited by Walter W. Powell and Patricia Bromley, 3rd ed., 171–91. Stanford, CA: Stanford University Press, 2020.

Lemos, Margaret, and Guy-Uriel Charles. "Patriotic Philanthropy? Financing the State with Gifts to Government." *California Law Review* 106, no. 4 (2018): 1129–93.

Lessig, Lawrence. *Republic Lost: The Corruption of Equality and the Steps to End It*. Rev. ed.. New York: Twelve, 2015.

List, John A. "The Market for Charitable Giving." *Journal of Economic Perspectives* 25, no. 2 (2011): 157–80.

Lister, Andrew. "Justice as Fairness and Reciprocity." *Analyze and Kritik* 33, no. 1 (2011): 93–112.

Locke, John. *Two Treatises of Government*. Edited by Peter Laslett. Cambridge, UK: Cambridge University Press, 2008.

Lomasky, Loren E. "Justice to Charity." *Social Philosophy and Policy* 12, no. 2 (1995): 32–53.

Lukes, Steven. *Power: A Radical View.* 2nd ed. London: Palgrave Macmillan, 2005.

Lynch, Cecelia. "Reconceptualizing Charity: The Problem with Philanthropy and 'Effective Altruism' by the World's Wealthiest People." *Critical Investigations into Humanitarianism in Africa Blog* (blog), January 11, 2016. http://www.cihablog.com/reconceptualizing-charity-the-problem-with-philanthropy-and-effective-altruism-by-the-worlds-wealthiest-people/.

MacAskill, William. *Doing Good Better: How Effective Altruism Can Help You Make a Difference.* New York: Gotham Books, 2015.

Madoff, Ray D. *Immortality and the Law: The Rising Power of the American Dead.* New Haven: Yale University Press, 2010.

Madoff, Ray D. "When Is Philanthropy? How the Tax Code's Answer to This Question Has Given Rise to the Growth of Donor-Advised Funds and Why It's a Problem." In *Philanthropy in Democratic Societies: History, Institutions, Values,* edited by Rob Reich, Lucy Bernholz, and Chiara Cordelli, 158–77. Chicago: University of Chicago Press, 2016.

Maitland, F. W. *Maitland: State, Trust and Corporation.* Edited by David Runciman. Cambridge, UK: Cambridge University Press, 2003.

Mansuri, Ghazala, and Vijayendra Rao. "Localizing Development: Does Participation Work?" Policy Research Report. Washington, DC: The World Bank, November 15, 2012. http://documents.worldbank.org/curated/en/461701468150309553/Localizing-development-does-participation-work.

Martin, Fiona. "The Sociopolitical and Legal History of the Tax Deduction for Donations to Charities in Australia and How the 'Public Benevolent Institution' Developed." *Adelaide Law Review* 38, no. 1 (2017): 195–221.

Martin, Nick. "Liberal Neutrality and Charitable Purposes." *Political Studies* 60, no. 4 (2012): 936–52.

Marx, Karl, and Friedrich Engels. "Manifesto of the Communist Party." In *The Marx-Engels Reader,* edited by Robert C. Tucker, 2nd ed., 469–500. New York: Norton, 1978.

Mauss, Marcel. *The Gift: The Form and Reason for Exchange in Archaic Societies.* London: Routledge, 2002.

Mayer, Jane. *Dark Money: The Hidden History of the Billionaires behind the Rise of the Radical Right.* New York: Knopf Doubleday Publishing Group, 2016.

McCaffery, Edward J. "The Political Liberal Case against the Estate Tax." *Philosophy and Public Affairs* 23, no. 4 (1994): 281–312.

McGoey, Linsey. *No Such Thing as a Free Gift: The Gates Foundation and the Price of Philanthropy.* London: Verso, 2016.

McKeever, Brice S. "The Nonprofit Sector in Brief: Public Charities, Giving and Volunteering, 2015." Washington, DC: The Urban Institute, October 2015.

Mill, John Stuart. "Considerations on Representative Government." In *The Collected Works of John Stuart Mill, Volume XIX: Essays on Politics and Society, Part II,* edited by John M. Robson, 371–754. Toronto: University of Toronto Press, 1977.

Mill, John Stuart. "Corporation and Church Property (1833)." In *The Collected Works of John Stuart Mill, Volume IV: Essays on Economics and Society, Part I*, edited by John M. Robson, 193–222. Toronto: University of Toronto Press, 1967.

Mill, John Stuart. "Endowments (1869)." In *The Collected Works of John Stuart Mill, Volume V: Essays on Economics and Society, Part II*, edited by John M. Robson, 615–29. Toronto: University of Toronto Press, 1967.

Mill, John Stuart. "On Liberty." In *The Collected Works of John Stuart Mill, Volume XVIII: Essays on Politics and Society, Part I*, edited by John M. Robson, 213–310. Toronto: University of Toronto Press, 1977.

Mill, John Stuart. *Principles of Political Economy*. Vol. 2. New York: D. Appleton, 1896.

Miller, David. "Justice, Democracy and Public Goods." In *Justice and Democracy: Essays for Brian Barry*, edited by Keith Dowding, Robert Goodin, and Carole Pateman, 127–49. Cambridge, UK: Cambridge University Press, 2004.

Mills, Pete. "The Ethical Careers Debate: A Discussion between Ben Todd, Sebastian Farquhar, and Pete Mills." Edited by Tom Cutterham. *The Oxford Left Review*, no. 7 (May 2012): 4–9.

Moore, Mick. "Empowerment at Last?" *Journal of International Development* 13, no. 3 (2001): 321–29.

Moriarty, Jeffrey. "Business Ethics." In *The Stanford Encyclopedia of Philosophy*, edited by Edward N. Zalta, Fall 2017. Stanford: Metaphysics Research Lab, Stanford University, 2017. https://plato.stanford.edu/archives/fall2017/entries/ethics-business/.

Murphy, Liam B. *Moral Demands in Nonideal Theory*. Oxford: Oxford University Press, 2003.

Murphy, Liam, and Thomas Nagel. *The Myth of Ownership: Taxes and Justice*. New York: Oxford University Press, 2002.

Musgrave, Richard A. *The Theory of Public Finance: A Study in Public Economy*. New York: McGraw-Hill, 1959.

Narayan, Deepa, Robert Chambers, Meera K. Shah, and Patti Petesch, eds. *Voices of the Poor: Crying Out for Change*. Vol. 2. New York: Oxford University Press for the World Bank, 2000.

Narayan, Deepa, Raj Patel, Kai Schafft, Anne Rademacher, and Sara Koch-Schulte, eds. *Voices of the Poor: Can Anyone Hear Us?* Vol. 1. New York: World Bank Publications, 2000.

Nelson, Kenneth. "Social Assistance and EU Poverty Thresholds 1990–2008. Are European Welfare Systems Providing Just and Fair Protection against Low Income?" *European Sociological Review* 29, no. 2 (October 5, 2011): 386–401.

Nozick, Robert. *Anarchy, State, and Utopia*. New York: Basic Books, 1974.

Nussbaum, Martha C. *Frontiers of Justice: Disability, Nationality, Species Membership.* Cambridge, MA: Belknap Press, 2006.

Ober, Josiah. "Classical Athens." In *Fiscal Regimes and the Political Economy of Premodern States,* edited by Andrew Monson and Walter Scheidel, 492–522. Cambridge, UK: Cambridge University Press, 2018.

Ober, Josiah. *Demopolis: Democracy before Liberalism in Theory and Practice.* New York: Cambridge University Press, 2017.

O'Halloran, Kerry, Myles McGregor-Lowndes, and Karla Simon. *Charity Law and Social Policy: National and International Perspectives on the Functions of the Law Relating to Charities.* Dordrecht: Springer Netherlands, 2008.

O'Neil, Megan, Brian O'Leary, and Peter Olsen-Philips. "Corporate Cash Giving Rises 5%, Exclusive Chronicle Survey Shows." *Chronicle of Philanthropy,* September 5, 2018.

Orts, Eric W. *Business Persons: A Legal Theory of the Firm.* Oxford: Oxford University Press, 2013.

Ostrower, Francie. *Why the Wealthy Give: The Culture of Elite Philanthropy.* Princeton, NJ: Princeton University Press, 1995.

Otsuka, Michael. *Libertarianism without Inequality.* Oxford: Oxford University Press, 2003.

Page, Benjamin I., Larry M. Bartels, and Jason Seawright. "Democracy and the Policy Preferences of Wealthy Americans." *Perspectives on Politics* 11, no. 1 (March 2013): 51–73.

Parijs, Philippe Van. *Real Freedom for All: What (if Anything) Can Justify Capitalism?* Oxford: Oxford University Press, 1995.

Patten, Alan. "Liberal Neutrality: A Reinterpretation and Defense." *Journal of Political Philosophy* 20, no. 3 (2012): 249–72.

Pettijohn, Sarah L. "The Nonprofit Sector in Brief: Public Charities, Giving and Volunteering. 2013." Washington, DC: The Urban Institute, 2013.

Pettit, Philip. "The Domination Complaint." *Nomos* 86 (2005): 87–117.

Pettit, Philip. *On the People's Terms: A Republican Theory and Model of Democracy.* Cambridge, UK: Cambridge University Press, 2012.

Pettit, Philip. *Republicanism: A Theory of Freedom and Government.* Oxford: Oxford University Press, 1997.

Pettit, Philip. "Three Issues in Social Ontology." In *Rethinking the Individualism-Holism Debate: Essays in the Philosophy of Social Science,* edited by Julie Zahle and Finn Collin, 77–96. Cham: Springer, 2014.

Pevnick, Ryan. "Democratizing the Nonprofit Sector." *Journal of Political Philosophy* 21, no. 3 (2013): 260–82.

Piper, Kelsey. "The Problem with Jeff Bezos's $2 Billion Gift to Charity." *Vox,* September 18, 2018. https://www.vox.com/2018/9/21/17880000/jeff-bezos-amazon-philanthropy-gift-2-billion.

Plato. "Laws." In *Plato: Complete Works,* edited by John Cooper, translated by Trevor J. Saunders, 1318–616. Indianapolis: Hackett, 1997.

Pogge, Thomas. "Are We Violating the Human Rights of the World's Poor?" *Yale Human Rights and Development Law Journal* 14 (2011): 1–33.

Pogge, Thomas. "'Assisting' the Global Poor?" In *The Ethics of Assistance: Morality and the Distant Needy*, edited by Deen K. Chatterjee, 260–88. Cambridge, UK: Cambridge University Press, 2004.

Pogge, Thomas. "How International Nongovernmental Organizations Should Act." In *Giving Well: The Ethics of Philanthropy*, edited by Patricia Illingworth, Thomas Pogge, and Leif Wenar, 46–66. New York: Oxford University Press, 2011.

Pogge, Thomas. "The Health Impact Fund: Boosting Pharmaceutical Innovation without Obstructing Free Access." *Cambridge Quarterly of Healthcare Ethics* 18, no. 1 (January 2009): 78–86.

Post, Robert. *Citizens Divided: Campaign Finance Reform and the Constitution.* Cambridge, MA: Harvard University Press, 2016.

Rakowski, Eric. "Transferring Wealth Liberally." *Tax Law Review* 51 (1995): 419–72.

Ravallion, Martin. "A Comparative Perspective on Poverty Reduction in Brazil, China, and India." *World Bank Research Observer* 26, no. 1 (2011): 71–104.

Ravallion, Martin. "Fighting Poverty One Experiment at a Time: *Poor Economics: A Radical Rethinking of the Way to Fight Global Poverty*: Review Essay." *Journal of Economic Literature* 50, no. 1 (2012): 103–14.

Ravitch, Diane. *The Death and Life of the Great American School System: How Testing and Choice Are Undermining Education.* New York: Basic Books, 2011.

Rawls, John. *Justice as Fairness: A Restatement.* Edited by Erin I. Kelly. Cambridge, MA: Harvard University Press, 2001.

Rawls, John. *The Law of Peoples: With "The Idea of Public Reason Revisited."* Cambridge, MA: Harvard University Press, 2001.

Rawls, John. *Political Liberalism.* New York: Columbia University Press, 1993.

Rawls, John. *A Theory of Justice.* Rev. ed. Cambridge, MA: The Belknap Press of Harvard University Press, 1999.

Rawls, John. "Two Concepts of Rules." *Philosophical Review* 64, no. 1 (1955): 3–32.

Raz, Joseph. *The Morality of Freedom.* Oxford: Clarendon Press, 1986.

Reckhow, Sarah. "More Than Patrons: How Foundations Fuel Policy Change and Backlash." *PS: Political Science and Politics* 49, no. 3 (2016): 449–54.

Reeve, Andrew. *Property: Issues in Political Theory.* Houndsmills: Macmillan International Higher Education, 1986.

Reich, Rob. "A Failure of Philanthropy." *Stanford Social Innovation Review* (Winter 2005): 24–33.

Reich, Rob. *Just Giving: Why Philanthropy Is Failing Democracy and How It Can Do Better.* Princeton: Princeton University Press, 2018.

Reich, Rob. "Philanthropy and Its Uneasy Relation to Equality." In *Taking Philanthropy Seriously: Beyond Noble Intentions to Responsible Giving,* edited by William Damon and Susan Verducci, 27–49. Bloomington: Indiana University Press, 2006.

Reich, Rob. "Repugnant to the Whole Idea of Democracy? On the Role of Foundations in Democratic Societies." *PS: Political Science and Politics* 49, no. 3 (2016): 466–72.

Reich, Rob. "Toward a Political Theory of Philanthropy." In *Giving Well: The Ethics of Philanthropy*, edited by Patricia Illingworth, Thomas Pogge, and Leif Wenar, 177–92. Oxford: Oxford University Press, 2011.

Reich, Rob, Lucy Bernholz, and Chiara Cordelli, eds. *Philanthropy in Democratic Societies: History, Institutions, Values.* Chicago: University of Chicago Press, 2016.

Reich, Rob, Lacey Dorn, and Stefanie Sutton. *Anything Goes: Approval of Nonprofit Status by the I.R.S.* Stanford, CA: Stanford University Center on Philanthropy and Civil Society, 2009. https://pacscenter.stanford.edu/publication/anything-goes-approval-of-nonprofit-status-by-the-irs/.

Ripstein, Arthur. *Force and Freedom: Kant's Legal and Political Philosophy.* Cambridge, MA: Harvard University Press, 2009.

Risse, Mathias. *On Global Justice.* Princeton, NJ: Princeton University Press, 2012.

Robson, A. Deirdre. "Industry: Art Angel? Pepsi-Cola's 'Portrait of America' Art Annual as an Early Instance of Corporate Art Sponsorship." *Journal of American Culture* 38, no. 4 (2015): 329–43.

Rodrik, Dani. *One Economics, Many Recipes: Globalization, Institutions, and Economic Growth.* Princeton, NJ: Princeton University Press, 2007.

Ronzoni, Miriam, and Laura Valentini. "Microfinance, Poverty Relief, and Political Justice." In *Microfinance, Rights, and Global Justice*, edited by Tom Sorrell and Luis Cabrera, 84–104. Cambridge, UK: Cambridge University Press, 2015.

Rossi, Enzo, and Matt Sleat. "Realism in Normative Political Theory." *Philosophy Compass* 9, no. 10 (2014): 689–701.

Rubenstein, Jennifer C. *Between Samaritans and States: The Political Ethics of Humanitarian INGOs.* New York: Oxford University Press, 2015.

Rubenstein, Jennifer C. "The Lessons of Effective Altruism." *Ethics and International Affairs* 30, no. 4 (2016): 511–26.

Rubenstein, Jennifer C. "The Logic of Effective Altruism: Response." *Boston Review*, July 1, 2015. http://bostonreview.net/forum/peter-singer-logic-effective-altruism.

Ruswick, Brent. "Just Poor Enough: Gilded Age Charity Applicants Respond to Charity Investigators." *Journal of the Gilded Age and Progressive Era* 10, no. 3 (2011): 265–87.

Samuelson, Paul A. "The Pure Theory of Public Expenditure." *Review of Economics and Statistics* 36, no. 4 (1954): 387–89.

Satz, Debra. "Some (Largely) Ignored Problems with Privatization." In *Political Legitimacy*, edited by Jack Knight and Melissa Schwartzberg, 9–29. Nomos LXI. New York: New York University Press, 2019.

Saunders-Hastings, Emma. "No Better to Give Than to Receive: Charity and Women's Subjection in J.S. Mill." *Polity* 46, no. 2 (2014): 233–54.

Saunders-Hastings, Emma. "Plutocratic Philanthropy." *Journal of Politics* 80, no. 1 (October 25, 2017): 149–61.

Saunders-Hastings, Emma. "Benevolent Giving and Philanthropic Paternalism." In *Effective Altruism: Philosophical Issues*, edited by Hilary Greaves and Theron Pummer, 115–36. Oxford: Oxford University Press, 2019.

Saunders-Hastings, Emma, and Rob Reich. "Philanthropy and the All-Affected Principle." Paper Presented at the American Political Science Association Annual Meeting. San Francisco, CA, September 2017.

Scheffler, Samuel. *Death and the Afterlife*. Edited by Niko Kolodny. Oxford: Oxford University Press, 2013.

Schlozman, Kay Lehman, Sidney Verba, and Henry E. Brady. *The Unheavenly Chorus: Unequal Political Voice and the Broken Promise of American Democracy*. Princeton, NJ: Princeton University Press, 2012.

Schmidtz, David. *The Limits of Government: An Essay on the Public Goods Argument*. Boulder: Westview Press, 1991.

Schneewind, J. B., ed. *Giving: Western Ideas of Philanthropy*. Bloomington: Indiana University Press, 1996.

Schrimpf, Anna. "The Politics of Empathy: A Study of INGO Attention and Neglect." PhD diss., Princeton University, 2016.

Sealander, Judith. "Curing Evils at Their Source: The Arrival of Scientific Giving." In *Charity, Philanthropy, and Civility in American History*, edited by Lawrence J. Friedman and Mark D. McGarvie, 217–39. Cambridge, UK: Cambridge University Press, 2003.

Semega, Jessica, Melissa Kollar, John Creamer, and Abinash Mohanty. "Income and Poverty in the United States: 2018." *Current Population Reports*. Washington, DC: U.S. Census Bureau, September 2019. https://www.census.gov/library/publications/2019/demo/p60-266.html.

Sen, Amartya. "Equality of What? Tanner Lecture on Human Values," May 22, 1979. https://tannerlectures.utah.edu/_documents/a-to-z/s/sen80.pdf.

Sen, Amartya. *Poverty and Famines: An Essay on Entitlement and Deprivation*. Oxford: Oxford University Press, 1983.

Sepinwall, Amy J. "Corporate Moral Responsibility." *Philosophy Compass* 11, no. 1 (2016): 3–13.

Sepinwall, Amy J. "Denying Corporate Rights and Punishing Corporate Wrongs." *Business Ethics Quarterly* 25, no. 4 (2015): 517–34.

Shapiro, Daniel. "Egalitarianism and Welfare-State Distribution." *Social Philosophy and Policy* 19, no. 1 (2002): 1–35.

Shue, Henry. *Basic Rights: Subsistence, Affluence, and U.S. Foreign Policy.* Princeton, NJ: Princeton University Press, 1996.

Simes, Lewis Mallalieu. *Public Policy and the Dead Hand: Five Lectures Delivered at the University of Michigan February 7, 8, 9, 14, and 15, 1955.* Ann Arbor: University of Michigan Law School, 1955.

Simmons, A. John. "Ideal and Nonideal Theory." *Philosophy and Public Affairs* 38, no. 1 (2010): 5–36.

Simmons, A. John. "Justification and Legitimacy." *Ethics* 109, no. 4 (1999): 739–71.

Simon, John, Harvey Dale, and Laura Chisholm. "The Federal Tax Treatment of Charitable Organizations." In *The Nonprofit Sector: A Research Handbook*, edited by Walter W. Powell and Richard Steinberg, 2nd ed., 267–306. New Haven: Yale University Press, 2006.

Singer, Abraham. "Rawls Well That Ends Well: A Response to Welch and Ly." *Business Ethics Journal Review*, February 16, 2018, 11–17.

Singer, Peter. "Good Charity, Bad Charity." *The New York Times*, August 10, 2013, sec. Opinion.

Singer, Peter. *The Most Good You Can Do.* New Haven: Yale University Press, 2015.

Skocpol, Theda. *Diminished Democracy: From Membership to Management in American Civic Life.* Norman: University of Oklahoma Press, 2013.

Solórzano, André. "Giving in Numbers." New York: Chief Executives for Corporate Purpose, 2019. http://cecp.co/home/resources/giving-in-numbers/.

Soskis, Benjamin, and Ray D. Madoff, eds. *Giving in Time: Temporal Issues in Philanthropy.* Lanham, MD: Rowman and Littlefield, forthcoming.

"Sponsorship Spending on the Arts to Total $1.03 Billion in 2018." *IEG Sponsorship Report*, March 12, 2018. https://www.sponsorship.com/Report/2018/03/12/Sponsorship-Spending-On-The-Arts-To-Total-$1-03-bi.aspx.

Sreenivasan, Gopal. *The Limits of Lockean Rights in Property.* New York: Oxford University Press, 1995.

Srinivasan, Amia. "Stop the Robot Apocalypse." *London Review of Books* 37, no. 15 (September 24, 2015): 3–6.

Steinberg, Richard. "Economic Theories of Nonprofit Organizations." In *The Nonprofit Sector: A Research Handbook*, edited by Walter W. Powell and Richard Steinberg, Second., 117–39. New Haven: Yale University Press, 2006.

Steinberg, Richard, and Walter W. Powell. "Introduction." In *The Nonprofit Sector: A Research Handbook*, 2nd ed., 1–10. New Haven: Yale University Press, 2006.

Stilz, Anna. "The Value of Self-Determination." In *Oxford Studies in Political Philosophy*, edited by David Sobel, Peter Vallentyne, and Steven Wall, Vol. 2, 98–127. Oxford: Oxford University Press, 2016.

Sulek, Marty. "On the Classical Meaning of Philanthrôpía." *Nonprofit and Voluntary Sector Quarterly* 39, no. 3 (2010): 385–408.

Sulek, Marty. "On the Modern Meaning of Philanthropy." *Nonprofit and Voluntary Sector Quarterly* 39, no. 2 (2010): 193–212.

Taylor, Robert S. "Donation without Domination: Private Charity and Republican Liberty." *Journal of Political Philosophy* 26, no. 4 (2018): 441–62.

Teles, Steven M. "Foundations, Organizational Maintenance, and Partisan Asymmetry." *PS: Political Science and Politics* 49, no. 3 (2016): 455–60.

Teles, Steven M. *The Rise of the Conservative Legal Movement: The Battle for Control of the Law*. Princeton, NJ: Princeton University Press, 2012.

Teles, Steven, and Mark Schmitt. "The Elusive Craft of Evaluating Advocacy." *Stanford Social Innovation Review* (Summer 2011): 39–43.

Temkin, Larry S. "Being Good in a World of Need: Some Empirical Worries and an Uncomfortable Philosophical Possibility." *Journal of Practical Ethics* 7, no. 1 (2019): 1–23.

Thompson, Janna. *Intergenerational Justice: Rights and Responsibilities in an Intergenerational Polity*. New York: Routledge, 2009.

U.K. Charity Commission for England and Wales. "Analysis of the Law Relating to Public Benefit," September 2013. https://assets.publishing.service.gov.uk/government/uploads/system/uploads/attachment_data/file/589796/Public_benefit_analysis_of_the_law.pdf.

U.K. Charity Commission for England and Wales. "Public Benefit: The Public Benefit Requirement," September 16, 2013. https://www.gov.uk/government/publications/public-benefit-the-public-benefit-requirement-pb1/public-benefit-the-public-benefit-requirement.

Uniform Law Commission/National Conference of Commissioners on Uniform State Laws. "Uniform Trust Code," 2010. https://www.uniformlaws.org/HigherLogic/System/DownloadDocumentFile.ashx?DocumentFileKey=3d7d5428-dfc6-ac33-0a32-d5b65463c6e3.

"Update on the E-2020 Initiative of 21 Malaria-Eliminating Countries." World Health Organization, June 2018.

U.S. Congressional Budget Office. "The Distribution of Major Tax Expenditures in the Individual Income Tax System, Pub. No. 4308." Washington, DC: U.S. Congressional Budget Office, May 2013. https://www.cbo.gov/publication/43768.

Valentini, Laura. "Ideal vs. Non-Ideal Theory: A Conceptual Map." *Philosophy Compass* 7, no. 9 (2012): 654–64.

Vallier, Kevin. "A Moral and Economic Critique of the New Property-Owning Democrats: On Behalf of a Rawlsian Welfare State." *Philosophical Studies* 172, no. 2 (2015): 283–304.

Viehoff, Daniel. "Democratic Equality and Political Authority." *Philosophy and Public Affairs* 42, no. 4 (2014): 337–75.

Vogel, Carol. "An Old Box Factory Is a Haven for New Art." *New York Times*, April 23, 2003.

Waldron, Jeremy. "Theoretical Foundations of Liberalism." *Philosophical Quarterly* 37, no. 147 (1987): 127–50.

Waldron, Jeremy. "Welfare and the Images of Charity." *Philosophical Quarterly* 36, no. 145 (1986): 463–82.

Walker, Darren. *From Generosity to Justice: A New Gospel of Wealth*. New York: The Ford Foundation/Disruption Books, 2019.

Walsh, Frank P. "Perilous Philanthropy." *The Independent*, no. 83, August 23, 1915.

Walzer, M. "The Moral Standing of States: A Response to Four Critics." *Philosophy and Public Affairs* 9, no. 3 (1980): 209–29.

Walzer, M. "Socialism and the Gift Relationship." *Dissent* 29 (1982): 431–41.

Walzer, M. *Spheres of Justice*. New York: Basic Books, 1983.

Watkins, Susan Cotts, Ann Swidler, and Thomas Hannan. "Outsourcing Social Transformation: Development NGOs as Organizations." *Annual Review of Sociology* 38, no. 1 (2012): 285–315.

Weber, Max. "The Profession and Vocation of Politics." In *Weber: Political Writings*, edited by Peter Lassman and Ronald Speirs, translated by Ronald Speirs. Cambridge, UK: Cambridge University Press, 1994.

Wenar, Leif. "Clean Trade in Natural Resources." *Ethics and International Affairs* 25, no. 1 (2011): 27–39.

Wenar, Leif. "Poverty Is No Pond." In *Giving Well: The Ethics of Philanthropy*, edited by Patricia Illingworth, Thomas Pogge, and Leif Wenar, 105–31. Oxford: Oxford University Press, 2011.

Werfel, Seth H. "Does Charitable Giving Crowd Out Support for Government Spending?" *Economics Letters* 171 (October 1, 2018): 83–86.

Werfel, Seth H. "Household Behaviour Crowds Out Support for Climate Change Policy When Sufficient Progress Is Perceived." *Nature Climate Change* 7 (2017): 512.

Wilde, Oscar. "The Soul of Man under Socialism." *Fortnightly Review* 49 (1891): 292–319.

Williamson, Vanessa. "The Philanthropy Con." *Dissent Magazine*, Winter 2019. https://www.dissentmagazine.org/article/the-philanthropy-con.

Wollstonecraft, Mary. *A Vindication of the Rights of Woman*. New York: A. J. Matsell, 1833.

Wolpert, Julian. "The Redistributional Effects of America's Private Foundations." In *Legitimacy of Philanthropic Foundations: United States and European Perspectives*, edited by Kenneth Prewitt, Mattei Dogan, Steven Heydemann, and Stefan Toepler, 123–49. New York: Russell Sage Foundation, 2006.

Woodruff, Paul, ed. *The Ethics of Giving: Philosophers' Perspectives on Philanthropy*. New York: Oxford University Press, 2018.

Wooster, Martin Morse. "On the Presidents of the Ford Foundation." *Philanthropy Daily*, June 27, 2016. https://www.philanthropydaily.com/on-the-presidents-of-the-ford-foundation/.

Wright, Karen. "Generosity vs. Altruism: Philanthropy and Charity in the United States and United Kingdom." *Voluntas: International Journal of Voluntary and Nonprofit Organizations* 12, no. 4 (2001): 399–416.

Young, Iris Marion. *Inclusion and Democracy*. New York: Oxford University Press, 2000.

Zacka, Bernardo. *When the State Meets the Street*. Cambridge, MA: Harvard University Press, 2017.

Zuehl, Jake. "Collective Self-Determination." PhD diss., Princeton University, 2016.

Zunz, Olivier. *Philanthropy in America: A History*. Princeton, NJ: Princeton University Press, 2014.

Index

For the benefit of digital users, indexed terms that span two pages (e.g., 52–53) may, on occasion, appear on only one of those pages.